AFRICAN PHILOSOPHY AS
CULTURAL INQUIRY

African Systems of Thought

General Editors
Charles S. Bird
Ivan Karp

Contributing Editors
James W. Fernandez
Luc de Heusch
John Middleton
Roy Willis

AFRICAN PHILOSOPHY
AS CULTURAL INQUIRY

Edited by
Ivan Karp and D. A. Masolo

Published in association with the
International African Institute, London

INDIANA UNIVERSITY PRESS
Bloomington and Indianapolis

This book is a publication of

Indiana University Press
601 North Morton Street
Bloomington, IN 47404-3797 USA

http://www.indiana.edu/~iupress

Telephone orders   800-842-6796
Fax orders   812-855-7931
Orders by e-mail   iuporder@indiana.edu

© 2000 by Indiana University Press

The paper used in this publication meets the minimum requirements of American National Standard
for Information Sciences—Permanence of Paper for
Printed Library Materials, ANSI Z39.48-1984.

Manufactured in the United States of America

**Library of Congress Cataloging-in-Publication
Data**
African philosophy as cultural inquiry / edited by
   Ivan Karp and D. A. Masolo.
      p.   cm. — (African systems of thought)
   Includes bibliographical references and index.
   ISBN 0-253-33808-5 (cl : alk. paper) — ISBN
   0-253-21417-3 (pa : alk. paper)
   1. Philosophy, African.   I. Karp, Ivan.   II. Ma-
   solo, D. A.   III. Series.

   B5305 .A373 2000
   199'.6—dc21   00-038870

   1 2 3 4 5 05 04 03 02 01 00

CONTENTS

Acknowledgments

From its inception as a seminar topic to its present form, this publication has been made possible through the contributions and efforts of several individuals and organizations, to whom we owe an immeasurable amount of gratitude.

Most of the material in this book originated from presentations given at the "Seminar on African Philosophy and Cultural Inquiry," which was held April 26–28, 1993, at the Methodist Guest House in Nairobi, Kenya. We are most grateful to the International African Institute of London, the Rockefeller Foundation in New York, the Carnegie Corporation and the Wenner Gren Foundation (also of New York), and the Smithsonian Institution in Washington, D.C., for the generous funding that made the seminar possible. We feel deeply and personally indebted to Elizabeth Dunstan and David Parkin of the International African Institute, to Alberta Arthurs and Lynne Szwaja of the Rockefeller Foundation, and to Patricia Rosenfeld of the Carnegie Corporation, all of whom supported this project through its different phases and its long period of gestation. In addition, the Rockefeller Foundation provided further material and financial support to D. A. Masolo during the summer of 1993, which enabled him to write first drafts of the part introductions, to organize the new material, and to write a draft of the general introduction.

We also extend our appreciation to each of the seminar participants, most of whom are also contributors to this collection, for their often timely and good work in revising their original papers for this publication. Special thanks to Peter Amuka for agreeing to contribute to this collection despite the post-seminar invitation. Last but not least, we are deeply indebted to Professor Corinne Kratz of Emory University and the staff of the Methodist Guest House in Nairobi for the indispensable organizational work that made hosting the seminar a reality.

AFRICAN PHILOSOPHY AS
CULTURAL INQUIRY

Introduction: African Philosophy as Cultural Inquiry

Since the early 1970s, a series of remarkable books and articles has been published that designates a subject matter called "African philosophy."[1] Much of this work is a response to earlier attempts to describe indigenous African belief systems and the content of their significant categories (such as time, causality, or personhood) as the expression of a collectively held "African" philosophy. This earlier literature, much of which was published between 1930 and 1960, was called "ethnophilosophy" by its critics. "Ethnophilosophy" shares two features with African philosophy; its texts are largely written by African scholars who seek to explain how African culture(s) resolve those key issues also posed in Western philosophical systems. In addition, both bodies of literature are shaped by a more or less self-conscious sensitivity to the imperial and colonial histories out of which African nations have emerged.

Ethnophilosophy still has its adherents, some of whom have forged ties with Afrocentric writers (Obenga 1995), but its claims have remained relatively unchanged since they were first formulated (Karp and Masolo 1998). The literature on African philosophy, on the other hand, has exhibited significant changes, many of which were caused by the social and historical contexts in which the literature was written. The first phase of African philosophy, which began in the 1970s, is largely a critique of how colonial categories are inadvertently reproduced in ethnophilosophical accounts of African cultures, and it seeks to establish standards through which African belief and custom can be evaluated. In this phase, African philosophy tends to defend the value of philosophy in the newly independent nations of Africa, arguing that philosophical training and tools provide rigor and method that are badly needed for the task of national development. In the 1980s, the second phase of African philosophy seeks to develop a "Philosophy of Culture," in Kwame Appiah's words, that can both account for and be critical of the cultural resources that Africans use in conducting their lives. This second phase has involved examining not only so-called "Traditional" African culture but also such topics as the role of African intellectuals as academics in the public life of African nations. Related topics have included how relations with the rest of the world affect the production of culture in Africa and its diaspora. This last topic includes accounts of the relationship between race and culture, of the differences between indigenous and global knowledge systems, and (not to mention that recursive theme of African writing) of defining the course and causes of "development."

The third phase of African philosophy is represented in Appiah's book (1992) and in the recent articles by Hountondji (1992a, 1992b) and by Wiredu (1996) and in some of the essays in this book. In the third phase, the politics of knowledge, always a significant theme in African philosophy, become much more the overt subject matter of philosophical writing, especially as these politics concern such pressing issues as freedom, responsibility and the conduct of life in civil society, and the role of the state in what Achille Mbembe (1992) has called the "Postcolony." As these topics have become more prominent, African philosophy has moved from the critique of how cultural differences are defined and valued to take a more critical stance toward such seemingly sacrosanct topics as nationalism and pan-nationalism, claims to racial solidarity, and the claim that the postcolonial period and scholarly writing about Africa exhibits a conceptual break from the themes and epistemological practices found in the colonial archive. This new phase of African philosophy is both a response to and an attempt to theorize the crisis of the postcolonial African state, and it coincides with the emergence of economic, social, and environmental problems that were not imagined to be possible in the utopian world of newly independent nations.

The convergences among African philosophy and other emergent forms of postcolonial writing and criticism are striking. We provide only one example here of another "third world discourse" that exhibits striking parallels. Subaltern studies in India began as a critique of Indian historiography and argued that the specificity of the subaltern voice has been systematically erased by both colonial and nationalist historians. For all the differences between the political projects of these two groups of Indian historians, Guha (among others) asserts that the ways in which they characterize the motives and culture of subaltern groups are extremely reductionist. In his essay "The Prose of Counter-Insurgency" (1988), for example, Guha shows that the narratives of both groups of historians are organized by their temporal distance from the events described and that both reduce cultural forms and religious motivations to political projects that they define and impose on the subjects of their research. During the colonial period, the historical project tended to support the colonial hierarchy of cultures and persons that opposed rational colonial rulers as an alternative either to natives bound by tradition or to insurgents who acted without recourse to any external guidance (see also Karp manuscript). The project that nationalist historians impose on the subjects of their research is the nascent nation—intuitively sought by untutored natives who are unconsciously acting on behalf of goals that will be achieved by the first leaders of independent nations (Chatterjee 1993).

At stake here are some of the same issues that emerge in the third phase of African philosophy: a respect for the complexity of the motives and cultures of subaltern agents; the complicit role of the intellectual in the power politics and crises of the postcolonial state; the role of criticism in the politics of knowledge; and the conflicts among cosmopolitan, nationalist, and indigenous forms of knowledge. Intellectual historians and sociologists of knowledge will have to work out the reasons why parallel critiques have developed in such different disciplinary locations and discursive spaces in Africa and India, and they will also have to work out the differences as well as the similarities in the ways in which postcolonial criticism emerges as a formation in two such different geographical and cultural locations.

Two factors that contribute to these differing discursive locations are relevant for our account of the development of African philosophy. African societies were among the last to be subjected to colonial rule by Europe, and educational institutions and disciplines in African societies were simply not as well established or prominent at the point of political independence as they were in India. From its beginning in the 1960s, the discipline of African history, for example, has set itself the task of recovering a "usable past" (Vansina et al. 1964; Jewsiewicki 1989)—that is, a past that is usable for the task of building national identity. African historians have yet to see themselves avoid writing across the boundary between the colonial and independence eras in their work; they also have yet to see that their concern with justifying nationalist movements puts them in the position of being judge and jury to the African masses, defining for these masses the purposes and ends of their cultures and actions.[2] In India, the time that has passed between independence and the present and the problems produced by nationalist movements have also resulted in powerful indictments of the ways in which Indian historians have justified nationalism (Nandy 1995). It may be that the era of nationalist historiography is coming to an end in Africa and that a new generation will feel more able to criticize national governments, but that has yet to happen both in Africa and among the senior generation of African historians in the United States. Hountondji's critique of ethnophilosophy and his demonstration of its association with nationalist politics has broken ground for this intellectual direction.

Just as history and politics have combined to affect the development of African historiography, ideas about race have shaped the ways that African philosophers have developed their critiques. The racially informed idea that African conceptual systems are the product of collective work rather than the elaborations of individuals is unthinkable with regard to Indian religion and philosophy, which early on became the subject of the civilizational discourse of Orientalist disciplines. By the end of the nineteenth century, European and Indian academics alike were asking how and to what degree Indian cultural forms exhibited the features of civilization (Chatterjee 1995). As a result, a large body of material about Indian philosophy and religion was written to challenge racially motivated assertions; such a body of material did not exist for African philosophers at the end of the colonial period. Indian philosophy was never asked to refute the idea that there were no analytic skills available in Indian culture, while African philosophy has always had to justify the very idea that African culture had anything remotely akin to philosophy, except at the level of a vaguely formulated collective unconscious.

However, like subaltern studies, African philosophy has moved toward a critical pluralism, especially in its latest phase, in which cultural and historical complexity become the subject of the writing rather than something that is irrelevant to the grand narratives of colonial and nationalist discourse. This pattern of development has some important consequences for how such typical topics of philosophy as personhood and agency or knowledge and discourse are treated in African philosophy and shows that African philosophy and anthropology now exhibit some real convergence, as we argue below in Part I.

FROM ETHNOPHILOSOPHY TO AFRICAN PHILOSOPHY

The history of African philosophy is a history of two contesting parties. The first of these parties has come to be known as ethnophilosophy, the study of collective forms of culture as manifestations of African philosophical systems. The second, now known as African philosophy, argues that philosophical practice, as a second-order critical evaluation of first-order thinking about nature, culture, and experience, must be a vital activity in Africa.

African philosophers themselves can also be divided into two camps— those who believe that technical and academic philosophy provides the tools for a much needed critique and revision of traditional African thought and those who argue that the critical skills and attitudes of Western philosophers can also be found in African cultures.[3] Both of these positions have roots in academic and social movements in the West, including Bergson's vitalistic philosophy, the philosophy of religion, Marxism, existentialism, and Freudian theory as it was incorporated into the surrealist movement in modern art.

The literature on ethnophilosophy is based largely on African materials and is written largely by Africans themselves, perhaps because anti-colonialist and nationalist movements affected them more than other peoples, who did not appear to exhibit the trappings of "civilization" and whose lives were encapsulated within settler states such as the United States and Australia. Ethnophilosophy's most immediate antecedents include Léopold Senghor's (1948, 1964) and Aimé Césaire's (1939) philosophy of "negritude" and the writings of the Belgian missionary Placide Tempels, who appears to have been greatly influenced by Henri Bergson's vitalist philosophy. Ethnophilosophy examines the systems of thought of existing and precolonial African communities in order to determine what might be the ideal forms of "authentically" African philosophy and praxis in the emerging postcolonial situation. In addition to the pioneering work of Senghor and Tempels, this school is represented in the writings of the anthropologist Marcel Griaule (1965), of the philosopher Alexis Kagame (1956), and of the theologians Vincent Mulago (1955, 1965, 1973), François M. Lufuluabo (1962, 1964a, 1964b, 1966), Basil J. Fouda (1967), and John S. Mbiti (1969), among others, many of whom were regarded as Tempels's disciples.

We also include the literature that defines "African socialism" in the ethnophilosophical approach. This is a body of disparate materials that combines Marxist social and economic theories with negritude's politics of difference—all in the service of creating culturally and politically independent states in postcolonial Africa. Julius Nyerere's theory of "Ujamaa" in Tanzania and Didier Ratsiraka's concept of "Fokonolona" in Malagasy are two of the best-known attempts to revalorize African culture in the terms of twentieth-century European social, economic, and political theory. Two works by Nyerere (1968a, 1968b) reveal that these political accounts share with other works of ethnophilosophy the thesis that Africans' central values are communal rather than individual.

Both African socialism and more strictly philosophical works of ethnophilosophy seek to subordinate the individual to the community. While this position seems to be non-Western and even opposed to the emphasis on the agonistic individual in Western thought and culture, it actually accepts a distinct opposition between individual and community that is itself not only Western but also utilitarian, even bourgeois, in character.

5

Various contradictions are characteristic of the ethnophilosophical writings. First and foremost, these writings remain profoundly descriptive and anti-normative—that is, non-critical—about African traditions and customs. But they generally do so in the service of a discourse that is powerfully critical of colonial rule and culture. This is the basis for the criticism aimed at ethnophilosophy by the African philosophers Paulin Hountondji and Kwasi Wiredu, which asserts that critical discourse cannot exempt one side from the criticism it levels at the other side.

Perhaps even more important, however, is the criticism that ethnophilosophy is so deeply counter-hegemonic—that is, oppositional without being radical—that its deep conceptual structure reproduces the order of colonial categories. On the surface, ethnophilosophy is robustly anti-colonial, yet it still accepts the basic categories in terms of which colonial culture defines other cultures and peoples. It attempts to revalorize them instead of seeking to criticize the grounds out of which colonial discourse emerges, such as the distinction between culture and civilization or the "traditional" and the modern.

Thus, it appears that ethnophilosophy has two contradictory aspects. It is a critical discourse that defines itself in opposition to colonialism. Yet it starts by accepting the colonial categories of "traditional" and "modern." The most significant difference between the original colonial categories and their use in ethnophilosophy is that instead of treating them as diametrically opposed, in the colonial fashion, ethnophilosophy tries to merge them by revalorizing indigenous values as worthy of attention and by then discovering the "traditional" in the modern. Thus, we argue that ethnophilosophers have attempted to create hybridized knowledge by arguing that characteristics of Western intellectual history can be found in African traditional thought, such as Kagame's argument that African thought utilizes Aristotelian and Thomistic elements.

In trying to identify the locus of philosophical discourse in the collective mind of Africans, ethnophilosophy also reproduces the ambiguities of the colonial culture, which is itself yet another hybridized formation. Once again ethnophilosophers also produce *sui generis* landscapes in which the indigenous and the imported simultaneously mix and separate, combining spaces and temporalities. Ethnophilosophy differs from colonialism in that it seeks to recover the traditional past as an instrument for reorganizing European cultural hierarchies. It also makes use of the Western notion that the universal is available to all people but is only found among some of them in order to reposition Africa within this hierarchical scheme.

The most notable characteristic of the ethnophilosophy school is its characterization of philosophy as a form of narrative—in fact, as a collective narrative. Ethnophilosophers treated African philosophy as a narrative whose content is revealed through various codes: through myths, through symbolic systems, and through religious and ordinary language. In this sense, African philosophy was represented as an innate form of indigenous expression. It could only be "recovered" and revalorized into a hybridized postcolonial present. The crucial point we are making is that the ethnophilosophers' ambiguous position indicates that they lack a location or identity in either the "traditional" or the colonial worlds. Even more important is the feature that ethnophilosophy shares with ethnographic practice—the assertion that meaning resides in collective practices. While true, this position is incomplete if it fails to show how change is produced by human agents.

Fundamentally, this ethnophilosophical literature is about the nature of change and the role of social and cultural criticism in formulating change, but it fails to specify the critic's role in African societies or in conceptual change. By emphasizing the collective nature of thought and the importance of the social leader who embodies this thought, ethnophilosophy reproduces colonial domination in a new form of authoritarianism. It gives voice to the leader but stifles the individual voices of the masses, who have not yet mastered this new cultural discourse. This attitude is all too familiar in the political ideology of some African states.

The idea that traditional knowledge is or was collectively produced and appropriated implies that the individual cannot be free and that religious, social, or cultural criticism is impossible. This in turn raises fundamental questions about personhood, agency, and the possibility of change (Giddens 1984; Jackson and Karp 1990). These questions lead us back to Popper's question about whether there is an intrinsic relationship between criticism and the growth of knowledge (Lakatos and Musgrave 1970). In ethnophilosophy there can be no growth of knowledge and change within the traditional context. In terms used by the Ghanaian philosopher Kwasi Wiredu (1980), traditional knowledge is doomed to self-damnation unless it is subjected to the therapeutic benefits of dialectical and critical reflection and re-evaluation. According to Wiredu, it is wrong to claim that people in the "traditional" settings lacked the inspiration for critical thinking about theoretical and practical matters of everyday life.

The idea that some aspects of African thought are collective and unchanging has been accepted even by the critics of ethnophilosophy. As Wiredu (1980) and Hountondji (1983) have proposed, the redemption of traditional knowledge systems will require precisely three elements of Western Enlightenment thought that ethnophilosophy appears to reject—individual agency, abstract theory, and openness (as suggested also by Crahay 1965; Horton 1967; and Pearce 1992). Wiredu (1980) sees hope for this redemption in the application of analytic practice (perhaps simplified to the level of pragmatic common sense) as people seek new methods and solutions to problems that old methods and solutions have failed to solve. Hountondji (1983) proposes that this redemption take as its foundation the Althusserian neo-Marxist notions which specify evolving relationships among power, ideology, and a constantly changing social world. Both Wiredu and Hountondji valorize the individual as the agent of change through social and cultural criticism. In other words, Wiredu and Hountondji defend the colonial and postcolonial as the new spatial and temporal realities that Africa should neither ignore nor pretend to be able to do without. Their views suggest that the superimposition of the colonial value system, its marginalization of African knowledge and techniques, but also Africans' preoccupation with the colonial, often give the false impression that Africans lack the appropriate skills for self-propagation.

This counter-critique valorizes critical rationalism over passive cultural nationalism and favors a selective approach to the valorization and uses of the past. Its point is that the past's influence on the present should be critically appraised in order to avoid both anachronism and a blind appropriation of everything from abroad. In effect, it offers an alternative representation of the (hybrid) postcolonial social and cultural condition.

Franz Crahay's neglected paper "Le Décollage conceptuel: conditions d'une philosophie bantoue" (1965) is among the most important critiques of ethnophilosophy. Crahay argues that the colonial distinction between the "traditional" and the "modern" is analogous to a distinction he draws between "constructing myth" and "practicing philosophy." This distinction is, in turn, similar to the metaphysical distinction between form and matter. Although form and matter make complementary contributions to the identity of things, they nonetheless remain conceptually distinct in nature and function. According to this perspective, philosophy, like form, is of the mind. It deals with those elements or categories of thought in which experience, as event and practice, is presented in and to our minds. It deals with ideas, those that are general and removed from the particulars from which they come. Though it is a human practice, philosophy is conceived as being essentially distinct from other human practices, such as folkways and traditional (or any) group behavioral patterns—i.e., customs, conventions, and mores.

But like matter, myths, traditions, customs, and mores are glued to the sensual. Their language remains "unabstracted" from the metaphors and experiences of everyday life; they are sociologically immediate and concrete. In this sense, then, Crahay argues that while philosophy frees itself from its conceptually limiting fixation with sociological conditions by "taking-off" to a free— i.e., universal—conceptual level, ethnophilosophy remains trapped in the (closed) confines of sociological structures and relativism, just like anthropology.

Robin Horton pushes this critique slightly farther. In his widely discussed essay (1967), he argues that religion does for traditional thought what abstract reasoning does for scientific knowledge. Trapped within the sociological immediacy of closed systems, he argues, religion—traditional religion—"explains" reality by appeal to personal and spiritual concepts. In this it differs from scientific explanation, which makes use of the abstract (non-human) concept of "particles" or forces. Myths, then, are to religious thought what philosophy is to science. And such pairs represent opposed and mutually exclusive models of knowledge. For Horton, the advent of philosophy in Africa must be predicated on a qualitative leap, that is, on an act of cultural transformation which begins with intellectual secularization and modernization.

AFRICAN PHILOSOPHY AS CULTURAL INQUIRY

African philosophy has criticized ethnophilosophy for simplistically transferring ethnographic data directly into philosophical terms and categories. But it has not altogether severed connections to the disciplinary field of anthropology. Since Crahay (1965), African philosophers have been arguing for a philosophical practice—explanations of reality or analysis of ideas in beliefs and languages—that focuses on and stems from the structure and experience of everyday life. This approach, according to Crahay, would not sidestep cultural experiences or avoid forms peculiar to Africans but rather would lift them out of narrative and description and make them "take off" (décoller) to become part of a second-order discourse. Hountondji (1983/1996) and Mudimbe (1988) take the same position as Crahay, but they place this position in the broader context of postcolonial criticism and competition among different systems of thought associated with both colonial and postcolonial realities.

Critical evaluations of the idea and uses of culture have been offered recently by several African philosophers, such as Kwame Appiah (1992), Paulin Hountondji (1992a, 1992b), Kwasi Wiredu (1980, 1996), and Kwame Gyekye (1987, 1997), among others. These critical accounts of cultural experiences and social forms in Africa open new avenues for comparative philosophical analyses; they also engage with ethnographic data derived from daily life in Africa. Mudimbe, for example, defines anthropology as part of the colonial archive but also as a means to escape the tyranny of the colonial (Mudimbe 1988: 198–200). In the wider context of working toward a definition of, to quote from Mudimbe, "an African gnosis and order of knowledge," recent works of African philosophers raise complex issues with multiple ramifications that cross the divide that customarily separates the work of the academy from life in society. In doing so, these works invoke what the Brazilian educator and theorist of education Paulo Freire wrote in his famous text *A Pedagogy of the Oppressed:* "We need to help people to read their reality and write their own history." Much like African intellectuals who write and work against colonial domination and who also theorize an ideal condition for the postcolonial subjects, the question of who it is that determines *how* the post-oppression reality is read and how its history will be written finds neither an obvious nor an easy answer, even if it be granted that the oppression is in the past. African philosophers ask themselves the following: Who is best placed to suggest which form of culture is best for African peoples? Who defines the needs of the people and the related epistemologies that best serve them? The debates on these issues obviously bear on the issue of the role of contemporary African intellectuals within the wider context of cultural discourse. In other words, they tend to question, to borrow from Wiredu, the legitimacy of their own "points of view." No doubt the discussions have produced a rich debate among African philosophers and other intellectuals today, and these discussions continue to define the key concerns of African intellectuals as they bring the social experiences of their peoples to the level of conceptual awareness. Although Wiredu and Hountondji share similar goals in their respective proposals for a critical recovery of indigenous knowledges, they propose different approaches for doing so. With his idea of knowledge as capital, Hountondji's strategy comes close to Freire's by means of their common reference to what Louis Althusser (1967: 116) calls the "reactivation of old elements" in the new (postcolonial) society. For both Hountondji and Freire, recognition of and dependence on the people's values form the basis for a cultural synthesis which restores subjectivity to locally situated individuals and groups. For both of them—Hountondji and Freire—overdetermination (of people's historical and cultural paths by external forces) must be replaced with self-determination in both theory and praxis. It is important to note, however, that the value of the debates lies not in who wins or whose representation of African cultures and their needs is more correct but rather in their shared sense that the existence of the debate is an index of the complex map of African cultural and historical awareness and inquiry.

Rather than dispute explicitly over the meaning or nature of the postcolonial field, the authors in this collection open up new discussions, some on persistent topics such as development, personhood, agency, and personal destiny. They connect these topics to the role of philosophy in the context of African people's definitions of their cultural or historical experiences and the complex social roles through which the practice of identity is defined and displayed. The essays presented here are not in agreement regarding these issues. Several of them utilize the idea of context as the crucial source for the construction of meaning or readings of reality. Wiredu, for example, continues on a universalist path, through which he challenges the political agenda addressed in postcolonial discourse, distrusting that "[t]he scope of the 'context' that [the others] mobilize in analysis is necessarily a closed frame, not an open-ended plenitude of meanings connecting . . . with other meanings and texts" (Mishra and Hodge 1994). Wiredu's fear is that postcolonial writing loses its chance to engage with the positive values of Western modernism, from which it can both learn and gain. He suspects that the nationalist brand of postcolonial critique is a dangerous manifestation of the exhaustion of Western rhetoric that expresses boredom with its own achievements rather than a movement devoted to developing pragmatically useful programs for development. This fear is legitimate but not new. Scholars' judgments have always differed with regard to the nature of historical events and with regard to the effects of crucial historical events on the evolution of historical thinking.[4] Likewise, African scholars have been divided over the question of the real value of colonialism. While some see it as a danger to which African societies and cultures were exposed, others, those who are more optimistic, while not endorsing colonialism, regard the period as disclosing the road to the future.

Few African intellectuals are known actually to have praised colonialism the way Herder, Hegel, or Droysen praised Napoleon.[5] Like the latter, however, some African philosophers accept the view that the precolonial/colonial divide separates qualitatively different historical periods, pointing out in particular the gains that have come as a result of the impact of Western education. They draw practical consequences from the cultural crisis that has been brought about by the effects of colonial rule on the traditional views and methods.[6] African intellectuals tend to agree that the years of colonial domination shook and changed the social structures, political institutions, self-perceptions, and thought and value systems of African peoples. But the period of critical restoration which defines the postcolonial practice for this perspective has inevitably led African intellectuals to look to history for an answer to the question, "What are the permanent forces on which society could be securely built?" Some African intellectuals are more optimistic than others. While not regarding colonialism as a period of splendor, they still view it as a turning point in the sense that it awakened the critical spirit necessary for sustaining cultural criticism and furthering social progress. This did not occur because the West is inherently better but because its culture illustrates the benefits of universal reason: that people can acquire a measure of wisdom by using their reason properly. They can be skeptical without hanging themselves on the gibbet of hyperskepticism. Though plagued by tempting and unanswerable questions,

11

people everywhere can safely assure themselves that "two and two make four," as claimed by Voltaire.[7] They can avoid gross error by using their senses prudently. With careful observation, discriminating argument, and constant testing, science can furnish a greater and more realistic understanding of the surrounding world.

The essays in this collection probe different sides, intellectual and social, of the attempts of African societies in the postcolonial condition to cope with the problems of social and cultural transformation. While some of them stress the restrictions which traditionalist thought sets upon any program of reform, others dramatize the ways that social actions can escape the limitations put upon them by their own cultural traditions. Together, they examine the extent to which the way we view our past affects our apprehension of the present. But not all the authors whose works are included in this collection view philosophy in this historical perspective, either in a direct manner or with the same intensity. Indeed, some of the authors included here belong to the analytic tradition in the sense that they share the view that the duty of philosophy is primarily analytic—as opposed to being either normative or phenomenological—entrusted with discovering the basic principles of knowledge through careful logical analysis. Yet this very vision is itself historically recent, both to the discipline of philosophy in general and in terms of its specific application to the understanding of concepts and ideas at work in the ordinary languages of different African peoples. Links to history, culture, and society are maintained through comparative analysis across linguistic and cultural worlds; this analysis places several non-Western philosophers in an interesting position as agents of cross-cultural communication and transfer of meanings. While this cross-cultural communication does not necessarily prove the existence of what Wiredu has elsewhere (1996) called "cultural universals," it certainly points to multiple horizons in the philosophical landscape. Furthermore, these links have helped to reveal two features of philosophy: the infinite number of questions and fundamental issues associated with philosophy as well as the proliferation and plurality of philosophy. We would say that there is a peaceful coexistence and mutual enrichment between the phenomenological francophone and the analytic anglophone perspectives in African philosophy, which provide the view, present here, that analytic philosophy, while being important and enlightening, is only one of many philosophical styles.

Finally, both this collection and the seminar on which it is based were predicated upon our belief that the first two phases of writing about African philosophy, accompanied by questions about the philosophical legitimacy of indigenous thought, have now run their course. We believe that there is now a need to move to a new theme—the nature of discourse in the multiple and multiplex settings that exist in contemporary Africa. Examining the relation-ships among discourse, knowledge, and everyday life is an inherently interdis-ciplinary endeavor, one that requires the skills and knowledge bases of both philosophers and anthropologists alike. This interdisciplinary mix enables us to study what people know and how they express their knowledge as well as how knowing and saying are contested or become authoritative. Anthropolo-gists bring to this problem skills in social analysis, experience with understand-ing the situational components of expression, and a long history of interpreting cultural idioms and symbolic forms. Philosophers bring to this set of issues skills related to understanding the logic and rhetorical basis of argumentation, an interest in analyzing and defining concepts exhibited in modes of thought and practices such as science and common sense, a concern for the implications of discourse, and sensitivity to a set of issues including personhood, ethics and morality, and metaphysics. The organization of this volume brings together and blends the approaches and materials of the two disciplines. Part I, "Power, Personhood, and Agency," combines studies of how concepts are used to achieve ends and to interpret experience with essays on the philosophical and logical status of assertions about the concept of the person in African societies. Part II, "Knowledge and Discourse," is about the pragmatics of verbal perfor-mance and the interpretation of how the changing life world is experienced. Finally, Part III, "African Discourses on Development," contains essays that are normative and prescriptive, essays that attempt to think through the ways in which development and modernity manifest themselves as fundamental concerns in the political and social worlds of African nations.

When we first conceived of this book, we called it *African Philosophy and Cul-tural Criticism,* but the writing of this introduction convinced us that we were placing the emphasis on the mental activities of the observer rather than on the collaboration between scholar and producer of culture, which the convergent histories of anthropology and African philosophy, as disciplines, seem to call for. After all, inquiry is a necessary prerequisite for critique. Almost all of the literature on African philosophy calls for sustained empirical investigation of African cultures and collaboration with the African producers of those cul-tures. This is a task that has just begun; the work of Hallen and Sodipo (1986/1997) and Odera's (1991) studies of "sage" philosophers are promising indica-tions that the discourse called "African philosophy" is entering a new phase. Perhaps the most important recent work is Kwame A. Appiah's widely debated *In My Father's House: Africa in the Philosophy of Culture,* a study that uses literary and philosophical tools to critique ideas about identity, ranging from Pan-Africanism and racial notions to the claims made by his father's matriclan in

Asante. This present book was conceived in a spirit that is akin to that of Appiah's work. We believe in African philosophy, more properly African philosophies, but we no longer feel able to live in a world defined in terms of departmental, ethnic, or national boundaries. The Academy, the Africanist profession, and Africans themselves are not well served by the residues of the nineteenth century that make such demands on our lives. African philosophy should refuse to recognize claims to ownership, whether these are based on race, ethnic identity, nationality, or academic discipline. African philosophy belongs not only to the Africans who "make" it and the scholars who inquire about it—it lives in all the parts of the world which Africans and scholars claim as their homes. Yet we are equally aware that the relationship between the makers and inquirers of African philosophy has been a delicate issue over the decades. We believe that although they are interrelated, the practice of the distanced inquirer is different from, yet also dependent upon, that of the engaged maker of cultural inquiry.

NOTES

1. The major works include Wiredu (1980, 1996), Hountondji (1983/1996), Mudimbe (1988), Appiah (1992), and Masolo (1994).

2. See Appiah (1992) on how philosophers can create works that envision a world with diverse and often competing ends and practices (in Mudimbe 1992).

3. Wiredu and Hountondji can be taken as representatives of the school of thought that considers "African philosophy as [a] propaedeutic for African culture," although their philosophical orientations are very different and although the remedies they propose have little in common. Hallen and Sodipo and Odera Oruka represent the "Africans as philosophers" approach, although here, too, the aims and methods of each are strikingly different. Odera Oruka relies entirely on interviews and adduces his own criteria for discriminating between the conventionally wise and those he calls "sage philosophers," while Hallen and Sodipo take naturally occurring discourses of Yoruba diviners as their units of analysis. Mediating between the two schools are Mudimbe and Appiah, whose views are again derived from different European philosophies. Mudimbe draws on Foucault to uncover an archeology of colonialism which organizes the thinking and writing about the Africa of Europeans and Africans alike, while Appiah takes a more analytic perspective and seeks to understand how certain assumptions form the basis for the construction of race and identity as it is applied to Africans and people of color. While both accept the critique of ethnophilosophy developed in the work of the other scholars, they would not exempt the work of African philosophy from the same critique, nor would they dispute that the dialectical skills of guild philosophers are also exhibited in "traditional" African cultures.

4. The diversity among German scholars in their interpretations of the effects of the French Revolution and of the Napoleonic invasions is a good case in point. While

some of these philosophers viewed those decades as a period of crisis that revealed the dangers to which their entire history became exposed, several German intellectuals— including, it is said, Hegel—gave this period of crisis a positive interpretation, viewing it simply as a radically different stage in their own history.

5. Ibid.

6. Despite the decisive influence that colonialism exerted on historical imagination, the reality of everyday African experiences and academic discourse clearly allows for another view—that colonialism's failure fully to destroy African social systems has revealed the capacity of the traditions to preserve bonds in social life, bonds that lie outside the new social institutions. This reality has also revealed history's capacity to build a bridge between the past and present, thus directing attention to factors that have shaped the similarities and differences among the various African societies.

7. *Dictionnaire* in *Oeuvres Complètes* XIX (p. 548) and XX (p. 120).

REFERENCES

Althusser, Louis. 1967. *Pour Marx.* Paris: Maspero.

Amin, Samir. 1989. *Eurocentrism.* New York: Monthly Review Press.

Arens, W., and Ivan Karp. 1989. "Introduction: The Creativity of Power." In *The Creativity of Power: Cosmology and Action in African Societies,* edited by W. Arens and Ivan Karp. Washington, D.C.: Smithsonian Institution Press.

Appiah, Kwame A. 1992. *In My Father's House: Africa in the Philosophy of Culture.* London: Oxford University Press.

Beck, Ulrich. 1994. *Reflexive Modernization: Politics, Tradition and Aesthetics in the Modern Social Order.* Stanford, Calif.: Stanford University Press.

Beidelman, Thomas O. 1993. "African Philosophy: Traditional Yoruba Philosophy and Contemporary African Realities—by Segun Gbadegesin." Book review in the *International Journal of African Historical Studies* 26: 690–91.

Césaire, Aimé. 1939. *Cahiers d'un retour au pays natal.* Reprint, Paris: Edition de Présence Africaine, 1956.

Chatterjee, Partha. 1993. *The Nation and Its Fragments: Colonial and Postcolonial Histories.* Princeton, N.J.: Princeton University Press.

———, ed. 1995. *Texts of Power.* Minneapolis: University of Minnesota Press.

Cooper, Frederick. 1994. "Conflict and Connection: Rethinking Colonial African History." *American Historical Review* 99, no. 5: 1516–45.

Crahay, F. 1965. "Le décollage conceptuel: conditions d'une philosophie bantoue." *Diogene* 52: 61–84.

D'Azevedo, W. 1962. "Uses of the Past in Gola Discourse." *Journal of African History* 3: 11–34.

Fortes, Meyer, and G. Dieterlen, eds. 1965. *African Systems of Thought.* Oxford: Oxford University Press.

Fouda, Basil. 1967. "La philosophie africaine de l'existence." Doctoral dissertation, Lille, Faculté des Lettres.

Freire, Paulo. 1970. *Pedagogy of the Oppressed.* New York: Continuum. New, revised 20th anniversary ed., 1999.

————. 1973. *Education for Critical Consciousness*. New York: Seabury Press.

Giddens, Anthony. 1984. *The Constitution of Society: Outline of the Theory of Structuration*. Berkeley: University of California Press.

Goody, Jack. 1986. *The Logic of Writing and the Organization of Society*. Cambridge: Cambridge University Press.

Griaule, M. 1965 (1948). *Conversations with Ogotemeli*. London: Oxford University Press.

Guha, Renegade. 1988. "The Prose of Counter-Insurgency." In *Selected Subaltern Studies*. Delhi: Oxford University Press, pp. 45–86.

Gyekye, Kwame. 1987. *An Essay on African Philosophical Thought: The Akan Conceptual Scheme*. Cambridge: Cambridge University Press. Revised 2nd ed., Philadelphia: Temple University Press, 1995.

————. 1997. *Tradition and Modernity: Philosophical Reflections on the African Experience*. New York and Oxford: Oxford University Press.

Hallen, Barry, and J. O. Sodipo. 1986. *Knowledge, Belief and Witchcraft: Analytic Experiments in African Philosophy*. London: Ethnographica. 2nd ed., Stanford: Stanford University Press, 1997.

Horton, Robin. 1967. "African Traditional Religion and Western Science." *Africa* 37, no. 1–2: 50–71, 155–87. Reprinted as "African Traditional Thought and Western Science," in B. R. Wilson, ed., *Rationality*. New York: Harper and Row, 1970, pp. 131–71.

Horton, Robin, and Ruth Finnegan, eds. 1973. *Modes of Thought*. London: Faber and Faber.

Hountondji, Paulin J. 1977. *Sur la "philosophie africaine": Critique de l'ethnophilosophie*. Paris: François Maspero.

————. 1983/1996. *African Philosophy: Myth and Reality*. Bloomington: Indiana University Press. 2nd ed., 1996.

————. 1992a. "Daily Life in Africa: Elements for a Critique." In V. Y. Mudimbe, ed., *The Surreptitious Speech: Présence Africaine and the Politics of Otherness 1947–1987*. Chicago: University of Chicago Press.

————. 1992b. "Recapturing." In V. Y. Mudimbe, ed., *The Surreptitious Speech: Présence Africaine and the Politics of Otherness 1947–1987*. Chicago: University of Chicago Press.

Jackson, Michael, and Ivan Karp, eds. 1990. *Personhood and Agency: The Experience of Self and Other in African Cultures*. Washington, D.C.: Smithsonian Institution Press.

Jewsiewicki, Bogumil. 1989. "African Historical Studies: Academic Knowledge as 'Usable Past' and Radical Scholarship." *African Studies Review* 32, no. 3: 1–76.

Kagame, Alexis. 1956. *La philosophie bantu-rwandaise de l'être*. Bruxelles: Académie Royale des Sciences Coloniales.

————. 1968–1969. "La Place de Dieu et de l'homme dans la religion des Bantu." *Cahiers des Religions Africaines* 4: 213–22; 5: 5–11.

————. 1971. "L'ethnophilosophie des Bantu." In Raymond Klibansky, ed., *La philosophie contemporaine*, vol. 4. Firenze: La Nuova Italia Editrice, pp. 589–612.

————. 1976. *La philosophie bantu comparée*. Paris: Présence Africaine.

Karp, Ivan. "Personhood and Development." Unpublished manuscript.

———. 1992. "Morality and Ethical Values According to the Iteso of Kenya." In Hermine G. De Sota, ed., *Culture and Contradiction: Dialectics of Wealth, Power and Symbol*. San Francisco: Mellen Research University Press, pp. 322–37.

Karp, Ivan, and C. S. Bird, eds. 1987. *Explorations in African Systems of Thought*. Washington, D.C.: Smithsonian Institution Press.

Karp, Ivan, and M. Kendall. 1982. "Reflexivity in Fieldwork." In P. Secord, ed., *Explaining Human Behavior*. Los Angeles: Sage Publications, pp. 249–73.

Karp, Ivan, and Dismas Masolo. 1998. "Ethnophilosophy: African." In *The Routledge Encyclopedia of Philosophy*, vol. 3. London: Routledge and Kegan Paul, pp. 446–50.

Kohn, Hans. 1967. *Prelude to Nation-States: The French and German Experience 1789–1815*. Princeton, N.J.: D. Van Nostrand.

Kratz, Corinne. 1993. "'We've Always Done It Like This . . . Except for a Few Details': 'Tradition' and 'Innovation' in Okiek Ceremonies." *Comparative Studies in Society and History* 35, no. 1: 30–65.

Lakatos, Imre, and Alan Musgrave, eds. 1970. *Criticism and the Growth of Knowledge*. Cambridge: Cambridge University Press.

Lufuluabo, Françoise Marie. 1962. *Vers une Théodicée bantoue*. Tournai: Casterman.

———. 1964a. *La Notion luba-bantoue de l'être*. Tournai: Casterman.

———. 1964b. *Orientation préchrétienne de la conception bantoue de l'être*. Léopoldville (Kinshasa): Centre d'Etudes Pastorales.

———. 1966. *Perspective théologique bantoue et théologie scholastique*. Malines, Belgium.

Masolo, D. A. 1987. "Alexis Kagame and African Socio-Linguistics." In Guttorm Floistad, ed., *Contemporary Philosophy: A New Survey*, vol. 5: *African Philosophy*. Dordrecht: Martinus Nijhoff, pp. 181–205.

———. 1994. *African Philosophy in Search of Identity*. Bloomington and Indianapolis: Indiana University Press.

———. 1995. *New Perspectives in African Philosophy*. Rome: Editrice Pontificia Università Gregoriana.

Mbembe, Achille. 1992. "Provisional Notes on the Postcolony: Obscenity and the Rites of Postcolonial Power." *Africa* 62, no. 1: 3–37.

Mbiti, John Samuel. 1969. *African Religions and Philosophy*. London: Heinemann.

Miller, Joseph C., ed. 1980. *The African Past Speaks: Essays on Oral Tradition and History*. Folkestone, United Kingdom: Dawson.

Mishra, Vijay, and Bob Hodge. 1994. "What Is Post(-)Colonialism?" In Patrick Williams and Laura Chrisman, eds., *Colonial Discourse and Post-Colonial Theory: A Reader*. New York: Columbia University Press.

Mudimbe, V. Y. 1988. *The Invention of Africa: Gnosis, Philosophy, and the Order of Knowledge*. Bloomington and Indianapolis: Indiana University Press.

———. 1991. *Parables and Fables: Exegesis, Textuality, and Politics in Central Africa*. Madison: University of Wisconsin Press.

———, ed. 1992. *The Surreptitious Speech: Présence Africaine and the Politics of Otherness 1947–1987*. Chicago: University of Chicago Press.

———. 1994. *The Idea of Africa*. Bloomington and Indianapolis: Indiana University Press.

———. 1995. *Les corps glorieux des mots et des êtres: Esquisse d'un jardin africain à la bénédictine*. Montreal: Humanitas, and Paris: Présence Africaine.

Mulago, Vincent. 1955. "L'Union vitale bantu chez les Bashi, les Banyarwanda, et les Barundi face à l'unité vitale ecclesiale." Doctoral dissertation, Rome, Propaganda Fide.

———. 1965. *Un visage africaine de christianisme.* Paris: Présence Africaine.

———. 1973. *La religion traditionelle des Bantu et leur vision du monde.* Kinshasa: Presses Universitaires du Zaïre.

Nandy, A. 1995. "History's Forgotten Doubles." *History and Theory* 34, no. 2: 44–66.

Nyerere, Julius K. 1968a. *Ujamaa: The Basis of African Socialism.* Dar es Salaam: Oxford University Press.

———. 1968b. *Ujamaa: Essays on Socialism.* Dar es Salaam: Oxford University Press.

Obenga, Theophile. 1995. *A Lost Tradition: African Philosophy in World History.* Philadelphia: The Source Editions.

Odera Oruka, Henry. 1983. "Sagacity in African Philosophy." *International Philosophical Quarterly* 23, no.4: 383–93.

———. 1991. *Sage Philosophy.* Nairobi: ACTS.

Pearce, Carole. 1992. "African Philosophy and the Sociological Thesis." *Philosophy of the Social Sciences* 22, no. 4: 440–60.

Senghor, L. S. 1948. *Anthologie de la nouvelle poésie nègre et malgache de langue française.* Paris: Presses Universitaires de France.

———. 1964. *Liberté 1: Négritude et humanisme.* Paris: Seuil.

Tempels, Placide. 1959. *Bantu Philosophy.* Paris: Présence Africaine.

Vansina, J., Raymond Mauny, and L. V. Thomas, eds. 1964. *The Historian in Tropical Africa.* London: Oxford University Press for the International African Institute.

Wiredu, Kwasi. 1980. *Philosophy and an African Culture.* Cambridge: Cambridge University Press.

———. 1996. *Cultural Universals and Particulars: An African Perspective.* Bloomington: Indiana University Press.

Wiredu, Kwasi, and Kwame Gyekye, eds. 1992. *Person and Community: Ghanaian Philosophical Studies,* vol. 1. Washington, D.C.: The Council for Research in Values and Philosophy.

PART I.
   POWER, PERSONHOOD, AND AGENCY

Introduction to Part I

Power, Personhood, and Agency

Both anthropology and philosophy share questions about how the concept of the person is defined and used in social interaction. These disciplines take rather different approaches to the answers they provide. Both are concerned with distinguishing between the continuity over time that enables agents to characterize an individual as a "person" and with the epistemological problem posed by the differences between social attribution and self knowledge. In the essays in this section, the anthropologists Parkin and Shaw as well as the philosopher Kaphagawani are concerned with defining and examining ideas about power, personhood, and agency, about how human beings in interaction with one another produce effects on the world. In general, anthropological research on these topics tends to be cross-cultural or comparative and sociological in outlook, while the philosophical literature is more definitional and analytic. Both Shaw and Parkin argue, for example, that notions of self are functions of social histories and explain how different societies cope with or adapt to their different social environments. Shaw uses a meticulous examination of Temne idioms of secrecy to critique the notion that there are essential differences between societies which can be drawn along the divides separating such dichotomies as individual versus society; self versus person; free versus constrained; and active versus passive, which have been used as models for understanding African notions of personhood and agency and for contrasting them with their Western opposites.

Through her gender-based examination of Temne interpersonal dynamics and discourses of personhood and self, Shaw argues that relational understandings of personhood attributed to African societies do not necessarily exclude the possibility that persons act as knowing "selves" in their capacity as social and political beings, that they engage in reflexive and critical monitoring of action and interaction. The latter understanding of personhood perhaps predates but runs close to the Enlightenment idea of the autonomous individual self as the seat of epistemological and moral agency, the subject of political and legal rights and freedoms (Mauss 1939; Carrithers et al. 1985; Fortes 1987). With time, these ideas were brought into radical contrast with what were presumed to be collective and communal senses of identity that were taken to be characteristic of rural and/or "primitive" folk. Thus, communalism came to signify backwardness, a sort of constraint on the individual sources and forces of progress.

Arguing against the received wisdom about folk societies Shaw, like Lienhardt and Fortes before her, demonstrates that writings on African personhood have overemphasized the communal model, that it is not true that the two variable understandings of self mutually exclude each other according to the society types in which they operate. Rather—and she refers to Carrithers et al. (1985: 236)—"the social circumstances of society in which a certain *moi* conception comes into being influence the form which the *moi* conception might take." Thus, the conception of self among the Temne of Sierra Leone clearly reflects their techniques of dealing with a social world rendered untrustworthy by its own history. The secrecy that surrounds the self and the Temne idiom "tok af, lef af" reflects a cultural alertness to the practice of social-economic predation during the slave trade and to the need to protect the self by partially concealing, disguising, and making it invisible in the face of the trappings of the public and historical arena, which came to be defined principally in terms of the fears and insecurity which it unleashed on its inhabitants.

Like Shaw, Parkin also argues that the separation and opposition of atomistic and relational conceptions of self so central to Western academic discourse do not always hold as contrasts in non-Western systems of thought. Thus, the coastal Swahili people of Kenya and Zanzibar hold a view of autonomous human agents that is not incompatible with their Islamic belief in divinely ordained human destiny. While they assert that an individual's human character is materially fixed and unalterable by virtue of their distinctive humorous balance as Muslims, they also believe that personal fate is shaped by the way a person and his environment respond and relate materially, morally, and religiously to this fixity of character. Parkin argues that in the idioms of the Swahili themselves, there seems to be no conflict between the demands of Islam and the healing techniques of Arabic- and Galenic-influenced medical science. They combine beliefs in the fixity of the mix of primary humors in the makeup of people's bodies and selves, in their propensity toward certain character traits and vulnerability to particular ailments, as well as in the healer's ability to change these.

The philosophical essay in this section (Kaphagawani) is an exercise in African metaphysics. Like Shaw and Parkin, Kaphagawani also argues against the reduction of African notions of self and personhood into the dual categories of communal and individualistic. All three authors criticize existing descriptions of the metaphysical components of African notions of personhood as being only partially correct due to misconceptions, poor translations, or the socio-geographic limitations of their ethnographic fields of reference. The outcome is the view that African notions of self and personhood are much more complex than the image of them provided in dualistic models that sharply discriminate between "West" and "non-West." Kaphagawani points out, for example, that the ideas about African concepts of personhood produced by Tempels are problematic precisely because Tempels tried to turn them into a sharp contrast to the Cartesian viewpoint. The result was something like the empiricists' indeterminate yet undeniable idea of personal identity, something like "a logical construction out of psychic events."

In Kaphagawani's view, Tempels's theory of the Bantu concept of force reproduces a fundamental ambiguity in the philosophical literature on personhood—viz., that the person is divided between the mind, defined as a collection of ideas, and a material body. According to Kaphagawani, Tempels did not realize that by framing this problem in this mode, he made it a linguistic issue more than a metaphysical problem. Kaphagawani's concluding view is that the analyses of African conceptions of personhood, self, or personal identity, which he deals with, have not done full justice to the full range of African discourses and diverse expressions on these issues.

In a sense, we have come full circle. The essays in this section of the volume recapitulate the arguments made against ethnophilosophy by African philosophers (Karp and Masolo, 1998). The same conceptual scheme that locates African philosophy as a collective enterprise located in a subject lacking the capacity for critical self reflection also eliminates the productive tension between two primary aspects of the self, the person and the individual (Lienhardt 1985; Riesman 1986; Fortes 1987; Jackson and Karp 1990; Karp 1997). The studies of personhood and its associations with power and agency contained in this volume demonstrate that understanding African cases requires careful description of contexts for social action; attention to such aspects of cosmology as ideas about nature, human nature, and society; and examination of the ends of actions themselves.

REFERENCES

Carrithers, Michael, Steven Collins, and Steven Lukes, eds. 1985. *The Category of the Person: Anthropology, Philosophy, History.* Cambridge: Cambridge University Press.
Fortes, Meyer. 1987. *Religion, Morality and the Person.* Cambridge: Cambridge University Press.
Jackson, Michael, and Ivan Karp, eds. 1990. *Personhood and Agency: The Experience of Self and Other in African Cultures.* Washington, D.C.: Smithsonian Institution Press.
Karp, Ivan. 1997. "Personhood, Concepts of." In John Middleton, ed., *Encyclopedia of Africa.* New York and London: Macmillan, pp. 342–46.

Karp, Ivan, and Dismas Masolo. 1998. "Ethnophilosophy: African." In *The Routledge Encyclopedia of Philosophy*, vol. 3. London: Routledge and Kegan Paul, pp. 446–450.

Lienhardt, G. 1985. "Self: Public and Private—Some African Representations." In M. Carrithers, S. Collins, and S. Lukes, eds., *The Category of the Person: Anthropology, Philosophy, History*. Cambridge: Cambridge University Press, pp. 141–55.

Mauss, M. 1939. "Une Catégorie de l'esprit Humaine: la Notion de la Personne, Celle de Moi." *Journal of the Royal Anthropological Institute* 68: 263–82.

Riesman, P. 1986. "The Person and the Life Cycle in African Social Life and Thought." *African Studies Review* 29, no. 2: 71–198.

1. "Tok Af, Lef Af": A Political Economy of Temne Techniques of Secrecy and Self

Rosalind Shaw

Studies of person and self in Africa have long been used as foils for Western concepts of person and self. In one of the best-known instances, Placide Tempels's *Bantu Philosophy* (1959), Western concepts of individuality are placed in opposition to Bantu concepts of the person as constituted genealogically:

> For the Bantu, man never appears in fact as an isolated individual, as an independent entity. Every man, every individual, forms a link in a chain of vital forces, a living link, active and passive, joined from above to the ascending line of his ancestry and sustaining below the line of his descendants. (1959: 108)

In studies such as Tempels's, characterizations of personhood have often drawn upon (largely implicit) ideas of agency. As a "link in a chain of vital forces," for

Fieldwork in Sierra Leone (in Bombali and Tonkolili Districts and in the cities of Freetown and Koidu) was carried out for fifteen months in 1977–78, for one month in 1981, for two months in 1989, and for ten weeks in 1992. I gratefully acknowledge financial support from the (then) Social Science Research Council in the United Kingdom, the Emslie Horniman Anthropological Research Fund, the University of London's Central Research Fund, the Carnegie Trust for the Universities of Scotland, the University of Edinburgh's Centre for African Studies, Tufts University, and the Wenner Gren Foundation for Anthropological Research. I would especially like to thank John Brooke, James Ennis, C. Magbaily Fyle, Paul Joseph, Paul Richards, and A. R. Vasavi for their comments on an earlier draft of this essay; the conveners and participants of the International African Institute/African Academy of Sciences' seminar on African Philosophy and Critical Inquiry in Nairobi in April 1993, at which an earlier draft of this essay was discussed; and both the Harvard University Women's Studies in Religion Program and the Bunting Institute of Radcliffe College for funding my travel to this seminar.

example, every person is both "active and passive," partially subsumed by the agency of the wider genealogical entity—"the chain"—of which he or she is a part. By contrast, it is implied that the individual as an "independent entity" has an unambiguous capacity to act as an autonomous agent. Tempels's opposition thus draws a contrast between types of agency as well as types of identity.

But where do the concepts in scholars' comparisons of "Western" and "non-Western" models of personhood come from? Tempels's famous passage above is a case in point. His contrast between Bantu and Western personhood has its precursor in (and includes almost the same language as) Tocqueville's critique of the weakening of social bonds under American individualism and democracy. According to Lukes, Tocqueville argued that

> In contrast to aristocratic society, in which men were "linked closely to something beyond them and are often disposed to forget themselves" and which "formed of all the citizens a long chain reaching from the peasant to the king," democracy "breaks the chain and sets each link apart" ... Democracy, Tocqueville concluded, "not only makes each man forget his forefathers, but it conceals from him his descendants and separates him from his contemporaries." (Lukes 1973: 13)

What this example makes clear is how historical ideas of "the individual" in Europe and North America—often constructed in opposition to prior understandings of personhood—have been drawn upon in comparisons between Africa and the West. Those who make such comparisons, however, usually seek to problematize African concepts while leaving unexamined the social and historical contexts in which Western concepts of persons and their agency have been constituted. Let me begin, then, by briefly outlining the notion of "the individual."

WESTERN CONSTRUCTIONS OF "INDIVIDUALS"

An understanding of agency as the capacity for autonomous individual action based upon discursively conscious "interior" intentions has informed dominant ideas of self and person in North America and England for several centuries.[1] Concepts of the individual and of personal agency have also been central to ideas about different kinds of society, and to discourses about the state in particular, in much of Western thought.[2] Such discourses are, of course, very diverse,[3] and I will only be able to sketch, very briefly, certain dominant dispositions among them.

In one strand of thought (prominent, for example, in nineteenth-century France), a "collectivist" definition of nation is envisaged that entails "the visionary elevation of the collectivity and collective purposes over the individual and individual purposes" (Carrithers 1985: 238; see also Lukes 1973: 3–16). Yet the very concept of this collectivity—envisioned as a new industrial social order that has broken with the feudal order of the past (Lukes 1973: 6)—is built upon the concept of the "individuals" who make it up. This concept forms a contrast with that of the "chain" of genealogical identity envisaged by both Tocqueville and Tempels, in which both person and community are defined relationally, in terms of a whole field of social relationships and roles (and see, for example, Kondo 1990: 26–43, on Japanese social personhood). In the idea of the nation as collectivity, individuals are instead defined in terms of inherent personal attributes, in keeping with another tendency in Western social thought to produce "attribute-based" models of personhood instead of "relational" models.

Durkheim and his colleagues drew heavily on this French strand in stressing social conceptions of the individual (Lukes 1973: 78; also pp. 111 and 120). According to Carrithers,

> A second assumption [of Durkheim's] is that modern society is moving toward a desirable recognition of all human beings' nature as human individuals . . . Therefore we are moving toward a new kind of sacredness, the sacredness of the human individual. (1985: 239; see also Lukes 1973: 12)

Thus, in Durkheim's vision of an ideal society, "society" and "the individual" are mutually constituted.

When Mauss wrote his famous essay on the person, "A Category of the Human Mind: The Notion of Person; The Notion of Self" (1985 [orig. 1938]), he followed his teacher, Durkheim, in stressing the social origins of the person and the self. But he also adhered to Durkheim's belief in the sacredness of the human individual as well as to his faith in progress (Carrithers 1985: 238–40), and therefore, he placed interior, individual selfhood on a higher developmental level than relational personhood. "A Category of the Human Mind: The Notion of Person; The Notion of Self" begins at one extreme with an account of Pueblo personhood, in which each clan consists of a limited number of "characters" (*personnages*), and each clan member's role "is really to act out, each insofar as it concerns him, the prefigured totality of the life of the clan" (Mauss 1985: 5). It is in the life of the clan, accordingly, that agency is located (Hollis 1985: 219). Mauss ends the essay at the other extreme with his characterization of the (modern Western) self (*moi*) as "the basic category of consciousness" and as "an echo of the Declaration of the Rights of Man" (Mauss 1985: 22). Agency is now located in "the self," on whom "all science and all action" are founded (ibid.). Mauss, then, traces an evolutionary trajectory from *personne* to *moi*, from a relational model of personhood as the exterior acting out of social roles to an "inherent attribute"–based selfhood in terms of an interior psychological essence. This trajectory, moreover, is viewed as a movement from socially "constrained" agency to political "freedom." And "freedom," finally, is understood in terms of "the Rights of Man"—rights that are themselves largely defined in terms of the absence of social constraints upon individual agency. A shift from "person" (*personne*) to "self" (*moi*) thus accompanies an emerging dichotomy between "society" and "individual" and the evolution of human beings as autonomous agents; Mauss's vision of modernity and liberty, moreover, excludes by definition relational understandings of personhood.

In contrast to the "collectivist" ideas of the individual, upon which Durkheim and Mauss drew, a more "atomist" strand of thought, derived from philosophers such as Hume and Hobbes, developed into nineteenth-century liberal and utilitarian ideas. This strand, in which human beings are defined as self-interested, "rational" calculators of individual advantage, has, according to Hollis (1985: 225), the strongest claim to be the precursor of modern individualism. This strand of thought has long been dominant in Britain and—especially—in the United States, where "'individualism' primarily came to celebrate capitalism and liberal democracy" and "became a symbolic catchword of immense ideological significance" (Lukes 1973: 26). Common to both collectivist and atomist strands of North Atlantic discourses about personhood, however, has been the mutually defining character of "the individual" and the nation-state. In atomist strands of thought prominent in the United States and Britain, this relationship has often been underscored by inversions in agency, in which it is viewed as desirable for agency to be located in "the individual" rather than in political structures —as in the Jeffersonian view that "that government is best that governs least."

One of the most important social and political contexts in which such discourses developed, in fact, was Jefferson's home, colonial Virginia (also the home of George Washington), among white tobacco planters in an environment of fiercely individualist and capitalist expansion. The relatively autonomous agency of these planters was based upon the dependent labor of others, initially that of indentured English servants and subsequently that of African slaves. Economic privatism, which had been established as the colony's central value by the Virginia Company (Breen 1980: 109), was translated not only into competitive individualism but also into weak political authority (Breen 1980: 112–15; Greene 1988: 26–27): "Virginia planters," observes one historian, "seem to have regarded government orders as a threat to their independence, almost as a personal affront" (Breen 1980: 115). Between 1680 and 1720, white indentured servants were replaced by African slaves, who were seen as a better long-term resource. This process of substitution of slavery for servitude solved a problem entailed by indentured labor, that of a growing population of disaffected white freedmen demanding land that was in increasingly short supply. One social consequence of this substitution was the development of white solidarity between the gentry and the small planters, a solidarity by which considerable differences in class and property were masked. It was, ironically, through the shift to African slave labor that white Virginian discourses of individualism developed into the rhetoric of the "equality" and "freedom" of individuals that became the hallmark of American republicanism. "Racism," argues Morgan, "became an essential, if unacknowledged, ingredient of the republican ideology that enabled Virginians to lead the nation" (1975: 386).

In both the United States and Britain today, the language of "freedom of speech," "freedom of choice," "individual opportunity," "the individual right to privacy," etc., is central to nationalist self-constructions as optimal societies for "individuals"—and "individuals" are thereby defined in terms of their capacity for autonomous action. Whereas attribute-based models of individuals and selves have been made integral to North Atlantic nationalist visions of modernity, relational models of personhood have often been part of dominant Western representations of "backwardness" and recur in images of "rural idiocy" and of "the primitive." The rhetoric of "the individual" thus proceeds based on the use of implicit contrasts with relational systems of personhood, in which such formulations as "the shackles of tradition," "unchanging social custom," "tribalism," "determinism," "fatalism," etc., construct negative, mirror-image descriptions of the kinds of societies in which both individuality and personal agency are supposedly erased.[4]

AFRICAN ALTERNATIVES TO THE MAUSSIAN *MOI*

The dichotomies examined above—individual/society; *moi/personne;* free/constrained; active/passive—have typically formed the premises on which studies of African concepts of self and personhood have been based. (John Mbiti's aphorism, "I am, because we are; and since we are therefore I am" [1992 (1969): 109], explicitly formulated in opposition to Descartes' "I think, therefore I am," is another well-known example [see Kaphagawani's critique in this volume].) Assumptions about African personhood as collective are part of an "invention of Africa" which derives primarily from Western discourses about historical transformations in Europe and North America.

More recently, however, a shift has occurred toward studies of African selfhood and individual identity—of the *moi* rather than the *personne*. Tempels's *Bantu Philosophy,* in fact, represents an early exploration of this focus on selfhood as well as on communalism: at one and the same time he stresses the submergence of the "individual" self within a broader social category or corporation and he draws attention to the idea of a hidden, "interior" self, which is indicated by an "interior name." Thus, immediately after the passage quoted at the beginning of this chapter, he writes:

> It may be said that among the Bantu the individual is necessarily an individual within the clan. This relationship is not regarded as simply juridical dependence, nor one of parenthood. It should be understood in the sense of real ontological dependence. In this order of ideas we may say that the "interior name" is the indicator of individuality within the clan. (Tempels 1959: 108)

This "interior" self is the subject, much later, of Lienhardt's argument that the "communal" model has been overstressed in writings on African personhood:

> [M]uch of what has been written about African ideas of self, rightly putting to the fore the importance of a person's group and status—the public self— for defining what and who he or she is, can deflect attention from [an] African concern . . . with individuals. . . . [This concern involves] the recognition of the importance of an inner, mysterious *individual* identity, comparable to what is meant by speaking in English of "what goes on inside" a person. (1985: 143, 145)

Similarly, Jacobson-Widding (1990) describes the shadow, for peoples of the lower Congo, as embodying an image of the self as elusive, secret, and fluid, distinct from jural, "collective" concepts of personhood.

But like the shadow (and *contra* Tempels), this hidden self is not necessarily seen as interior. Earlier, in his major monograph on Dinka religion, Lienhardt argued that the concept of a reified inner entity such as "the mind" is foreign to the Dinka.[5] Building on Lienhardt's insight, Jackson (1989) makes the telling observation that whereas in the West, the self is ordinarily conceived of as internal, in many West African contexts it tends to be closely identified with that which is *external:* it is often associated with the undomesticated danger and fertility of the bush and is opposed to the civilizing space of the town. For example, typically the individuating achievements of the questing hero are only possible in the wilderness—away from the established conventions of the social community (Jackson 1989: 40). The sources of illness and insanity, too, are located not "inside" but rather are described in terms of invasion from the bush. "The unconscious," accordingly, "is not so much a region of the mind as a region in space, the inscrutable realm of night and of the wilderness filled with bush spirits, witches, sorcerers, and enemies" (Jackson 1989: 45).

A similar connection between "external" forces and individuation is made in Horton's comparison of four West African societies: Tallensi, Asante, Yoruba, and Kalabari (1983). Horton finds "forces of nature" such as the bush and the river to be involved in the constitution of selfhood and individual accomplishment among the latter three peoples, for whom status is acquired partly through achievement. By contrast, the "forces of nature" are not regarded as a positive source of personal accomplishment and identity among the Tallensi because, Horton argues, this is a strongly ascription-based society which does not stress individuating achievement. In fact, we can extend Horton's argument here, since agents of the "outside" *are,* in fact, central to the one category of people whose individuation is socially encouraged: senior Tale men. The external entities that contribute to the individuation of senior men are not "forces of the wild," however, but rather are forces of the outer reaches of what Horton characterizes as "forces of society": matrilateral kin and ancestors. Although, as we know from Fortes (1949), membership of the agnatic lineage provides the basis for formal, legal personhood, matrilateral kinship enables senior men to extend a widely cast net of less formal contacts outside the confines of the lineage. This net of kin is unique to each senior man and thereby enables him to develop influence as an "individual." In addition, a mature Tale man who consults a diviner because of sickness or misfortune may be told that he has been sent the affliction by a personal configuration of cognatic—and mostly matrilateral—ancestors, called the *bakologo* ancestors. Once he acknowledges them by establishing a shrine in his compound, they will help him to develop individual achievements; for example, he might become a diviner himself (Fortes 1949, ch. 11; Horton 1983).

These tropes of the external, the wild, and the hidden trace understandings of self that might have more in common with the *moi* than the *personne,* as they define selfhood outside of and apart from formal social roles. But it would be more true to say that they confound this dichotomy altogether since, unlike the Maussian *moi,* they are relational. They involve not only "external" kinship links, as among the Tallensi, but also relationships between humans and spirits of the bush or river, which, although outside *human* society, are nonetheless still conceptualized as social relationships (Jackson 1982: 17). There is a danger, then, that merely shifting the emphasis in studies of African personhood from *personne* to *moi* may do no more than replace one spurious comparative term for another, since this Western dichotomy is a socially constituted, historically situated construct that does not necessarily translate into understandings of personhood as they exist elsewhere (see Kondo 1990: 34). This is certainly not to say that socially constructed concepts closely approximating "selves" and "individuals" are restricted to contexts of Western individual*ism* (e.g., Carrithers 1985). It is simply to bring us back, once again, to problems of comparison and to the importance of understanding differences in the social and historical construction of such concepts.

THE SLAVE TRADE AND POLITICAL ECONOMIES OF SELF

What social histories, then, might we find associated with West African concepts of a hidden self or of the individuating qualities of a relationship with a bush or river spirit? This question directs us to a second important reason for drawing connections between Western and African models of self and personhood: the historical relationship between them.

We have seen that in the United States, the United Kingdom, and France, the construction of "individuals" has been linked to the construction of national identities. It has also, of course, been linked to an unprecedented capitalist expansion, in which individuating concepts such as "self-improvement" underscored the virtues of hard work, progress, and enterprise upon which capitalism depended.[6] Since this era of capitalist penetration was largely built upon the Atlantic slave trade, its political economy connected the (re)construction of Western individualism at this time with a system in which the personhood of Africans was erased. Olaudah Equiano's *Interesting Narrative* (1969 [orig. 1789]), the celebrated eighteenth-century autobiography of a freed Igbo slave, provides a graphic personal account of this erasure. As well as the violation and destruction of the person through acts of murder, rape, flogging, and other forms of violence (e.g., 1969, I: 73–74, 214, 224), slavers split up families and herded people together regardless of distinctions in age, gender, status, and language—thereby obliterating African relational foundations of personhood (e.g., 1969, I: 85–91). They then reclassified captives as objects and commodities by weighing, measuring, and exchanging them for sums of money (e.g., 1969, I: 93). Those subjected to these forms of social death reconstituted themselves as subjects, however, by building new, creolized foundations of personhood. Equiano, for example, combined Igbo and Western techniques of self-construction in trying to make those with power over him into "fathers" or "brothers" (e.g., 1969, I: 139, 172–73; II: 33) and in embracing a form of Protestant Christianity that drew upon Igbo understandings of personal destiny (see Edwards and Shaw 1989).

The Atlantic slave trade had different consequences for constructions of personhood for those who remained on the African side of the Atlantic, living in communities from which slaves were liable to be taken. I shall try to outline some of these consequences for Temne-speaking communities in northwestern Sierra Leone, in which the hidden and the secret are important in many forms of social practice—including the constitution and defense of the self.

A HABITUS OF WAR

For more than four hundred years of its history, Sierra Leone and the upper Guinea coast of which it is a part were a major site for the slave trade and its associated wars. The Portuguese, who first arrived at the part of the coast they named "Serra Leoa" in the mid-fifteenth century, began exploiting the area for slaves immediately (Rodney 1970: 95). As in other parts of Africa, their captives were mostly acquired through wars: the sale of captives to slavers was initially a by-product of but subsequently a motive for conflicts and raids. In the second half of the sixteenth century, for instance, the Portuguese described what they saw as an "invasion" (which historians have subsequently interpreted as a gradual imposition of domination) of the area by a Mande-speaking group they called the "Mane." During this period the slave trade flourished, the Mane eventually regarding the sale of slaves to the Portuguese as an end in itself (Rodney 1970: 102–103). Some Temne groups acquiesced and took their place in a centralized political structure under Mane rulers; in so doing, they acquired skills in Mande techniques of warfare, iron working, and government (Rodney 1970: 46–56). Other communities resisted such incorporation through concealment and guerilla warfare. Manuel Alvares, a Jesuit missionary in Sierra Leone in the early seventeenth century, wrote of some who had not been discovered by the Mane: "The fearful respect these savages have for the conquering (Manes) has made them so careful and cunning that, in order to conceal the path to their secret villages, they walk it backwards" (Alvares 1990 [trans. Hair, c. 1615], II, Ch. 2: 2). His account of resistance among the neighboring Limba describes other techniques of concealment: "They are astute and clever, and inclined to be warlike, hence their villages have underground places, in which they live with all the necessities of life when besieged. This is how they have preserved their independence (and avoided conquest by) the Mane" (II, Ch. 2: 3).

During the seventeenth century, the participation of other Western European powers in the slave trade grew, and during the eighteenth century, dominance shifted to English private traders (Rodney 1970: 248). This was an era of unprecedented slaving that reached a peak in the middle of the eighteenth century, when between four and six thousand slaves were dispatched from Sierra Leone annually (Rodney 1970: 250–51). These figures bespeak an environment of precariousness among communities in the region, in which practices of concealment and protection had become integral to everyday life:

"They never care to walk even a mile from home without firearms," wrote John Atkins in 1721. This testimony clearly points to a state of insecurity bordering on anarchy. Another graphic illustration of this was to be seen in

the dislocation of villages in Sierra Leone, and their re-siting in almost inaccessible hideouts, away from the main waterways and the slave-raiding chiefs.
(Rodney 1970: 259)

In 1807, the British had made the Atlantic slave trade illegal for all British
subjects and had turned their attention to what they termed "legitimate trade"
in produce such as groundnuts, timber, and palm products. However, because
this "legitimate" trade depended on slave labor within the interior for production and transportation of the goods the British wanted, the latter allowed
slavery to continue in the hinterland for more than a century, until 1928
(Lenga-Kroma 1978: 76–78; 153ff). Slave-raiding therefore intensified, and
the external slave trade continued, slaves being taken to French Guinea to the
north and to Sherbro and Gallinas to the south (ibid.). In addition, new "trade
wars" were fought over access to the river depots which were crucial for the
"legitimate trade." As Lenga-Kroma describes for southern Temneland:

> The result of this situation was the occurrence of frequent wars, and nine-
> teenth century Southern Temne country was thus characterized by profes-
> sionalism in warfare, making both life and property insecure throughout the
> first three quarters of the century. (1978: 83)

People traveled in armed bands, and stockaded towns were more necessary
than ever (Lenga-Kroma 1978: 156).

The British colonial government in Freetown saw these conflicts as "tribal
wars," failing to see their commercial rather than "tribal" origins in the "legitimate trade" that they themselves had promoted (Lenga-Kroma 1978: 157). In
order to acquire a share of this interior trade, the Colonial government pro-
claimed the establishment of a British Protectorate over the hinterland of Sierra Leone in 1896. They did so before consultation with its chiefs, however,
who found that their authority had been considerably eroded (Lenga-Kroma
1978: 178–202). In 1898 there followed a rising, called the "Hut Tax War"
(due to its precipitation by the government's attempts to collect a house tax),
which was led in Temneland by the warrior-chief Bai Bureh (Denzer 1971).
The imposition of the Protectorate was thus the occasion for further warfare
generated by European economic interests. There followed ninety years of
"peace" under colonial rule and independence before the outbreak in 1991 of
the rebel war along Sierra Leone's border with Liberia.[7]

Historians have (for the most part) been careful not to sensationalize the
history of warfare in the region, mindful of racist colonial stereotypes that attributed this history to the "warlike nature" of the "natives" (Abraham 1975:
121–23). The Temne, in fact, did not suffer as much as many other groups

during the era of the slave trade, as they had the role of middlemen. In the eighteenth century, for instance,

> The wars that loom so large in Temne traditions were probably not as destructive as often made out . . . The intention was to incapacitate, not to kill, and success in battle was reckoned on the number of captives and the amount of plunder . . . As well entrenched middlemen [of the slave trade, the Temne] constituted, with the Mande traders among them, "the entrepreneurs in the business." Nevertheless, there was a lot of movement of peoples—exiles on the run from war infested areas—to avoid capture and enslavement. (Ijagbemi 1968: 73–74)

But although major devastation was usually avoided, personal security was precarious and alliances were fluid and shifting. The fact that warfare had become "normalized," at least in the eighteenth and nineteenth centuries, was insidious in itself. It had become part of the environment in which social and cultural reproduction went on, in which crops were grown, marriages contracted, and rituals performed. Historians describe how, as part of the *habitus* of war and raiding, certain forms of leadership, hierarchy, settlement, and production were produced and reproduced. These included the professionalization of warfare, the emergence of leaders known as "war chiefs," an economy in which chiefs were dependent on slave labor for agricultural and (later) cash crop production, the construction of stockaded towns ringed with several defensive barriers, and the location of settlements in concealed places (e.g., Denzer 1971; Abraham 1975 [on Mende warfare]). Today, many Temne towns still bear the name *ro-Mankane*, "the hiding place."

"DARKNESS"

In this *habitus* of war, techniques of concealment, disguise, and invisibility were prominent forms of defense and attack. Associated with these were tropes of invisibility and practices of secrecy that were highly elaborated and that were understood in terms of a polysemous concept known in Temne as "Darkness" (*an-sum;* see Shaw 1991). "Darkness" is a concept that seems to be common to Mande-speaking peoples, who traded with, intermarried with, and in some areas imposed themselves as rulers over Temne-speaking peoples. Darkness has particular relevance for those living in a context of war, since it can be embodied in the form of medicines that enable warriors to disappear (= *dine*) by creating a visual "darkness" that conceals the user from detection. In the early seventeenth century, Alvares mentions the use of such a medicine, called *nebrina*, which was said to have been brought by the Mane rulers:

> A village is approached by those bent on war. A fog then arises which prevents one man seeing another, and hence, God willing, the attackers have the victory. (Alvares 1990 [c. 1615], II, Ch. 12: 5)

Bai Bureh, the hero of the 1898 Hut Tax War, is sometimes described today as having had such powers and was said to have used them to surprise the enemy and evade capture. Today, to protect themselves in the rebel war on Sierra Leone's southern border, many soldiers go to diviners for medicine that will produce Darkness, thereby allowing them to see enemy soldiers before they themselves are seen. Such medicines take many forms: some wear a small horn filled with medicine sewn into their cap; some wear an amulet around their arm; some bite a special ring; some rub liquid medicine over their body; some simply repeat potent Islamic verses. Stories circulate about soldiers who are suddenly obscured by a kind of visual chaos—strikingly similar to the "fog" described nearly four centuries ago by Alvares—as one or more deploy their Darkness medicines. In 1992, my friend Michael related an account told to him by a soldier he knew: "A Fula soldier from Guinea and a famous rebel leader were in combat, shooting at each other. The Fula grew tired of the shooting and used his medicine. Suddenly, everything became confused, and he disappeared."

Other dominant strands in this political economy of knowledge include the cult associations—principally the Temne *ra-Gbenle, an-Poro,* and *an-Bondo*—termed "secret societies" because of their restrictions on knowledge of medicines, rituals, and speech discourses that are known as their "secrets" (*e-gbundu*; Dorjahn 1959, 1961; Dalby and Kamara 1964; Lamp 1978, 1985). These secrets are "owned" by a particular association and are described as creating Darkness between initiates and non-initiates. Through the practice of secrecy, members describe themselves as sharing in the knowledge that underpins claims to power by these associations (see Bellman 1984 for Kpelle).

Islam has been another such strand since its introduction into Sierra Leone via Mande-speaking "strangers" in the sixteenth century (Skinner 1978) and via Fula "strangers" in the eighteenth century (Fyle 1988). Although concepts of Islamic knowledge in terms of powerful secrets (*sihr*) are found all over Islamized parts of West Africa, these concepts acquired particular salience in Sierra Leone, where Islam was viewed as the secret basis of the military power of Mande states to the north and east, of the skills of Susu, Fula, and Kuranko warriors who took over many Temne chiefdoms prior to the nineteenth century (Ijagbemi 1968: 1–75), and of the wealth of Muslim Mande traders. On the basis of their claims to powerful hidden knowledge, successful Islamic teachers and diviner-healers (*an-more* in Temne) acquired the patronage of chiefs (Skinner 1978) and—since independence—of politicians.

AGENCY AND "WEALTH-IN-PEOPLE"

These understandings of power and knowledge have developed within what has been described as a "wealth-in-people system" (Bledsoe 1980). The upper Guinea coast is a region in which land has been relatively plentiful but labor problematic. Successful cultivation of the staple crop—rice—depends on the capacity of the farmer to control the labor of others; this control is accomplished by building up ties of dependency and indebtedness through kinship, marriage, parenthood, wardship, pawnship, and, in the past, slavery (e.g., Bledsoe 1980: 46–79 for Kpelle; Richards 1986 for Mende). "Wealth-in-people" is not only a function of the ecology of the region, however. It is also rooted in the history of the slave trade and its associated warfare, in which leaders built up followings of supporters, whose security in turn depended on the ability of these leaders to protect them from the slave-raiding of other groups (Denzer 1971; Bledsoe 1980: 63).

In such a historical context, personal agency is not located in "the autonomy of the individual." As Kopytoff and Miers argue,

> In most African societies, "freedom" lay not in a withdrawal into a meaningless and dangerous autonomy but in attachment to a kin-group, to a patron, to power—an attachment that occurred within a well-defined hierarchical framework. It was in this direction that the acquired outsider had to move if he was to reduce his initial marginality. Here, the antithesis of "slavery" is not "freedom" qua autonomy but rather "belonging." (1977: 17)

It is *through* such attachment that subordinates—junior men, women, and, formerly, slaves—exercise agency. For those in positions of dominance, the most powerful forms of agency consist, in fact, of the capacity to act indirectly. Temne chiefs (*an-bay*), for instance, have the capacity to see, hear, and act at a distance through their subchiefs (*e-kaper*), who are called "the eyes and ears" of the chief. Formerly, war chiefs did not fight themselves but had the capacity to fight *through* others, as Dorjahn describes:

> In each chiefdom there were a number of men, usually heads of lineages and often but not invariably subchiefs, who were sufficiently powerful and wealthy to supply men, weapons, food, and magical protection for a war party. Such a man was known as a "war chief," *obai urafa*, even though he himself did no fighting and apparently rarely accompanied his men on actual raids. The forces in the field were led by warriors, *ankurgba*, hired by the war chief for this purpose. (Dorjahn 1960: 121)

Similarly, successful farmers are those who have the capacity—through control of dependents and of resources—to get others to work for them.

Women are pivotal here, not only because men are dependent on the labor of their wives but also because men can control the labor of other men through women. Women's agency tends to be mediatory in relation to men, enabling or constraining men's capacity to act through them. Through his wives' cooking, for instance, a successful farmer will be better able to persuade a cooperative work group (*an-konp*) to work for him. And through the marriage of a daughter (usually through his wife's mediation), a man is able to make claims on the labor of his son-in-law. This mediatory agency of women is expressed in a Temne proverb: "The woman is the 'means' of the man" (*ow-uni bom, kono yi an-sababo ka w-an duni*). She is the means through which he will either become a "big person" or a "useless person." Some women become "big persons" themselves, but this is rare because they are dependent on men for access to land and for the labor required to clear the bush in order to make a farm.

Wealth-in-people, then, implies different kinds of agency for those who have different kinds of power. It also implies the practice of secrecy, since relationships of dependency and subordination involve asymmetries of knowledge. The authority of chiefs over their subjects, of elders over juniors, of initiates over non-initiates, and of husbands over wives is underscored by their right to know more about those underneath them than the latter know about them. Wealth-in-people implies wealth-in-*knowledge*-of-people (see Guyer 1994). What this means, therefore, is that for dependents—as for warriors using Darkness medicine—secrecy is part of their own capacity to use Darkness for personal defense and for the contestation of those who have power over them.

TOK AF, LEF AF

Most studies of secrecy in West Africa have been focused on cult associations, particularly in the Sierra Leone/Liberia area, where such associations are termed "secret societies" (e.g., Little 1965, 1966; Cohen 1971; Bellman 1984). But secrecy is also important as part of a discourse of power and personhood in everyday situations. The Krio proverb in the title of this essay, *tok af, lef af* (talk half, leave half), refers to the importance of defending yourself by always keeping something back from others as a precaution against their using what you tell them against you. Some practices of *tok af, lef af* are typical of responses to domination throughout the world. To take an example from my 1992 visit to Sierra Leone, Pa Alfa, whose taxi I hired to take me from Freetown to the Makeni area, was a master of *tok af, lef af.* He charmed the police and the soldiers at the frequent checkpoints along the road, greeting them well and chatting with them, concealing his (in fact, considerable) irritation at their orders to search the car and at their constant demands for "gifts." He evaded their requests to give their girlfriends a ride in his already-crowded car by fabricating circuitous and time-consuming routes which he claimed we were taking: "No, we are not going straight to Makeni. We are branching first to Mabole, then to Mabont."

Such strategies of evasion and concealment are almost universal "weapons of the weak" against intimidation—especially intimidation by those backed by the power of the state (and, in the above example, often driven by economic desperation). But practices of *tok af, lef af* have to be placed not only in the context of the political and economic situation at the time during which they occur and not only in the context of the previous sixty years of British colonial rule over the Protectorate but also in the context of the four-hundred-year history of wars generated or exacerbated by the Atlantic slave trade, by the nineteenth-century British colony in Freetown, and by the "legitimate trade" that the latter promoted. Social relationships were influenced by this historical context, in which it could often be the case, as a contemporary lorry proverb affirms, that "your best friend is your secret enemy." Such a disposition toward one's friends and relatives does not derive from some inherent psychological attribute of mistrust or from an essentialized "cultural paranoia" (as foreign visitors to Sierra Leone sometimes claim). It is a necessary and reasonable response to the shifting alliances and enmities, as well as to the use of spies, which characterized the *habitus* of war.

In the time span of my fieldwork in Sierra Leone—from the late 1970s to the early 1990s—attacks by "secret enemies" often took intangible forms, such as gossip and the destructive use of ritual and medicine, often through a diviner. Like the Darkness medicine that warriors used (and still use) for protection, secrecy is also described as creating a Darkness. Since, as I was sometimes told, "You can only fight your enemy when you know his/her secrets," discretion about oneself and silence about one's past and future actions are often seen as necessary forms of defense, as in the following situation.

Alusine is a young man in a family I knew in Freetown. After struggling for a few years on an impossibly low clerical salary, he decided to try to join his brother in the United States and find work there. Since at that time the U.S. Embassy in Freetown granted so few visas that it had become almost impossible for an ordinary Sierra Leonean to obtain one, diviners and leaders of independent churches developed a minor industry in ritual and medicine to assist their clients in their applications. So before applying for his visa, Alusine took his passport to a prophet in an independent church that he and his family often consulted. For two weeks the prophet prayed over the passport, consecrating it each time with the sign of the cross. Alusine's visa application was successful. Within three days, he left the country without telling anyone but the prophet and his closest family members that he was going. His in-laws and more distant relatives were initially offended that he had not come to them to say good-bye before leaving. But ultimately they understood his reasons: if too many people knew about Alusine's extraordinary good fortune, someone might have tried to spoil his luck. Even though Alusine was seen as an exemplary person—the kind of person who is least likely to have enemies because of his kindness and generosity—someone might nevertheless have been jealous and nursed a "bad heart" (*ke-buth ke-les*) for him. As his brother told me, "It's not everyone that likes your progress." Such a person could have gone to a diviner and hired him to use medicine against Alusine, which (perhaps by causing an accident or by making him ill) would have turned his good fortune into disaster.

SECRECY, SELF, AND PERSON

As well as being a means of defense against others, secrecy is integral to the construction of selfhood and personhood. This may seem paradoxical since, as the full Temne term for "person"—"town-person" (*w-uni ke-pet*)—suggests, personhood entails connection with others in a community. Temne evaluations of a person often use parts of the body as tropes for the capacity to relate to others: even though these tropes describe attributes, they are attributes that derive from a relational rather than an essentialist, attribute-based understanding of personhood.[8] Contrary to certain Western assumptions that relational models of personhood erase personal attributes and differences, thereby obliterating "the individual," Temne concepts of the "town-person" *do* enable the description of personal differences in terms of attributes—but these are attributes that derive from the capacity for relationships rather than from inner essences. Such attributes are, then, subsumed within a relational model of personhood (while attributes that refer to the capacity for social relationships in many Western contexts—as in the English term "hard-hearted"—tend, in contrast, to be subsumed within attribute-based models of "personality traits").

A generous person, for instance, has "an open heart" (*ke-buth ke-kanthe*), while a stingy, jealous person has "a bad heart" (*ke-buth ke-les*) or "strong eyes" (*baki re-for*). A stubborn, insubordinate person who does not listen to his or her seniors has "deaf ears" (*e-lens e-tana*). The responsible keeping of secrets is also a necessary condition of personhood, since membership in a social category and in a community entails respect for the secrets that define this membership—especially those of the cult associations. If you treat secrets appropriately, you will be respected and trusted as someone with "a closed mouth" (*ke-sen ke-faker*); if, on the other hand, you have "an open mouth" *(ke-sen ke-kanthe)*, no one will trust you, as he will know that you are liable to "pull secrets outside" (*wura e-gbundu do-kan*). In addition, for a woman to be a "town-person," she also has to have been initiated into the *Bondo* society and she has to have given birth, both of which incorporate her into a structured community of women through her acquisition of women's secrets. They also integrate her into her husband's community in that they are, respectively, the precondition for marriage (in the case of initiation) and the confirmation of marriage (in the case of childbirth).

The ability to keep secrets is also an attribute of selfhood. The term that most closely approximates "the self" (*an-yethe*), however, is not widely known. It is part of "deep Temne" (*ka-themne ke-bolon*), an esoteric form of speech often used by male elders and ritual specialists on ceremonial occasions. Unlike the "town-person," *an-yethe* is developed by placing Darkness between oneself and one's own community. But like town-personhood, *an-yethe* is nevertheless a relational concept, since one cannot develop it without establishing relationships with forces of the "outside." To have a "good self," *an-yethe fino*, is to have powerful knowledge (*ka-tenp*), especially knowledge of medicines and rituals that has been revealed by spirits of the bush or river. *An-yethe*, then, is constituted through stocks of hidden knowledge that are unique for each person, since different people will acquire such knowledge through different experiences and different relationships with spirit patrons. Development of *an-yethe* also entails being able to keep secrets (*bene gbundu*): if you do not keep secrets well and if you "pull secrets outside" (*wura e-gbundu do-kan*), you are a fool and have a "bad self" (*an-yethe les*). You will be vulnerable because others will know too much about you and may be able to use that knowledge against you—especially by going to a diviner to hurt you. The admonition to "know your self" (*tara an-yethe na mu*) is used if someone is about to reveal a secret or is using medicines inappropriately. To "know your self," then, means to know the specific secrets upon which your particular capacities—to become invisible, to see the spirit world, to be a chief, to heal—are based. This does, I would argue, describe a construction of individuality—due to the stress on unique personal capacities—without the notion of autonomous agency that is constitutive of Western individualism. Those who "know themselves" do not act alone, even if they act with spirit rather than human partners.

Although *an-yethe* is not a generally known term, we have already seen that practices of secrecy are widely exercised as forms of self-defense as well as being established techniques for defining and promoting the membership of a group. Littlejohn (1973) has drawn attention to the duality of right and left in everyday Temne practices, a duality which carries meanings of inclusion in and exclusion from normal community life, of "being in proper relation with others" and "not being in proper relation with others." Although the right hand is preeminent in conditions of sociality and has superior moral strength, the left hand's association with the hidden, the solitary, and the extra-social gives it, in some contexts, a strength and a capacity for truth that subsume those of the right hand. Littlejohn concludes that for Temne, "not-being-in-proper-relation-with-others is . . . a condition of perception of truth" (1973: 298).

The constitution of human beings places them, in fact, in this hidden realm of the left side. All human beings consist of flesh (*an-der*), life/breath (*an-esem*), and shadow or spirit (*an-mompel* or *an-yina*). *An-esem*, life/breath, is a cognate for the word for "name" (*n-es*). It is located particularly in the left side of the body, where it is concentrated in the heart, *ka-buth*: because of this, the heart is the site of the mind, *an-mera*, of memory and of knowledge. The term for "shadow," *an-mompel*, has been largely replaced by the Muslim Mande loan word for "spirit," *an-yina* (which derives from the Arabic *jinn*). A person's *an-yina* is that part that dreams at night and that goes to the place of the ancestors (*ro-kerfi*) after death; it is active in the sphere of extra-human agents, outside ordinary human society. Most of a human being, then, is hidden: as a popular Temne funeral song explains, "To see a person is not to know them" (*ke-nenk w-uni ke ye ke tara ko*).

It is for this reason that there is so much stress placed upon having "an open heart" and upon the constitution of the "town-person" through social relationships in Temne moral discourse. It is also for this reason that those in a subordinate position in any asymmetrical relationship—wives, juniors, commoners, non-initiates—are enjoined to be "open" to their seniors, while those in a senior position—husbands, elders, chiefs, initiates—are expected to retain their own secrets and, thereby, their own personal power.

WOMEN AND SECRECY

This obligation to be "open" to their seniors can create contradictions for women. On the one hand, men often represent women as being prone to "pull secrets outside." They are, men often say, liable to reveal confidential knowledge through gossip, and they are unable to control secrets of their own medicines as thoroughly as men control secrets of men's medicines. Their capacity to be "town-persons" is diminished by this weakness. On the other hand, in the context of the relationship between husband and wife, women are also represented by men as being "too secretive." This again reduces women's capacity for personhood, since (from the husband's perspective) it undermines the proper relationship of marriage. What is particularly important for a husband is that his wife does not keep secrets from him that concern his "wealth-in-people" rights over her reproductive and productive capacities. If she has a lover and keeps this a secret, for instance, she will block fertility in several areas until she tells her husband. Her husband's ancestors will withdraw their blessing and protection. He will suffer misfortune. The rice crop will fail. The woman herself will also have birth problems, and her children will fall ill unless she confesses to her husband by "calling the name" of her lover.

But for a woman as a wife, to tell your husband or your co-wife too much is foolish. "If you tell your husband or your 'rival' [o-res, 'co-wife'] about your money," Yan Safi, an elderly woman in Petbana, the village in southern Temneland in which I conducted most of my fieldwork, told me, "your husband will take it from you. If you don't agree, he will beat you and take it and share it between your rivals. And your rivals, if they know you have money, they will go to the diviner to destroy it. Or they will tell your husband." Men see certain women's secrets—such as the women's *Bondo* society, birth, and menstruation—as legitimate. For women, however, there is not always such a clear divide between "legitimate" and "illegitimate" secrets. Ya Nandewa, an official of the *Bondo* society with whom I was discussing secrecy, said, "It's good to have secrets. Women give birth, and men don't, so that is a secret for men to go there. If you're married, and your husband has a girlfriend, he would hide it from you, so why shouldn't you do the same to him?"

In order to defend themselves in their marital home, then, women often see it as necessary to *tok af, lef af.* Although they do not use the term *an-yethe*, in their use of secrecy and in certain ritual practices, their strategies are similar to those of ritual specialists and senior men who "know themselves." Women who want children sometimes cultivate a personal relationship with a river spirit. To do this, they search for a pebble that attracts them along the side of a river: it will attract them precisely because it is inhabited by a spirit. They take it home and keep it secretly in a small box, offering it a libation or an egg and promising it a sacrifice of a sheep or chicken if it enables them to have a child. They also (again, usually secretly) consult diviners—whose special knowledge is imparted by a patron spirit from the river—and apply the ritual and medicine the diviners prescribe in order to solve problems they have in their husbands' households. Like those who "know themselves," then, women acquire certain capacities from "external" spirits, and they defend these capacities through secrecy.

Their association with spirits of the river is fitting, since women's fishing activities and their domestic tasks of washing and carrying water bring them into frequent contact with streams and rivers. But it goes further than this: since the Temne practice virilocal marriage and lineage exogamy, women who marry into the lineage come, like rivers, from outside the community and connect communities together. From the standpoint of the lineage a woman marries into, this is both beneficial and potentially dangerous since, like the river, women are unknowable. As two equivalent proverbs often quoted by men claim, "if you know a woman, you know a thing under the water" (*man tara w-uni bom e, n tara are i ro-mant rata*), and "if you know a woman, you know a thing in darkness" (*man tara w-uni bom e, n tara are i ka an-sum e*).

WOMEN AND PRIVATE DIVINATION

Women's secret consultation of diviners is in particular a major source of suspicion and contention for men. The majority of diviners' clients are women, who consult diviners in private sessions. Both the divination sessions themselves and the rituals prescribed in them usually have to be kept secret because a wife has no authority to use a diviner's diagnosis in her husband's household; she would, in fact, be the one who would be accused of wrongdoing (Shaw 1985). This is because (as we have seen) women are already viewed by men as "too secretive," and a woman's access to hidden knowledge in the closed space of a diviner's room, without the knowledge of her husband, is regarded as an erosion of her husband's authority over her. Men view this as sinister and draw upon stereotypes of women as jealous and prone to witchcraft in order to argue that women are liable to hire diviners to use bad medicine against their husbands and co-wives. Usually, in fact, women go to diviners to seek help with their children's illnesses and with their own health or reproductive problems as well as to redress problems in their marriages.

For instance, Mariama, a young married woman in Freetown, has consulted diviners ever since she married. She first did so when her husband, Ibrahim, stopped giving her money for food and other household expenses. She complained to a friend of hers in the market, who took her to see Pa Yamba, a diviner the friend had used herself. Mariama consulted Pa Yamba, and when she used the medicine he gave her to wash with, Ibrahim started giving Mariama money again. Later, when Ibrahim was out of work, she returned to Pa Yamba to help Ibrahim find a job. Pa Yamba told her to make an offering of four kola nuts in a bowl of water. She bought the kola nuts and gave them away to passersby as she was walking home from Pa Yamba's house, receiving their invocations of God's blessings in return. Ibrahim got a job in the army without knowing of the consultation and of the offering Mariama had made on his behalf.

Women's experiences with divination generate stocks of knowledge that become important resources, because for those who "know themselves," secret knowledge of rituals and medicines gives protection and power. Through secret divination, women also subvert their husbands' knowledge of them: Mariama's use of divination, for instance, reversed the direction in which knowledge and secrecy were supposed to flow in the relationship between husband and wife, even though—or perhaps especially because—she had got her husband a job without his knowledge. Instead of using her mediatory agency as a wife in a way that her husband could see and control, Mariama used a form of indirect action through others—in this case, the diviner and the people who consumed her kola nuts, as well as the spiritual agencies behind her sacrifice and the medicine she used. She thereby used the kind of "action at a distance" to which husbands and "big persons" regard themselves exclusively entitled.

Thus, on the western side of the Atlantic, the slave trade fed a political economy that promoted "individualism" and "autonomy." But for Temne-speaking communities on the African side, the *habitus* of war that the slave trade engendered was associated with the development of Mande concepts of Darkness into a means of self-construction and self-defense that supported a relational form of individualism. This did not, however, involve "autonomy." The different capacities and powers of Temne persons and selves all involve acting through others or being acted through in what Karp (1988) and Jackson and Karp (1990: 21) have described as a "paradox of agency"—a situation in which an apparent loss of agency is a precondition for regaining it, or vice versa.

The agency of Temne husbands and "big men" is similarly paradoxical, because their most powerful actions are those accomplished indirectly (and often invisibly) through others. The agency of Temne wives and junior men, on the other hand, is also paradoxical, because their manifest actions are often subsumed by the agency of another, who acts through them. Yet this mediatory capacity of subordinates also enables the subordinates to block the agency of those who act through them: women, for example, can do this by refusing to cook or farm for their husbands. The indirect and often hidden agency claimed by senior men can, moreover, be appropriated, as it is by women who secretly consult diviners about problems in their husband's household, seeking to redirect a situation in which they are subject to the direction of others.

Yet it could be argued that these notions of indirect or mediatory agency and of women being both controlled and controlling are paradoxical only according to a Western construction of the individual in terms of autonomous agency. Temne understandings of person, self, and individuation have a different social history. In the context of relational concepts of person and self, such as those of "town-person" and *an-yethe*, personal agency *cannot* involve autonomy. The paradox, from the perspective of a relational concept of self, would lie instead in the idea of someone acting alone.

NOTES

1. MacFarlane (1978) argues that English individualism, together with capitalism and the nuclear family, can be traced back at least as far as the thirteenth century. Unlike the situation in other parts of Europe, its historical origins are unclear:

> it is no longer possible to "explain" the origins of English individualism in terms of either Protestantism, population change, [or] the development of a market economy at the end of the middle ages. . . . Individualism, however defined, predates sixteenth-century changes and can be said to shape them all. The explanation must lie elsewhere, but will remain obscure until we trace the origins even further than has been attempted in this work. (1978: 196)

2. As Jean La Fontaine observes, "What has been overlooked in discussions of the Western notions [of self, person, and individual] is that they exist in the context of a particular concept of society as a whole: the idea of the nation-state" (1985: 136–37).

3. See Lukes (1973) for an excellent synopsis of the distinctions in meaning and the historical divergences among different forms of Western individualism.

4. Such "othering" was also a recurring theme of North Atlantic Cold War discourse about the nature of communist societies, which were often represented as reducing their inhabitants to social automata. This theme has now been replaced by a very similar rhetoric, in which Muslim societies are frequently characterized as hidebound by tradition, maintained by "fanaticism," and/or crippled by "clannism," a rhetoric which gained particular force in the United States and the United Kingdom during the 1991 Gulf War and during Operation Restore Hope in Somalia.

5. Lienhardt writes, in what has become a famous passage,

> The Dinka have no conception which at all closely corresponds to our popular modern conception of the "mind" as mediating and, as it were, storing up the experiences of the self. There is for them no such interior entity to appear, on reflection, to stand between the experiencing self at any given moment and what is or has been an exterior influence upon the self. So it seems that what we would call in some cases the "memories" of experiences, and regard therefore as in some way intrinsic and interior to the remembering person and modified in their effect upon him by that interiority, appear to the Dinka as exteriorly acting upon him, as were the sources from which they derived. (1961: 149)

6. Such concepts as "self-improvement" were based on a hierarchical opposition between a "lower," "animal" condition and a "higher," "moral," "civilized" condition (closely linked to the binary pair "passion" and "reason"), in which a person was supposed to "progress" from one to the other in a direction that was conceived as "upward." At the same time, this opposition was used as the basis for hierarchical distinctions between male and female, upper class and lower class, and white and black, in which distinctions there was a limit to how far those in the "lower" category could, in fact, "progress." See Costanzo 1987; Masur, n.d.

7. As Paul Richards (1995) argues, the recent rebel war has had much in common with the trade wars of the nineteenth century. As in earlier conflicts, communities were raided. New techniques of slavery replaced those of previous centuries: children and

teenagers were conscripted into rebel armies, and those who resisted were forced at gunpoint to mutilate and kill members of their families, thereby ensuring that they could not return to their communities. Also like the trade wars, Richards argues, were the external economic interests involved. Backed by shadowy international interests, rebel leaders used their armies as a labor force in order to exploit timber and minerals (especially diamonds) (Paul Richards, personal communication, September 2, 1993).

8. Jackson's discussion of concepts of person among the neighboring Kuranko clarifies this use of "relational attributes":

> *Morgoye* [personhood] is quite unlike the English word *personality*, which connotes personal identity, a "distinctive individual character especially when of a marked kind" (OED). *Morgoye* refers to moral qualities which ideally characterize social relationships. While *personality* implies an individual who stands out against his or her social background, *morgoye* connotes abstract qualities of social relations. In particular, *morgoye* denotes altruism and magnanimity, virtues which Kuranko set at the foundation of social order. . . . A true person thus does more than merely conform to social rules; he realizes or exemplifies social ideals. (1982: 15)

REFERENCES

Abraham, Arthur. 1975. "The Pattern of Warfare and Settlement among the Mende of Sierra Leone in the Second Half of the Nineteenth Century." *Kroniek van Africa* 2: 130–40. Reprinted as Occasional Paper No. 1, Institute of African Studies, Fourah Bay College.

Alvares, Manuel. 1990 [c. 1615]. *Ethiopia Minor and a Geographical Account of the Province of Sierra Leone.* Translated by P. E. H. Hair, Department of History, University of Liverpool. Mimeograph.

Bellman, Beryl. 1984. *The Language of Secrecy: Symbols and Metaphors in Poro Ritual.* New Brunswick, N.J.: Rutgers University Press.

Bledsoe, Caroline H. 1980. *Women and Marriage in Kpelle Society.* Stanford, Calif.: Stanford University Press.

Breen, T. H. 1980. *Puritans and Adventurers: Change and Persistence in Early America.* Oxford: Oxford University Press.

Carrithers, Michael. 1985. "An Alternative Social History of the Self." In M. Carrithers, S. Collins, and S. Lukes, eds., *The Category of the Person: Anthropology, Philosophy, History.* Cambridge: Cambridge University Press, pp. 234–56.

Carrithers, Michael, Steven Collins, and Steven Lukes, eds. 1985. *The Category of the Person: Anthropology, Philosophy, History.* Cambridge: Cambridge University Press.

Cohen, Abner. 1971. "The Politics of Ritual Secrecy." *Man,* n.s. 6: 427–48.

Costanzo, Angelo. 1987. *Surprising Narrative: Olaudah Equiano and the Beginnings of Black Autobiography.* New York: Greenwood Press.

Dalby, David, and Abdul Kamara. 1964. "Vocabulary of the Temne Ragbenle Society." *Sierra Leone Language Review* 3: 35–41.

Denzer, La Ray. 1971. "Sierra Leone—Bai Bureh." In M. Crowder, ed., *West African Resistance: The Military Response to Colonial Occupation.* New York: Hutchinson.

Dorjahn, Vernon R. 1959. "The Organization and Functions of the *Ragbenle* Society of the Temne." *Africa* 29: 156–70.

———. 1960. "The Changing Political System of the Temne." *Africa* 30: 110–40.

———. 1961. "The Initiation of Temne *Poro* Officials." *Man,* o. s. 61: 36–40.

Edwards, Paul, and Rosalind Shaw. 1989. "The Invisible C*hi* in Equiano's *Interesting Narrative.*" *Journal of Religion in Africa* 19: 146–56.

Equiano, Olaudah. 1969 [1789]. *The Interesting Narrative of the Life of Olaudah Equiano, or, Gustavus Vassa the African.* Edited by Paul Edwards. 2 vols. London: Dawson of Pall Mall.

Fortes, Meyer. 1949. *The Web of Kinship among the Tallensi.* London: Oxford University Press.

Fyle, C. Magbaily. 1988. "Fula Diaspora: The Sierra Leone Experience." In *History and Socio-Economic Development in Sierra Leone.* Freetown: Sierra Leone Adult Education Association.

Greene, Jack P. 1988. *Pursuits of Happiness: The Social Development of Early Modern British Colonies and the Formation of American Culture.* Chapel Hill: University of North Carolina Press.

Guyer, Jane. 1994. "Wealth in People as Wealth in Knowledge: Accumulation and Composition in Equatorial Africa." *Journal of African History* 36: 91–120.

Hollis, Martin. 1985. "Of Masks and Men." In M. Carrithers, S. Collins, and S. Lukes, eds., *The Category of the Person: Anthropology, Philosophy, History.* Cambridge: Cambridge University Press.

Horton, Robin. 1983. "Social Psychologies: African and Western." In Meyer Fortes and Robin Horton, *Oedipus and Job in West African Religion.* Cambridge: Cambridge University Press.

Ijagbemi, E. Ade. 1968. "A History of the Temne in the Nineteenth Century." Doctoral thesis, University of Edinburgh.

Jackson, Michael. 1982. *Allegories of the Wilderness.* Bloomington: Indiana University Press.

———. 1989. "Ajala's Heads." In *Paths toward a Clearing: Radical Empiricism and Ethnographic Inquiry.* Bloomington: Indiana University Press.

Jackson, Michael, and Ivan Karp eds. 1990. "Introduction." In *Personhood and Agency: The Experience of Self and Other in African Cultures.* Washington, D.C.: Smithsonian Institution Press.

Jacobson-Widding, Anita. 1990. "The Shadow as an Expression of Individuality in Congolese Conceptions of Personhood." In M. Jackson and I. Karp, eds., *Personhood and Agency: The Experience of Self and Other in African Cultures.* Washington, D.C.: Smithsonian Institution Press.

Karp, Ivan. 1988. "Laughter at Marriage: Subversion in Performance." *Journal of Folklore Research* 25: 35–52.

Kondo, Dorinne. 1990. *Crafting Selves: Power, Gender and Discourses of Identity in a Japanese Workplace.* Chicago: University of Chicago Press.

Kopytoff, Igor, and Suzanne Miers. 1977. *Slavery in Africa: Historical and Anthropological Perspectives.* Madison: University of Wisconsin Press.

La Fontaine, Jean S. 1985. "Person and Individual: Some Anthropological Reflections." In M. Carrithers, S. Collins, and S. Lukes, eds., *The Category of the Person: Anthropology, Philosophy, History.* Cambridge: Cambridge University Press, pp. 123–40.

Lamp, Frederick. 1978. "Frogs into Princes: The Temne Rabai Initiation." *African Arts* 11, no. 2: 38–49.

———. 1985. "Cosmos, Cosmetics, and the Spirit of Bondo." *African Arts* 18, no. 3: 28–43, 98–99.

Lenga-Kroma, James Samuel. 1978. "A History of the Southern Temne in the Late Nineteenth and Early Twentieth Centuries." 2 vols. Doctoral thesis, University of Edinburgh.

Lienhardt, Godfrey. 1961. *Divinity and Experience: The Religion of the Dinka.* Oxford: Clarendon Press.

———. 1985. "Self: Public and Private—Some African Representations." In M. Carrithers, S. Collins, and S. Lukes, eds., *The Category of the Person: Anthropology, Philosophy, History.* Cambridge: Cambridge University Press, pp. 141–55.

Little, Kenneth. 1965. "The Political Functions of the Poro: Pt. 1." *Africa* 35: 349–65.

———. 1966. "The Political Functions of the Poro: Pt. 2." *Africa* 36: 62–72.

Littlejohn, James. 1973. "Temne Right and Left: An Essay on the Choreography of Everyday Life." In R. Needham, ed., *Right and Left: Essays on Dual Symbolic Classification.* Chicago: University of Chicago Press.

Lukes, Steven. 1973. *Individualism.* Oxford: Basil Blackwell.

———. 1985. "Conclusion." In M. Carrithers, S. Collins, and S. Lukes, eds., *The Category of the Person: Anthropology, Philosophy, History.* Cambridge: Cambridge University Press.

MacFarlane, Alan. 1978. *The Origins of English Individualism: The Family, Property and Social Transition.* Oxford: Basil Blackwell, and Cambridge: Cambridge University Press.

Mauss, Marcel. 1985 [1938]. "A Category of the Human Mind: The Notion of Person; the Notion of Self." Translated by W. D. Halls. In M. Carrithers, S. Collins, and S. Lukes, eds., *The Category of the Person: Anthropology, Philosophy, History.* Cambridge: Cambridge University Press, pp. 1–25.

Mbiti, John. 1992 [1969]. *African Religions and Philosophy.* London: Heinemann.

Morgan, Edmund S. 1975. *American Slavery, American Freedom: The Ordeal of Colonial Virginia.* New York: W. W. Norton & Co.

Richards, Paul. 1986. *Coping with Hunger: Hazard and Experiment in an African Rice Farming System.* London: Allen and Unwin.

———. 1995. "Chimpanzees, Diamonds and War: Debating Local–Global Interaction on the Liberia–Sierra Leone Border." In H. Moore, ed., *The Changing Nature of Anthropological Knowledge.* London and New York: Routledge.

Rodney, Walter. 1970. *A History of the Upper Guinea Coast 1545–1800.* Oxford: Clarendon Press.

Shaw, Rosalind. 1985. "Gender and the Structuring of Reality in Temne Divination." *Africa* 55: 286–303.

———. 1991. "Splitting Truths from Darkness: Epistemological Aspects of Temne Divination." In P. Peek, ed., *African Divination Systems: Ways of Knowing.* Bloomington: Indiana University Press, pp. 133–52.

Skinner, David E. 1978. "Mande Settlement and the Development of Islamic Institutions in Sierra Leone." *International Journal of African Historical Studies* 2: 32–62.

Tempels, Placide. 1959. *Bantu Philosophy.* Paris: Présence Africaine.

2. Islam among the Humors: Destiny and Agency among the Swahili

David Parkin

In the burgeoning literature on human agency produced over the last two decades, there has been a progression away from concerns that simply addressed the issue of methodological individualism. These early concerns presupposed a contrast between two overarching forms of determinism—between what Hollis characterized as "autonomous man" and "plastic man" (Hollis 1977). Methodological individualism presented the rational individual as having played a decisive role in shaping society through the decisions and plans that he or she undertook in conjunction with various others (Lukes 1977). These various others constantly redefined social interaction and precluded, in the eyes of methodological individualists, any fixed notion of an overall determining "society." Society was, indeed, persons in interaction who were exercising influence on each other in such a way that (social) tendencies could be discerned and yet that did not prevent individual initiative, a process laboriously outlined in Giddens's concept of "structuration" (1976) and Bourdieu's "*habitus*" (1977). A generalized notion of "intersubjectivity" was another early

Fieldwork among Swahili-speaking peoples has been carried out on the Kenya coast over the last fifteen years and in Zanzibar during December 1992 and January 1993. Acknowledgment of funds (provided for some of these periods of fieldwork) is made to the British Academy, the Nufield Foundation, the Economic and Social Research Council, and the School of Oriental and African Studies. A French version of this essay was first presented on April 13, 1993, during a seminar of the Ecole des Hautes Etudes en Sciences Sociales in Paris, convened by Dr. Mary Picone; I thank Dr. Picone and members of the seminar for their interest and comments. I would also like to thank Susan Beckerleg for her comments.

attempt to describe social process as emanating from individuals that were interacting on the basis of shared and newly created understandings, although as Ricoeur argues (1981: 182–93), social process becomes, in the end, another form of objectivity.

Later attempts at understanding human agency have sought to dissolve the dichotomy of society versus the individual or other such opposed forms of determinism. I am most in sympathy with Charles Taylor's reinvestigation of Hegel's philosophy of mind (1985), which offers a more dialectically constituted notion of the person, who operates among other consciousnesses in public space, so creating and recreating his/her own consciousness of self.

These are approaches which display a self-evident concern with epistemological issues characteristic of so-called Western philosophical thinking, and they turn, in the end, on reworked ideas of the relative autonomy of individual rationality and divine destiny, in relation to each other, as factors shaping perceptions of the person and of human agency.

Non-Western views may not so easily regard divinely ordered destiny as contestable. Preordained human character and destiny may indeed be absolute and unquestionable presuppositions, to which other views, within the culture, of human agency have to be adapted or at least refashioned in such a way that they seem to be compatible (or at least not incompatible) with a central religious precept. Among the people I now describe, a theory of bodily humors combines with cosmological and religious assumptions to assert that an individual's human character is fixed and unalterable. His/her personal fate is shaped by the way the person and his/her environment respond and relate materially, morally, and religiously to this fixity of character. This fact is a local starting point for any discussion of how people make choices, recover from illnesses, and turn misfortune into good fortune. But it is a starting point that has to be altered and even forgotten as discourse proceeds through the creation of what we might call deliberate category mistakes.

SWAHILI ISLAM AND MEDICINE

There appears at first sight to be a tension in Swahili ideas about the physical and mental makeup of a person and about the fact that he or she is also a Muslim. As a Muslim, a person is expected to practice lifelong moral improvement by following the dictates of Islam. As with the Prophet himself, a person should therefore be able to change his or her moral character and hence their destiny both in this world and the next.

One the other hand, certain major principles of Swahili medicine are derived from the Greek and later Arabo-Galenic theory of the four humors which make up the body-mind of a person and which fix his character (*tabia*) at birth. This was a view offered by both medical practitioners and laypeople during my fieldwork in Kenya and Zanzibar. It is confirmed by Beckerleg, who says that "The basic *tabia* . . . cannot be changed, and is the main determinant of emotional response" (1990: 107) but that "weather, food, drugs, or other factors may modify a particular characteristic" (1994: 305). Swartz, quite independently, also asserts that "character traits are fixed and, although controllable, cannot be changed" (1991: 167).

Despite this tension in theory between the fixity of character and the possibility of self-improvement—that is to say, between the way in which persons are prescribed and are yet given agency—it does not become heightened as either a theological or conceptual conflict in everyday affairs. At one level, we should not be surprised at this. After all, none of us in any society consistently follows the many expectations of behavior to which we are variously subject. Or, at least, we can behave differently in situations which are cordoned off from each other and which are never compared. We see ourselves as being "free" to choose in some situations but as constrained in others. At another level, however, the tension constitutes a set of parameters within which variations in people's conduct are both created and yet controlled, or at least limited. I wish to describe this set of controls and to suggest ways in which healers appear to circumvent them.

The setting for much of this discussion is Zanzibar (Unguja Island), with special reference to the period from 1964, the year of the Zanzibar political revolution, to the present. Some of the patterns described can be found in other Swahili-speaking communities, but others appear to be distinctive to Zanzibar. I first present some facts about Swahili medicine, as recorded elsewhere.

Beckerleg, writing of Watamu, north of Mombassa on the Kenya coast, notes that "The concept of the unchanging tabia (human character) is a Swahili version of the classical (Galenic) theory of temperament based on the interplay of the four humors. . . . Swahili practitioners . . . link tabia to the balance of the humors, which have the properties of heat (*haar*), cold (*baridi*), dryness (*yabisi*), and dampness (*rotba*). Each person has a particular temperament depending on the balance of the humors of blood (*damu*), yellow bile (*mandano*), phlegm (*balghamu*), and black bile (*sowda*) found in all people. Blood is hot and wet, yellow bile hot and dry, phlegm cold and wet, and black bile cold and dry" (Beckerleg 1994: 305). The character or temperament of each individual is made up of his/her own distinctive balance of the four humors, which reacts distinctively to variations in diet, weather, the seasons, and, when unbalanced (i.e., ill), to the particular properties of herbal treatments.

Foods and medicines are themselves classified according to degrees of heat, cold, moisture, and dryness: the incorrect proportions that cause illness and the correct ones that restore balance and health again vary by individual. The above are mainly Arabic-derived Swahili terms (and there are others), but sometimes, Bantu-derived terms may be used instead (e.g., heat, *joto;* dryness, *ukavu;* and moistness, *unyevu*).

For comparison, the classical Galenic correspondence between humoral combination and temperament is outlined as follows:

Humor	*Temperament*
Blood (warm and moist)	Sanguine
Phlegm (cold and moist)	Phlegmatic
Choler (hot and dry)	Choleric
Black bile (cold and dry)	Melancholic

Expressed thus, this classical Arabo-Galenic schema comes across as limited and static. Beckerleg's account of the Swahili version, however, shows the vast number of permutational possibilities which can be derived from cross-cutting classifications of character, illness, foods, winds, seasons, and the possible causes and cures relating to any one individual who presents himself to a healer. It is also evident that classificatory variations occur between different Swahili communities along the East African coast and even between neighboring healers, thereby increasing the overall number of permutations. I would speculate that this virtual infinity of classificatory possibilities, by which any one human being may be described or diagnosed, means that, in practice, a person's character is always being modified, despite its theoretical fixity. Most talk, then, is likely to be more about changing personal circumstances and dispositions than about pre-destined expectations.

Yet the role of Islam is ever present in Swahili society, and members of religious congregations and orders are constantly berated for falling short of proper and pious behavior, and their moral characters are called to account. Yet, given the fact that a person's humorally based temperament predisposes him to particular emotional responses (a "hot" character inclines toward "hot" tempers and may commit terrible acts under certain unpropitious circumstances), this temperament must also be part of the individual's moral character. Yet, the individual is enjoined to control the latter according to Islamic moral precepts. Islam and an individual's distinctive humoral balance appear to be in conflict.

I want to argue that in Swahili medical diagnosis, classificatory proliferation is an ongoing process and that this militates against the rigid moral classification of particular individuals. As an example of a local case of further classificatory proliferation, I take the use of astrology by a well-known Zanzibar healer. Astrology, or *falaki*, as it is known, is not mentioned by either Beckerleg or Swartz as part of the criteria by which a person's character is determined at birth. Indeed, Beckerleg notes that *falaki* is often forbidden by Islamic clerics and is sometimes even seen as a form of witchcraft (1990: 268) and that, in answer to her question, an informant scorned the "popular western idea of astrology" as indicating that the stars and planets have an influence on an individual's character.

The Zanzibar healer to whom I now refer appears to have combined such popular Western ideas with existing Arab-derived Swahili astrological cosmology and in fact insists that a person's humorally based character is astrologically determined. The healer begins with a fourfold designation of elements in the world, broadly familiar to Western astrology, from which the humors are derived, namely water (*maji*), earth/flesh (*udongo*), fire (*moto*), and air (*upepo*). The signs of the zodiac are grouped under these humors: fire is Aries, Leo, and Sagittarius; earth or flesh is Taurus, Virgo, and Capricorn; air is Gemini, Libra, and Aquarius; and water is Cancer, Scorpio, and Pisces. The healer sees himself as a specialist in that branch of *falaki* which discovers a person's astrologically determined humoral makeup and, hence, that person's temperament and proclivity for certain sicknesses. He is ostensibly able to gather such initial information from a person's birth date. In practice, few people in Zanzibar know their birth dates, and so the healer divines a person's astrological signs through calculations based on the letters of the person's name and those of his/her mother, converting these into a numerical formula which indicates the individual's humorally based temperament and which can be applied to a table of possible states of sickness.

The humors combine differently from person to person according to variations of food and season and therefore of external heat (*joto*), cold (*baridi*), dryness (*ukavu*), and moistness (*unyevu*) (known respectively in Arabic as *hararatun, burudatun, yubasun,* and *rotubasun*). In this context, herbs and other medicines may also be defined as being of water, flesh, fire, or air, and they may be applied in appropriate combinations. Thus, a patient complaining of, for example, a stomachache may be said to have an elemental makeup (*miyongo*) containing too much heat (*moto*). An herbal remedy itself designated as hot will only cause further suffering, while one regarded to belong to the category of water (*maji*) will cure the stomachache. Another patient's sickness may be diagnosed as *yabisi,* with symptoms of constipation. Chafed lips and skin, which are caused by too much dryness in the person's elemental state, for which an herbal medicine that is described as falling within either the category of air (*upepo*) or that of water will be relieved. "Air" medicines will not, however, treat conditions caused by too much heat, which only become more inflamed, though "earth" is good for heat, as is "water" (provided the water does not boil away and become "dryness"), and so on.

In Mombassa, Mkangi (1990) found that the combinations of internal and external factors can give rise to four main conditions of ill health or humoral imbalance: *adamawi, balghami, safarawi,* and *saudau,* each of which is derived from Arabic terms and each of which is based on hot/cold and dry/moist combinations which reproduce those making up the Galenic humors of blood, phlegm, choler, and black bile but which do not much reproduce the Galenic equations of temperament. We may consider Beckerleg's identification (above) of the four humors, namely blood (*damu*), phlegm (*balghamu*), yellow bile (choler) (*mandano*), and black bile (*sowda*), found in Watamu, Kenya, and her remark that two, at least—phlegm and yellow bile—"are sometimes mentioned as symptoms of illnesses but are not linked by lay people to the schema of tabia (temperament) and bodily substance" (1994: 306). Once again, we see here variation in the terminology of the humors, with laypeople (at least) using them to indicate imbalance or excess—agents that cause sickness.

Thus, Mkangi's informants report that excessive body heat accompanied by moistness produces a sallow skin and is called *adamawi,* a condition to which large, flabby people are said to be prone. *Balghami* is the condition that results when cold and moistness combine to lower the body temperature, thereby creating a sense of dryness in the patient. One's movements and thinking are slowed down, one's skin loses its color, and one's lungs and respiratory system are especially affected (cf. Galenic phlegmatic). Dryness and an excess of body heat, precipitating feverish restlessness and shivering, will point to *safarawi.* A lowering of the body temperature and dehydration, with attendant loss of skin color, also occur in the condition of *saudau,* but in this case, the patient is hyperactive, with apparently uncontrollably high energy, and is said to be prone to infection by sexually transmitted diseases, which may lead to impotence in a man. This condition is caused by a prevalence of dryness in the body (over moistness) (Mkangi 1990).

Regardless of the variability in terminology and symptomatology, healers need a starting point for their diagnosis, and again, this tends to result in a mix of the generally held and the idiosyncratic beliefs. The Zanzibari healer to whom I have been referring is like others in that he asks the patient to give a description of the sensation and duration of the sickness and to describe what part of the body is affected. He commonly takes the patient's pulse. This, together with the patient's own comments and his physical appearance, will determine into which of the above four categories (or their equivalent) the healer will place the patient's condition.

What is distinctive about this healer, however, is that he does start by as-certaining the patient's astrologically determined humoral makeup by using his own and his mother's names in the way I have described. Unashamed *falaki* is, then, his starting point, but it is by no means shared by others, who may regard *falaki* as contrary to Islam.

Just as their starting points may vary, healers need not be consistent in their actual diagnoses, preferring to treat each case in the way that best satisfies the patient and that produces beneficial results. It is, moreover, questionable as to whether a healer is ever required to demonstrate, as a complete process, the full logic of humoral theory, temperament, and predisposition to particular kinds of ill health.

Indeed, I suggest that built into Swahili methods of diagnosis and cure are the possibilities for deliberate inconsistency of theory and practice, which provides for a fragmentary rather than a coherent method of therapy. I further suggest that a demonstrated, coherent theory would be against the interests of Islam, which urges moral self-improvement as a lifelong endeavor and as the best protection against ill health. I do not think that this is simply a matter of the demands of Islam and of Arabo-Galenic medical science being in conflict with each other. After all, it is often claimed, as in other Muslim societies, that all scientific knowledge has been predicted by God in the Koran (which one can check if one interprets it correctly) and that since no new technology is new to Him, He already has anticipated and made possible the means by which humans can overcome apparent conflicts between Islamic practice and such new knowledge.

I would argue rather that Islamic-based moral piety tends to be the most general and, to that extent, consistent presupposition of balanced health among Swahili and that what we identify as medical assumptions and practices are built around it, variously providing the local differences that are evident in, for example, Watamu, Mombassa, and Zanzibar (and most certainly elsewhere in the Swahili world). I see this relationship between Islam and the variations of medical theory and practice as another way of talking about the fixity of indi-vidual character and the possibilities for its modification. Let me follow this suggestion with special reference to Zanzibar.

ZANZIBARI HISTORY AND ISLAMIC MORALITY

The centrality of Islamic morality might be said to characterize all Swahili throughout the East African coastal area. At a general level, this is indeed so, especially since in both the Kenya coastal areas and Zanzibar, there has recently developed a raised Islamic consciousness of quite radical proportions. In Zan-zibar, however, Islamic morality has developed a distinctive relationship to traditional medical knowledge as a result of the political changes occurring in Zanzibar from 1964 until the present.

The Zanzibar revolution of 1964 resulted in the death and exile of a large but unspecified number of Zanzibari of so-called Arab descent, mainly those of Omani origin. Karume, the first president of the newly formed Revolutionary Government of Zanzibar, carried out a number of measures aimed at transforming Zanzibar from a feudal, formerly slave-based society into a socialist one. First, Karume encouraged the use of Swahili, regarded as an indisputably "African" language, in all spheres of official and daily life, banning the teaching of both English and Arabic in schools. He also banned the use of such ethnic terms as "Shirazi," as he felt they were divisive of what was regarded as an essentially African Zanzibari population. Second, Karume sought to secularize the new Zanzibari state, and although he did not ban the role of Islam in private and public life, which would have been impossible, he minimized it, as evidenced by the conversion of the important and specially built Muslim Academy in Zanzibar Town into a secular, nondenominational orphanage. Third, he brutally purged town and country of traditional healers, regarding them as dealers in sorcery, of which he is reported to have a great fear, although one can also see this measure as part of his modernization–secularization policy. Discovered healers were, as a minimum measure, deprived of their medical wares and perhaps imprisoned, and there are reported instances of killings at the hands of the special police charged with carrying out the purge. (It has to be mentioned that Karume carried out other measures for which local people continue to give him credit. These include nationalizing of land, much of which formerly comprised plantations owned by "Arabs"; permitting poor people to occupy the houses in Zanzibar Town, houses that had formerly been occupied by owners who had died or been exiled during the revolution; attempting to institute universal primary education and a policy of housing for all; and trying to create economic self-sufficiency.)

As far as my argument here is concerned, the effects of Karume's policies on healers who escaped imprisonment or death were twofold. Some quietly settled on the Kenya coast, sometimes reaching it after a prior period on the Tanzanian mainland. Others, who had had a lower profile to begin with, simply stopped practicing. A further effect was to discourage Islamic discussion and learning, theological as well as medical and scientific. It has often observed in Zanzibar that generations of Islamic scholarship simply disappeared or went underground. Life histories testify to this. Zanzibar was once a, perhaps *the*, great center of such learning, but despite the rapid recent revival, it still lacks the spontaneity of discussion and learning opportunities that exist today in, say, Lamu and Mombassa in Kenya.

The Zanzibari renaissance is of very recent origin, perhaps about ten years, and is evidently linked to the circumstances that occurred in November 1989, when the wall between West and East Germany was broken down and when Zanzibar lost the ideological and financial support of its staunchest communist ally, the former German Democratic Republic (East Germany).

From this time onward, various policies were reversed, resulting in (1) a renewal of ties with Middle Eastern states, including Oman: (2) a joining (without first consulting the Union government) with the powerful international Association of Islamic Societies, the principal members of which are financially well-endowed Islamic republics; (3) the allowing of the teaching of English and, to some extent, of Arabic either in schools or institutes, private as well as state; (4) the permitting of the practice of private medicine and of the set up of private pharmacies and small "hospitals," nearly all of which are so far based on modern biomedicine; and (5) the "liberalizing" of the Zanzibari economy, with talk of establishing a "free economic zone," both of which represent unambiguous steps in the direction of capitalism despite the fact that, as late as December 1992, the Union government still insisted it was a revolutionary socialist government.

Since about 1990, there has been a proliferation of private chemists and small hospitals, especially in Zanzibar Town, that are set up and staffed on a part-time basis by doctors, nurses, and nursing orderlies who normally work in the island's major state hospital, Mnazi Mmoja, formerly called the V. I. Lenin Hospital. Returning Zanzibari businessmen have plans to set up a pharmacological factory on the island, and other medical-related investments are expected. Alongside this new development of modern biomedical facilities traditional healers have started practicing again or more openly, although by comparison with Mombassa and Lamu in Kenya, they remain cautious and unadvertised, preferring to be recommended by word of mouth. As yet, no major medical exiles in Kenya have returned to Zanzibar, but it is a likely possibility.

Similarly, and in tandem, perhaps, with comparable movements elsewhere in the world, Islam has become much more openly central in the lives of Zanzibaris. So-called radicals or fundamentalists, identified under the rubric of the Halali Sunna, are spoken of by the pro-government clerics as a minority, but in fact, they have considerable influence, as instanced, for example, by their opposition in 1992 to the government encouragement of a Zanzibari tourist industry; they protested on the grounds that white tourists dress scantily and have no respect for (or are at least ignorant of) either Islamic or Zanzibari local customs. These radicals are in turn opposed, of course, by local traders, who benefit from tourists, as well as by the government, which, through the pro-government Sheikhs, counter-argues that Islam has always encouraged travel for learning and that in the end, Islam benefits from contact with those outsiders who are willing to appreciate the benefits of Islam. Accompanying these changes, Swahili remains the rich language of discourse and of some literature, especially religious literature, but Arabic is now sought as well.

In short, then, ideas of Islamic propriety and knowledge have now once again become the open yardsticks by which persons in Zanzibar measure themselves. Islam is not hidden but is vibrant, advertising itself publicly in the literature sold in the Town's streets by young Muslim men; by the posters which contrast tourist dress unfavorably with Muslim women wearing the *bui-bui* and *hijabu;* by the regularly broadcast Friday mosque sermons, which combine political and social comment and criticism with prayers and conversions to Islam (cassettes of which may be bought in a special shop); and by demonstrations and discussion related to Islamic issues.

By contrast, traditional (as distinct from modern) biomedicine is still re-emerging, so to speak. Some of its finest scholars are no longer in Zanzibar, and new apprentices have yet to make their mark, while older practitioners are for the moment content to limit their clientele to people of a given local circle. The difference between Zanzibar and Kenya and the Tanzanian mainland is striking, for in the latter areas, healers widely advertise their skills in newspapers and outside their surgeries.

HEALERS, IMAMS, AND THE DISPLACEMENT OF CULPABILITY

Under the circumstances of Zanzibar's recent history, the standard Islamic postulate that piety before God is the best protection against ill health is highlighted by the higher profile that Islam enjoys in relation to traditional healing.

It is not surprising that much traditional healing starts with appeals to the Koran and to holy Arabic texts, despite the fact that few healers have much more than a recitational knowledge of Arabic. Although there is a range of different healing specialists, with herbalists at one end of the spectrum and bone- or joint-setters and diviners and geomancers at the other end, all at least make some reference to verses of the Koran and to the legitimacy of statements from the Koran or from the Hadithi about the Prophet's life.

Then in this sense also, Islam is the governing context for diagnosis and cure, within which problems of sickness are moral as well as physical and mental and within which the person, although deemed, according to Swahili humoral theory, to have a fixed character, perhaps set astrologically at birth, is nevertheless expected to be personally responsible for his or her morality and health.

Islam is held up constantly as a faith that offers individuals the choice to develop themselves. They can choose to observe as many of the five pillars of the religion as they can (declaration of faith, prayer five times daily, alms-giving (*zakat*), fasting during Ramadan, and going on a pilgrimage to Mecca at least once in their lifetime); they can opt to renounce so-called *bi'da* practices (regarded by Wahabi and other fundamentalists as unacceptable innovations brought into Islam since the Prophet's death); they can join a radical or fundamentalist Islamic movement or a *tarika* brotherhood; they, both women and men, can choose to dress in any one of a number of distinctively Islamic ways and give up Western dress; they can also give up smoking hashish (*bangi*) or tobacco, drinking alcohol, and sexual "promiscuity"; they can improve their management of conjugal and family relations and increase their respect for other persons; and they may act upon the Islamic ruling that every individual should widen his or her knowledge of the world through his or her experience, including travel and questioning, and interpret it through the Koran and Hadithi.

In Zanzibar, formal sermons given by *imams* and Sheikhs as well as sermons given at men's evening *baraza* and in family contexts are examples of ways in which individuals can improve themselves and the Islamic society and the wider world in which they live. They may be contested, as in the conflicts over the acceptability (or otherwise) of practices (as being *bi'da*) or of joining a brotherhood, but in fostering theological debate, they illuminate the possibility of religious choices in the creation of personal destiny. But lest we begin to think of such self-improvement as incremental in the sense that a lifetime spent in such piety will automatically ensure entry into heaven at death (and perhaps even sainthood), such accumulated virtue can be annihilated by a single act of behavior that is deemed to be a sin. Thus, at the very point of death, a person who has been pious all his or her life can ruin it all by knowingly abusing the religion or the name of the Prophet.

The latter may be explained as the result of the person's inherent deficiencies of character, which have eventually overcome the individual's piety: try as he might, he could not overcome his intrinsic personality shortcomings, which arose from his humoral makeup. But Swahili discourse appears to allow for a kind of compensatory process by which individuals can choose to overcome their intrinsic personality defects by pious acts, although these individuals are always threatened by the possibility that their defects may overcome their virtuous intentions. It is a theory that is reminiscent of the battle of personal wills described by European post-Enlightenment thinkers, but, unlike the latter, Islam places emphasis on greater or lesser amounts of individual propensity for sin. Recognizing the great emphasis placed by local people on the unchanging nature of "bad" character, the Halali Sunna reformist movement insists that an individual can overcome his or her personality weaknesses through the exercise of willpower, and proponents of this movement claim some success in having in this way brought some "sinful" individuals back into the fold of Islam.

Imams or *maalims* are the constant judges of a person's scale of religious worthiness, although the final arbiter is presumed to be God. But how do diviners and healers fit this moral pivot of Islam to their own diagnoses and attempts at cure? I suggest that they do so by casting most, perhaps nearly all, sicknesses and misfortunes in terms of ultimate social and interpersonal causation, whatever may be the particular physical symptoms which need to be treated immediately.

Although the recasting (as we might call it) of the physical in terms of the social is widespread throughout Africa and elsewhere in the world and is not confined to Islam, the form it takes in Zanzibar occurs for the two reasons I have mentioned: (1) the hesitancy or guarded manner with which healers practice their craft (despite and perhaps because of the recent privatization of modern biomedicine), for fear of a return to the days when they might be accused of sorcery and so suffer harm; and (2) the heightened consciousness of Islam as a complete moral and social system.

My point with regard to the latter is that traditional Islamic healing has for centuries been practiced as a science which first accommodated Islam and then sought legitimation for it, whereas (as nowadays in Zanzibar) it is Islam which accommodates the work of healers, who constantly refer to the Koran and other sacred texts for therapy and not just for legitimation. In this, the intrinsic humoral properties and personality of the patient serve as a reminder to the patient that he or she has to overcome his or her defects and that this can only be done through correct Islamic behavior, but that given the possibility that the symptoms and sickness may nevertheless persist, such defects and Islamic inadequacy may become displaced onto malevolent social and cosmic others, such as witches and possessory spirits.

In other words, it would become impracticable for a healer to have to constantly blame a patient's sinfulness for her sickness. Such a perspective may provide an overall starting point and framework for questioning by *maalims* and *imams*. But the healer, who may of course also be a *maalim* or *imam* in other contexts, can alternatively blame witches and spirits and so relieve the patient of intrinsic culpability. The Halali Sunna Islamic reformists reject witchcraft and spirit possession as causes of illness, but many healers nevertheless continue to invoke them, sometimes excusing the measure because it gives the patient the reassurance of an explanation that he or she understands and perhaps seeks before moving on to more humoral-based therapy. The explanations thus move the patient from intrinsic personal badness or weakness, which is laid bare through inadequate religious observance, to ideas of his or her innocence in a world of evil others, one that includes witches and spirits. A person is thereby reminded in turn of his inherent human moral frailty, offered salvation through Islam, and then excused the accusation of being sick (through being a bad Muslim) by having the blame transferred to others.

In practice, healers rarely address the question of the adequacy of a person's piety, although it may be referred to obliquely in divination beforehand. Impiety as the governing cause of ill health is thus part of an agenda which is revealed through the public mosque sermons and, privately, by religious clerics, but this cause is kept out of the surgery. At first, we might think that this indicates a separation of the religious and the medical, of the moral and the therapeutic. But, as mentioned above, healers often are or were once also *maalims*, and they receive the gift of healing through their own piety—sometimes, as in the case of Sharifs, through the *baraka*, which is conferred on them by descent from the Prophet Mohamed. In the days since the revolution in Zanzibar, many healers who did not leave the island turned their spiritual energies directly to matters of the mosque, turning back again, in the recent past, to treating individual patients outside the mosque. This illustrates the interpenetrability of diagnosis, cure, worship, and proselytization, which can certainly be broadly distinguished as activities, as indeed they are in the Swahili language, but which are not separately constituted as "systems." Even the place where the healer practices, usually his home in Zanzibar, may include a room which serves both as a mosque and as a resting room, as is the case in Kenya in the so-called surgeries or clinics.

Although not normally spoken of as such in the surgery, we can think of Islamic-based moral piety as a generalized spiritual force which converts things into diagnostic methods and preventive and curative medicine. Because this spiritual force inheres in or is "fed" into things, the healer can draw on it and need not blame the patient for being impious (and so for lacking spiritual defenses). The patient need not be judged, because the piety comes to belong to objects rather than persons, except, of course, for the healers themselves. Thus, healers must be pious and worthy of the name of Islam. Ordinary Muslims ought to be pious, and in religious contexts they are exhorted to be, but in the domain of medicine, they can be allowed to draw on the piety in things through the help of the healer.

Well-known examples of such spiritually imbued objects are the *hirizi*, an amulet containing sacred Koranic verses written in Arabic on paper and sewn into the leather or other pouch worn on the arm; the *kombe*, the water (often rosewater) which has been used to wash off Koranic verses also written in Arabic on a plate in saffron and which is drunk to cure sickness or to repulse the effects of evil spirits or witchcraft; and the very medicines themselves, ranging from plant parts to animals and insects, which only have effects through Islamic knowledge. It is often said, for example, "everything is (potentially) medicine" (*yote ni dawa; kila kitu ni dawa*). For instance, according to the Zanzibari healer with whom I began this account, plant and animal parts, including insects, can only be made beneficial in the light of the healer's knowledge of the client's elemental or humoral makeup (which he variously called *miyongo, mizaja,* and *hali*), and the basis (*msingi*) of this makeup is the planetary position (*nyota zake*) under which the client was born. "You can't just take a plant and say it is medicine. You have to know the patient's elements through his stars."

Given that the hot/cold and dry/moist distinctions frame the form taken by these elements and the sicknesses which derive from their imbalance, it is only foods of an appropriate kind which redress the balance. Thus, foods also partake of this ultimate Islamic spirituality through their elemental properties. For instance, a person diagnosed as having arthritis of, say, the foot and leg should not eat beef, which is a cold food, one that would worsen arthritis, which is also a cold sickness. He or she should eat hot foods so that the healer can, through massage of the legs, open up the narrowed blood vessels which cause the coldness of arthritis. Conversely, prawns or lamb/mutton, both hot foods, are more likely to worsen a condition, while unlike objects are more likely to restore balance, although excess in the latter case may be harmful. The all-embracing object imbued with medical spirituality is the Koran itself. A common expression—in fact, a verse taken from the Koran—is that the Holy Book *is* medicine, a description that is taken in two not-incompatible senses. The first is that the physical book itself is curative, as in healing rituals in which the book is held and moved above and around the head of a patient or in rituals in which verses are taken from the Koran and written in Arabic on paper or on a plate, as in the examples of the *hirizi* and *kombe* given above. A second sense is that the Koran contains all past, present, and future knowledge and so can be used by those with sufficient understanding to cure any affliction and even to work miracles: hence, the shading of the qualities of sainthood into those of healing. The two senses in which the Koran can be regarded as medicine point up the ambivalence in ideas of material spirituality: Halali Sunna reformists accept that the Koran is holy but reject curative objects like the *hirizi* or *kombe*, despite the fact that Koranic verses are used in their making.

Most healers, however, hold to the generalized idea of spiritually imbued materiality, namely that everything is created by God and can be realized as such through faith and correct procedure, especially when, as in the case of some plants and foods used in cures, they are mentioned in the Koran. This explains why healing sessions contain an early phase which purges the patient's body of evils caused by spirits or witchcraft. For although the so-called white, good, or Rohani jinns may be harnessed in the cause, the non-Islamic spirits are not imbued with Islamic spirituality and must be driven out. They are not humans; they are satanically constituted and so are the obverse of divine objects, as is witchcraft. At one level, dispersing non-Islamic spirits clears the ground for medicines, including *kombe* and *hirizi*, to work; at another level, focusing on them as the cause of affliction deflects blame for his or her unfortunate condition away from the patient, or at least enables the healer to give advice that does not impugn the person's moral behavior, such as suggesting that the patient change his or her diet and eat fewer hot or cold foods according to the nature of his or her elemental makeup.

It is not too much to say, in conclusion, that the Swahili theory of personal humoral makeup avoids classifying persons as intrinsically good or bad but instead sees them as beings that are remade constantly. They are remade by changes in their diet and by their changing exposure to cold, heat, and seasonal changes and sometimes even by the aging process itself: a baby is born "hot" but may "cool" when older. Where astrology is used, individuals may also be remade by the fact that a person may have a number of different names: since in practice a healer uses names rather than a fixed birth date to determine a person's planetary sign and elemental makeup, a patient may reveal different personal and mother's names to different healers, so altering the way that individual is constituted by each healer. In these different ways, patients do in theory have some say in the medical discourse by which they are diagnosed and made well. They thus have the potential (again, in theory) to change their elemental makeup. The key question is which among them are the empiricists who consciously experiment in this manner in order to get the best for their well-being that the elements offer? It is unlikely that persons would admit to such attempts to change their elemental makeup by, say, switching names from one healer to another, but it would be strange if some had not tried it and so sought to alter their possibilities of being. They certainly follow prescriptions to take different foods and herbal medicines and to desist from situations in which they are exposed to heat and cold. That they can seek to alter their possibilities of being by switching names from one healer to another is permitted by the interpretive flexibility in the methods of diagnosis and cure available in Swahili culture. This flexibility arises from the play between the central presupposition of Islamic moral piety (as that which determines health) and the impracticability of this being the only basis of a healer–patient relationship.

REFERENCES

Beckerleg, S. 1990. "Maintaining Order, Creating Chaos: Swahili Medicine in Kenya." Doctoral dissertation, University of London.

———. 1994. "Medical Pluralism and Islam in Swahili Communities in Kenya." *Medical Anthropological Quarterly* 8, no. 3: 298–313.

Bourdieu, P. 1977. *Outline of a Theory of Practice.* Cambridge: Cambridge University Press.

Giddens, A. 1976. *New Rules of Sociological Method.* New York: Basic Books.

Hollis, M. 1977. *Two Models of Man.* Cambridge: Cambridge University Press.

Lukes, S. 1977. "Methodological Individualism Reconsidered." In S. Lukes, *Essays in Social Theory.* London: Macmillan.

Mkangi, K. 1990. "A Preliminary Report on the Basics and Principles of Swahili Therapeutics." Presentation to seminars at the School of Oriental and African Studies, London, May 1990.

Ricoeur, P. 1981. *Hermeneutics and the Human Sciences.* Edited and translated by J. B. Thompson. Cambridge: Cambridge University Press.

Swartz, M. 1991. *The Way the World Is.* New Haven, Conn.: Yale University Press.

Taylor, C. 1985. "Hegel's Philosophy of Mind." In C. Taylor, *Human Agency and Language: Philosophical Papers, vol. 1.* Cambridge: Cambridge University Press, pp. 77–96.

3. Some African Conceptions of Person: A Critique

Didier N. Kaphagawani

The editors regret to announce that Didier N. Kaphagawani passed away July 28, 2000 in Malawi after a long illness.

Since Tempels, discussions of African conceptions of reality make a basic yet questionable assumption that such conceptions must be in contrast to their Western equivalents. This has been most evident in the discussions of the concepts of person and personhood. This trend often gives the impression that after such a long time, human nature has been laid bare to enable the exact knowledge of its constituting parts. Thus, it has been argued, much in line with Tempels's speculations, that while Western philosophy defines personhood and personal identity in fairly static terms, African peoples think of personhood as more dynamic. Yet it is not hard to realize that Tempels's eagerness was itself only driven by a questionable ambition to draw sharp contrasts between African conceptions and the Cartesian *res cogitans* which he believed to be analytically and scientifically more acceptable or, in the idioms of his goals, "more philosophical." The result was the false impression that the concept of person and personal identity in rationalist and empiricist texts has some greater objective basis than what he had come to learn from the Baluba.

One can identify at least three basic attempts to define personal identity in Western philosophy since the Enlightenment. First there are those who explain personal identity in mentalistic terms. According to this group, our identity through time is considered to be a function of the continuity of our thoughts, beliefs, and feelings. Second, there are also those who explain personal identity in terms of the continuity of our bodies. They argue that despite the changes we undergo in the process of growth and development over time, it is the basic unity of our identity which is responsible for our remaining the same "person." Finally, some philosophers have argued that personal identity is just an illusion without an independence of existence or substance. Exponents of the first theory extend far back into the history of philosophy. This theory is grounded especially in the medieval religious theory of the soul as the seat of personal identity, as the element in which resides reason and will as the basic faculties of the soul. Descartes preferred the term "mind" to the medieval "soul," and since his time, several philosophers have substituted the term "mind" for "soul." Opponents of the Cartesian and older forms of dualism have emphasized the view that our identity is a function of nothing more than the identity of our bodies. This view includes the position of Gilbert Ryle as well as that of more recent materialists who advocate the identity theory.

The British philosopher John Locke defended the view widely referred to as the *memory theory*, that personal identity is based on self-consciousness, particularly on memories of one's former experiences. According to Locke, personal identity is due not to the identity of substance but merely to the identity of consciousness.[1] Thought is always accompanied by consciousness of the fact that we are thinking. It is impossible, he says, "for any one to perceive without *perceiving* that he does perceive. When we see, hear, smell, taste, feel, meditate, or will anything, we know that we do so."[2] The identity of the self is so completely dependent upon the subject's consciousness of past and present states that to deny this identity because of the time that has intervened between one state and another or because of the change of substance is as absurd as claiming that someone is not the same person because he is wearing different clothes than he did yesterday.

What is said of the identity of the person can be applied equally well to the identity of the self, for both terms have the same denotation for Locke, although they differ in connotation. But Locke makes a distinction between the ideas of "self" and "person" on the one hand and the idea of "man" on the other. The "man," in his view, is made up not of soul alone but also of "body and shape." Hume, on the other hand, came to the conclusion that nothing is responsible for our identity through time because our identity is only an illusion. Where Locke admitted the inference of the subject of consciousness, Hume claimed to identify only perception. "I never can catch myself at any time without a perception," he says, "and never can observe any thing but the perception."[3] It is obvious from this comment and the related passages from Hume that he was looking for a simple, independent, and immutable self in the form of a substance, and having "failed" to trace it apart from perceptions, he thought the self and perceptions to be one, as neither could survive the other.

Recently, Gilbert Ryle has argued that mentalism commits the category mistake by suggesting that there must be a separate substance called mind merely on account of the functional evidence of those activities that we contrast to the physical ones. This mistake, he contends, originates in improper use of language, leading inevitably to the impression of the mind as the ghost in the machine, which ascribes mind to a category to which it does not belong. But what is important here is to note that all these ideas cast a non-uniform Western view of the notion of personal identity and self. The ones we have seen can hardly be summed up in a single notion, to which can be contrasted another notion which is also assumedly uniform in its rendition. Perhaps a useful summarizing view is the one suggested by Jackson and Karp, who argue that Western notions of personhood and self can be referred to as being more egocentric than African ones, which tend to be more sociocentric.[4]

I wish to argue in this essay that although several scholars of African philosophy have suggested notions of personhood which they purport to contrast to Western ones, such notions, like the Western ones to which they are contrasted, give only a partial view of how persons are regarded under different and often changing points of focus. As suggested by Shaw in the essay contained in this volume, concepts of personhood and of constitutions of selves as social entities or agents are functions of ever-changing economic histories and historical economies. They are not constant, even if philosophical definitions tend to fix them as unchangeable substances. Analysis of the ways in which various African peoples talk of persons and their capacities equally reveals that representations of personhood shift within the context of discourse without negating or diminishing the importance of other views that are not in equal focus at any given time and discourse form. Similarly, I do not believe, so long after they have been so widely discussed, that the concepts of personal identity or self propounded by Western rationalists and empiricists (in their different configurations since the Enlightenment) necessarily supersede or contradict one another in any significant manner. Rather, they depict different angles and approaches to the understanding of the multi-sided (expressive and substantialist) manifestations of the human condition. I shall base my critique of such theories of African ideas of personhood on linguistic evidence that often opposing views do exist and are expressed when and where appropriate. My main linguistic resource shall be Chichewa, the language I understand best by both birth and conscious use. The theories I have chosen to critique are those advanced by Tempels, Kagame, and Mbiti, or, as they have been called, respectively, the concept of personhood based on the idea of force, that based on the idea of shadow, and that based on the idea of communalism.

TEMPELS'S THESIS

As I said above, Placide Tempels strongly believed in a radical conceptual difference between the Bantu and Western philosophers in terms of the essential nature of beings in general and of human beings in particular. According to him, the Bantu think of being in terms of essential energies or forces. Building his thesis on his perception of Luba modes of speech and speech genres, Tempels concluded that "In every Bantu language it is easy to recognize the words or phrases denoting a *force*, which is not used in an exclusively bodily sense, but in the sense of the integrity of our whole being."[5] For the Bantu, according to Tempels, it is not enough to have life; rather, what is even more important is that life be lived in degrees of force. The stronger one's force, the more meaningful and complete his/her life is perceived to be. Thus, he says, "We need not be surprised that the Bantu allude to this vital force in their greetings one to another, using such forms of address as: 'You are strong,' or 'you have life in you,' 'you have life strongly in you.'"[6] And, as life is lived in terms of degrees of the vital force, so too it is lost in similar degrees of the diminution of force. Yet Tempels warns that it would be quite erroneous to translate the Ciluba terms *kufwa* and *kufwididila* as "to die" and "to die entirely," respectively. Misfortune diminishes one's vital force, and all those natural conditions which are perceived to contribute to the diminution of one's vital force are classified as morally bad simply because they do not sustain or augment the vital force. According to Tempels, the idea of diminishing and augmenting the vital force marks a significant difference between how the Bantu and Westerners think and talk of beings. While the Bantu idea of being, as based on their notion of the vital force, is essentially dynamic, that of Westerners is typically static.[7] It is hard for the Bantu to separate the idea of force from that of being. For them, force is being and being is force.[8] But to claim only that the idea of the vital force is inseparable from that of being does not in itself lead to claiming the identity of the two. They may be inseparable in terms of mutual entailment of one by the other, but they still remain separate and distinct from each other. Thus, while the vital force might indeed be a necessary condition for being, Tempels still fails to explain that it is a sufficient condition. Hence, being could have other properties besides that of the vital force. But faced with this possible objection, Tempels expeditiously explained that for the Bantu, the vital force is not merely an adventitious and accidental reality. Rather, he argued, the vital force is more than being just a necessary attribute of being; rather, it *is* being. "Force is the nature of being, force is being, being is force."[9]

But this position raises quick questions. First, if being is defined in terms of force—that is, if the Bantu think of the ordinary idea of force (as capacity for action) as substance—then we need an explanation of how the Bantu think and talk of action, of performance. As we know them, the Bantu—and I assume most other African peoples I have known too—talk vividly of people and things as having or lacking the capability to perform in varying degrees with respect to expectations. Thus, they talk of people as having or lacking the necessary physical force to perform certain functions requiring physical strength. Hence, for them, as for all people of sound common sense, there are weak and strong people and weak and strong animals. Likewise, they talk of strong and weak medicines, strong and weak building timber and/or stones, strong and weak clothing texture (in terms of the clothing's capacity to withstand adverse strength or the physical force exerted on it). In most of these cases, reference to force is purely in terms of someone's or something's capacity to either resist opposing forces or to produce effects, meaning they talk of force as capacity of an agent rather than as substance itself. Tempels's thesis thus portrays the Bantu as extraordinary in their conceptual and linguistic representations of reality, and his thesis indicates that their concepts and languages lie outside the normal and common sense, as defined by their corresponding Western examples. Using an old but controversial theory about the relationship between thought and language, Tempels aimed to show that the Bantu thought in perverse ways, as, in his view, was evidenced by the perversity of their language. But a close study of a Bantu language like Chichewa reveals no evidence of the alleged confusion or incapability of the Bantu to conceptually distinguish substance from its properties. It is thus not surprising that Tempels himself fails to offer any example, even from Ciluba, his primary reference.

Tempels's second problem arises from his claim that it is erroneous to translate *kufa* as "to die" and *kufadi* as "to die indeed," for if there are any words and phrases which lend themselves to easy translation, these two are such words. To say "X akufa" in Chichewa does not indicate that one is defining or regarding death or the act of dying as being more than "the process of dying is occurring to X" or "X is in the process of losing life," as is meant by the English "X is dying." Similarly, to say "X akufadi" is not so much to ascertain the ultimate degree of loss of life as it is to claim that one is certain of his claim—that the claim "X is dead" is true—that "X died already." It is merely a truth claim in reference to what has happened to X. To impute to these expressions metaphysical references denoting degrees and intensities of the vital force is to take far too literally an ordinary mode of expression. Cannot the Bantu talk like ordinary, everyday people who pass information between themselves in manners that use simple ways of setting aside the skepticism and surprise of their listeners?

Third, Tempels's insistence on the distinction between "man" and "person" raises similar questions of translation. He claims, rather surprisingly, that *munthu* in Chichewa, for example, should not be translated as "man" but rather as "person," because, according to his interpretation of Ciluba, "'*Muntu*' signifies, then, vital force, endowed with intelligence and will."[10] Although this double translation may be required in some Bantu languages, Chichewa has only one term, *Munthu,* which signifies both "person" and "man." It is noted that in Kiswahili, another Bantu-based language, there are two terms, *binadamu* and *mtu,* which can be translated to refer to "man," as in "human being," and "person," respectively. But even in Kiswahili, both *binadamu* and *mtu* are assumed both to have body and to possess intelligence and will, concrete properties which separate them from other beings by virtue of their specific bodily and cognitive attributes. Again, the Bantu, like all people with sufficient common sense, do not think of humans as having intelligence and will only at some times and not at others. In Chichewa, *munthu* denotes as much a "human being" as it does a "person."

There are, however, some occasions when the Chewa use the term *munthu* in such a manner that clarification is called for, as Chewa can be prone to misinterpretation; Tempels has evidently fallen prey to this problem. Such misinterpretation may occur, for example, when the Chewa say "Azungu siwanthu," literally translatable as "Whites are not humans." Yet, with only little analysis, it is not hard to see that this expression is not uttered to assert the nonhumanness of white people. Rather, it is used as a critical expression to indicate disapproval of the epistemological and moral principles which underlie some aspects of Western comportment that are observed to consistently negate what the Chewa consider ideal epistemological and moral values. Hence, the statement does not translate into "Whites are not humans" but rather "Whites do not behave as people are expected to do." But to the extent that only concrete "persons" are both epistemological and moral agents, Tempels might be right in advising against translating *munthu* as "human;" rather, it might be translated as "person."

Yet certain situations warrant translating *munthu* as "human." To say, for example, "Achewa ndi wanthu" is to assert the humanness of the Achewa; this statement emphasizes their humaneness or ideal social and moral qualities rather than expressing the metaphysical idea that they possess intelligence and will. Similarly, the Achewa may say, as they often do, "Azungu ndi wanthu" in order to express appreciation for certain qualities which they may believe to be shared by white folks as part of their culture. These expressions reveal how the Achewa describe their appreciation of the everyday qualities of social and moral values without driving wedges between their own conceptions and those of other people with regard to the metaphysical constitution of personhood. The use of the term *munthu* outside these specific contexts may shift attention to other modes of speech and may shift focus to other aspects of human life and its multiple expressions. In other words, for the Achewa, as for most people with sound common sense, humans are simultaneously several things at the same time, but speech and thought may pay attention to only one or a few of these things at any given time.

Finally, Tempels's theory of the Bantu conception of the world of forces borders on the impossible. Tempels's emphasis on strict metaphysical differences between Bantu and Western conceptions of personhood is thus overblown by an ambitious project to draw a divide between the two traditions in the hope that he would thus elevate systems of thought to levels previously denied them. It should sound a little ridiculous to anybody, for example, that a major difference between the Bantu and other people is that the Bantu think humans to be metaphysically distinct from other beings on account of their possession of reason and volition. What do peoples of other cultures think humans are? One does not need much rational effort to realize Tempels's exaggerations. As a result, his theories of an African worldview result in pushing African systems of thought even further into mystical realms than he had intended.

MBITI'S THESIS

As is well known, John Mbiti excelled as one of Tempels's chief disciples. Like Tempels, Mbiti too was greatly driven by the zeal to reveal another way in which he believed African modes of thought to be characteristically distinct from their Western counterparts. What he claims—that while Western social systems and thought view persons primarily as atomic individuals, Africans view persons as constituted by and constituting a social world which is primarily communal—has come to be regarded as a fundamental difference between African and Western social systems and thought. Tempels himself had been quite explicit in claiming that in Bantu thought, persons or humans are defined and individuated communally. According to Tempels, "This concept of separate beings, of substance . . . which find themselves side by side, entirely independent one of another, is foreign to Bantu thought. Bantu hold that created beings preserve a bond one with another, an intimate ontological relationship, comparable with the causal tie which binds creature and Creator. For the Bantu there is interaction of being with being, that is to say, of force with force."[11] But while a sense of African communalism is prompted by his notion of the interaction of the vital forces as a necessary element of the "dynamic" African worldview, Mbiti's is a more direct claim to the primacy of the community over the individual as the basis of African social theory, which, according to him, places emphasis on the social good, on the unity of the group, over the free agency and freedom of the individual. Thus, as pointed out earlier in this volume by Shaw, Mbiti sees in African social theory the exact opposite of what Western Enlightenment theory attributed to the individual as the seat of moral, economic, epistemological, and legal values. As Tempels claims, "The child, even the adult, remains always for the Bantu a man, a force, in causal dependence and ontological subordination to the forces which are his father and mother. The older force ever dominates the younger."[12]

This is by far the most influential aspect of Tempels's idea of a Bantu system of thought. One finds its roots in the political thought of the leading African ideologues: i.e., Leopold Sedar Senghor, Julius Nyerere, Kenneth Kaunda, and even Kwame Nkrumah. To these leaders, African communalism presented a desirable alternative to the Western framework of individualism, which, in their view, was the underlying premise of exploitative and conflictual Western capitalism. Communalism was thus not only a metaphysical principle of social existence but also a sort of critique of the social order, one derived from the European Enlightenment.

Of the leaders mentioned above, perhaps Senghor and Nyerere became the best known exponents of the idea that African communalism can be seen as a form of humanism or, as Nyerere frequently put it, as an antidote to the predatory Western evil. For Senghor, whose thought was formed in Europe during and in the company of the great neo-Kantian champions of the framework which privileges simultaneity and the ontological coexistence of opposites over contrariness and opposition of opposites, the idea of negritude is all about binding opposites together in an aesthetic interplay of complementarity that brings the universe to its fulfillment. African art, like African knowing, ethics, and ontology, transcends the dichotomies and disparateness of shapes, colors, subject–object, good and evil, and being and non-being. Africans, according to Senghor, see these elements of reality as signs to be interpreted for the establishment of harmony and rhythm. They see reality as being made up of these elements, which may seem contradictory in appearance but which are really complementary. Nyerere took this sense of communalism far afield into the world of realpolitik, a new socio-political order in which all are different but equal producers and consumers. *Ujamaa* is a socio-economic framework which avoids the conflictual antagonism of both capitalism and doctrinaire socialism.

Mbiti's defense of communalism thus traces its roots deep into both cultural and intellectual histories of the preceding times. Since the time of his own writing, several others have toed this line in search of an African difference and uniqueness. But this endeavor has found as much welcome as controversy. What the points that I have made above show is that the scholars of African difference were so much steeped in articulating the ideological divides between African and Western worldviews that they lost the real self in their analyses in pursuit of something else, perhaps an esteemed value such as community. The concepts of the self adopted by these scholars are chosen strictly with this goal in mind: they are concerned not with what concept best captures the manifold experiences of the self but with what concept best allows them to both promote difference and derive the ontological values of the vital forces as well as communalism. Their position rejects that of Tempels in an interesting way. Tempels, eager to represent the African experience of the self as a sort of pathology by virtue of its "deviation" from the supposedly "scientific" psychologism of European Enlightenment, went on to describe the African self as ineffable precisely because, for him, it lacks precise location; it is non-substantive. The African self is neither a mental nor a material substance or unity of both. By contrast, the communalists have tried to counter this ineffability of an African self by arguing that while they accept the radical difference between Africans' and Western philosophers' ideas of self, the difference is not present because the former is pathological. Rather, like Lacan, they think that the sense of being an active subject is not merely analogous to but also dependent on the use of the term "I." Just as the term "I," known as a "shifter" in linguistics, belongs to no one and in a conversation moves around among the participants, so the sense of being a subject, a self, is not a realism of self that is transmitted from one level to another through the transmission of "nanny," as the Dogon say. The self becomes a shifter, the "I" that appears and disappears in the linguistic and ontological roles of various participants. No one can therefore be greater than the communal good. Rather, it is the communal good that is greater; it uses the individuals. What a striking similarity with Lacan's assertion that "I identify myself in language, but only by losing myself in it like an object"![13] Mbiti and others decenter the self from the psyche to the relational body and shifting "nanny." The self of their conception is one that is constituted by an objective relational expression; it transcends the reification of self in the specificity of substance in the Cartesian sense.

The communalist thesis thus sets itself up as the antithesis to the Cartesian individualist notions of self and of subjectivity. But, as Shaw argues in the essay included in this collection, both perspectives are reflections of changing circumstances in the histories and political economies of the societies in which they respectively acquire status as both intellectual and ordinary expressions of value choices and institutional frameworks. They are, on that note, just "philosophies and theories [which], like political opinions, should be regarded as part and parcel of the world in which we live rather than transcendent views that somehow escape the impress of our social interests, cultural habits, and personal persuasions."[14] Individual theories, even at their best, often bear the tendency of failing to match the products of intellectual reflection with the manifold and ambiguous character of lived experience. Thus, although the substantive Enlightenment theories of the self may be justified as functions of specific historical social transformations, they make sense only in the context of their contrast to and competition with a rival perspective. The same applies to the communalist theories in African social science. Indeed, such Chewa proverbs as "Mvula ikakuona litsiro siikata" ("The rain does not stop pouring after it sees your individual dirtiness") and "Wanthu ndi mchenga saundika" ("Human beings are like sand out of which one cannot make a mountain") clearly indicate their awareness of both individuality and social system as different but mutually interdependent elements in the constitution of the world of real persons and selves. Similarly, the practice of privileging the opinions of some members of society over those of other members (i.e., giving disproportionate status to the opinions of elders over those of the young) does not necessarily amount to a non-cognizance of the epistemological value of youth. Rather, like in every orderly distribution of roles in a system of production, this privilege is given to individuals who show and sustain the ability to perform the roles apportioned to them by the social system. No one is held *a priori* to be an expert in any domain of knowledge merely on the ground of his age. Everyone must prove his worth by the measure of an established norm. And furthermore, the Chewa believe that old knowledge quickly loses its worth and validity unless it is constantly renewed and rejuvenated. So, while they say that *Mau wa akuluakulu akagonera* (the elders' words are sweet after a year), the Chewa also say that *Tsobola wakale sawawa* (old pepper is never hot forever), pointedly meaning that what held sway previously need not necessarily continue to do so even after it falls into obsolescence and irrelevance. It does not require extra effort to see the variance between the romanticized representations of African worldviews in the texts of Tempels's school and those of another, which starts with the assumption that Africans of the pro-colonial (as pre-missionary) period were as ordinary a people as those anywhere else and which so postulates the complexity, ambiguity, and multifacetedness of the "human consciousness in its lived immediacy."[15]

KAGAME'S THESIS

Kagame, for his part, followed the Aristotelian metaphysical path in arguing that the Bantu sense of self is to be found in their separation of specific human nature from the rest of created beings; this separation is achieved by identifying in humans an element which is the seat of the distinctive qualities of intelligence and will. Ostensibly, Kagame's goal was to restitute what Tempels had denied of the Bantu conception of the ontological constitution of personhood by going back to the functional nature of the self. As is well known, his analysis led him to the postulation of universal function-based characteristics that he identified as the seat of human essence. Like Descartes, Kagame argued that the Bantu belief in the immortality of some aspect of personhood was enough ground to support the idea that they believed in humans as entities that were partly made of "shadows," or, as he calls it, "the vital principle of animality known as shadow." A human (person) differs from other animals because "he is animated by a second vital principle which is immortal and in which are anchored the intelligent operations proper to man."[16] But the definition of these capacities suggests, as Wiredu has opined about the Akan, that having intelligence and being (morally) free are not universal attributes. According to Wiredu's analysis of parallel beliefs among the Akan, "neither free will [and intelligence] nor the lack of [them] is a universal feature of the human condition; some people have free will [and intelligence], others do not. Second, one and the same individual may have free will [and intelligence] with respect to one sphere of conduct but not some other."[17] In fact, Kagame's own definition of the Bantu notions of these features suggests that they are attributed to individuals at some times and not at others. A person in considered intelligent not only when he is capable of reflecting and meditating "upon the data of his senses" but also when he shows in practice the ability to "compare the facts of the knowledge he has acquired" and "to invent something new by combining previously acquired knowledge."[18] These definitions mean that although these operations are open only to humans, being free and/or intelligent is not an automatic ontological attribute. This is why old age is not an automatic repository of either wisdom or moral excellence, even if there is a general (normative) expectation of the ideal that old age, as an indicator of biological maturity, be matched by a corresponding optimal maturity in intelligence and social and moral responsibility.

According to Kagame, humans are further distinguishable from other animals by their possession of an element that is only roughly translatable into English as "heart" (*roho* in Kiswahili)—the disposition to act in morally qualifiable ways. To say that a person "has a bad heart" (*fulani ana roho nzuri* in Kiswahili) means to describe their actions as having a habitual inclination to be repulsive to others (i.e., being ill tempered or quarrelsome). Some people have "bad hearts" and others "good" ones. Note that such "hearts" are regarded as acquirable from specific social conditionings through upbringing and that not all individuals exposed to the same conditioning context acquire similar dispositions of "heart." Consequently, people are considered to differ from each other in terms of their individuality with reference to their emotional dispositions as well as to their intellectual and moral qualities. All these factors—that is, dispositions and qualities—combine with the manner in which an individual appeals to others to make up the individual's personality. Some individuals have a striking presence in the midst of others, while others can frequently go unnoticed. Because of this, appeal is "read" in people by others; they themselves might not be aware of it. Appeal is not learned and cannot be improved or lost, so no one is praised or blamed for this appeal. And it is also not "read" equally by all those with whom one comes into contact. In a rather loose translation, people with "striking presence" or "strong appeal" are said to "drown with their blood" those with whom they come into contact. They have *mbi*, as the Luo of Kenya say; they simply stand out. What should be noted as a flaw in Kagame's thesis is his propensity to articulate these appraisals of human behavior by assigning them to substances or substantial elements (principles) in the Aristotelian and Cartesian fashions of grading beings by virtue of their "higher functions," which are (naturally) revealed at every "higher stage."

In conclusion, I hope that the reader has been able to identify a number of points from this analysis of the recent representations of African perceptions of self. First, I have tried to show the growth of the assumed gap between Western conceptions of self and those in use in African "traditional" expressions. While showing the artificial divides assumed to separate these two traditions of thought, I have also tried to expose the rift between theory and lived experience, the distance between the products of intellectual abstraction and, as Michael Jackson aptly calls it, "the manifold and ambiguous character of the immediacy of a *lebenswelt*." I have concurred with Parkin and Kratz that the idea of African communalism, which is regarded with such reverence by a section of African scholars, is itself real only because it is produced by individuals whose actions and behaviors validate and fix norms as much as they violate and change them. As stated by the nineteenth-century German neo-Kantian philosopher Georg Simmel, "A BASIC DUALISM . . . pervades the fundamental form of all sociation. The dualism consists in the fact that a relation, which is a fluctuating, constantly developing life-process, nevertheless receives a relatively stable external form. The sociological forms of reciprocal behavior, of unification, of presentation toward the outside, cannot follow, with any precise adaptation, the changes of their inside, that is, of the processes that occur in the individual in regard to the other."[19] In other words, community is not an ontologically stable entity. It is a collaborative life-world which brings into sociation forces, meanings, and agents of varying gender, age, and influence to construct their space, their *habitus*.

NOTES

1. John Locke, *Essays Concerning Human Understanding*, vol. 2, pp. xxvii, 23.
2. Ibid., pp. xxvii, 9.
3. D. Hume, *A Treatise of Human Nature*, vol. 1, pp. iv, 6.
4. Michael Jackson and Ivan Karp, *Personhood and Agency*, p. 18.
5. Placide Tempels, *Bantu Philosophy*, p. 45.
6. Ibid., p. 47.
7. Ibid., p. 51.
8. Ibid., pp. 50–51.
9. Ibid., p. 51.
10. Ibid., p. 55.
11. Ibid., p. 58.
12. Ibid., p. 60.
13. Jacques Lacan, *Écrits*, p. 86.
14. Michael Jackson, *Things as They Are*, p. 1.
15. Ibid., p. 2.
16. Alexis Kagame, "The Problem of 'Man' in Bantu Philosophy," p. 35.
17. Kwasi Wiredu, *Cultural Universals and Particulars*, p. 130.
18. Kagame, "The Problem of 'Man' in Bantu Philosophy," p. 36.
19. Georg Simmel, *On Individuality and Social Forms*, p. 351.

REFERENCES

Bourdieu, P. 1977. *Outline of a Theory of Practice*. Cambridge: Cambridge University Press.
Danto, A. C. 1980. *Nietzsche as Philosopher*. New York: Columbia University Press.
Floistad, G., ed. 1987. *Contemporary Philosophy. African Philosophy*. Vol. 5. Dordrecht: Martin Nijhoff.
Gwengwe. 1970. *Kukula ndi Mwambo*. Limbe: Publications of Malawi Literature Bureau.
Gyekye, K. 1984. "The Akan Concept of a Person." In R. Wright, ed., *African Philosophy: An Introduction*. Lanham, Md.: University Press of America.
Hume, D. 1974. *A Treatise of Human Nature*. London: Dent.
Jackson, M., ed. 1996. *Things as They Are: New Dimensions in Phenomenological Anthropology*. Bloomington: Indiana University Press.
Jackson, M., and I. Karp, eds. 1990. *Personhood and Agency: The Experience of Self and Other in African Cultures*. Washington, D.C.: Smithsonian Institution Press.
Kagame, A. 1989. "The Problem of 'Man' in Bantu Philosophy." *Journal of African Religion and Philosophy* 1.
Kumakanga, S. 1970. *Nzeru Zakale*. Nairobi: Longman.
Lacan, Jacques. 1966. *Écrits*. Paris: Éditions du Seuil.
Locke, J. 1947. *Essays Concerning Human Understanding*. London: Dent.
Mbiti, J. 1969. *African Religions and Philosophy*. London: Heinemann.
Menkiti, J. 1984. "Person and Community in African Traditional Thought." In

R. Wright, ed., *African Philosophy: An Introduction*. Lanham, Md.: University Press of America.

Nothomb, D. 1965. *Un Humanisme Africaine: Valeurs et Pierres d'Attente*. Brussels: Lumen Vitae.

Onwuanibe, R. 1984. "The Human Person and Immorality in Ibo Metaphysics." In R. Wright, ed., *African Philosophy: An Introduction*. Lanham, Md.: University Press of America.

Perry, J. 1975. *Personal Identity*. Berkeley: University of California Press.

Schacht, R. 1983. *Nietzsche*. London: Routledge.

Simmel, G. 1971. *On Individuality and Social Forms*. Chicago: University of Chicago Press.

Tempels, P. 1959. *Bantu Philosophy*. Paris: Présence Africaine.

Vesey, G. 1974. *Personal Identity*. London: Macmillan.

Wiredu, K. 1980. *Philosophy and an African Culture*. Cambridge: Cambridge University Press.

Wiredu, K. 1984. "The Concept of Mind with Particular Reference to the Language and Thought of the Akans." In R. Wright, ed., *African Philosophy: An Introduction*. Lanham, Md.: University Press of America.

Wiredu, K. 1996. *Cultural Universals and Particulars: An African Perspective*. Bloomington: Indiana University Press.

Wiredu, K., and K. Gyekye, eds. 1992. *Person and Community: Ghanaian Philosophical Studies*. Washington, D.C.: The Council for Research in Values and Philosophy.

Wright, R., ed. 1984. *African Philosophy: An Introduction*. Lanham, Md.: University Press of America.

PART 2.
KNOWLEDGE AND DISCOURSE

Introduction to Part 2

Knowledge and Discourse

The chapters in this section of the book analyze local forms of discourse to show how different media of expression, such as the use of proverbs and metaphor, are primary aspects of vernacular idioms for understanding and managing misfortune and for effecting social and personal transformations as well as for developing ways of knowing the world. These essays share a goal of narrowing the gap between linguists and social scientists with respect to the study of language use. They confirm that the social nature of language and linguistically conditioned social phenomena are related in such a way that they bring closer together sociolinguists and other social scientists; they do so by revealing how language not only depicts but also constitutes social hierarchies and differences among its speakers, their identities, and their relations to one another. These essays center on the questions of who speaks what language form to whom, on what occasion, and for what purpose? But these essays are also concerned with the contributions that the analysis of speech can offer to other disciplinary areas through the examination of such face-to-face interactions as marriage negotiations. They also reveal the role of language as an artistic tool in social processes (i.e., praise-naming games) or as part of wider categories (i.e., the sociology of knowledge and social change).

In Peter Amuka's essay, we see how the Luo people, using the genres of *pakruok* and *ngero*, assert their status as individuals by relating themselves to other persons. *Pakruok* is a genre of speech in which an individual identifies him or herself by affiliating his or her identity with a significant other. In praising an other, one praises oneself. *Ngero* is a subgenre of *pakruok* in which one praises oneself by taking the name of a significant status. Here the play of words is complex and ambiguous, referring to numerous attributes of the person holding that status. Audiences revel in the multilayered complexity of *pakruok* and *ngero* performances. At one and the same time, these performances invoke shared attitudes and beliefs and assert the achievement and distinctiveness of individuals. What is at stake is not the truth value of these assertions but rather the skill with which they are performed. Individuals recount familiar virtues by describing other people or statuses that possess them. By recounting the attributes of others and the relationships of friendship or kinship between self and other, individuals can assert virtues and achievements not directly but rather through associations they have made with other persons and roles. Thus, they raise their own social or moral standing to the same level as that of the others that they praise in their speech. Either these individuals are already known and admired for the qualities attributed to them or the person engaging in *pakruok* creates such status for them through his language art.

Through skilled and playful performances, important persons and characters are defined and presented to any number of audiences as these performances are repeated again and again. In the process, a community that shares a set of verbal devices, that delights in the skill of the performances—which are extremely competitive—and that is composed of marked and differentiated individuals is created and expressed in *pakruok* and *ngero* performance events. In *pakruok* and *ngero* performances, Luo show and tell themselves both to their community and to themselves. The acts of self-fashioning manifested in performance are simultaneously occasions for the construction of a moral community of shared values and references. Social ideals are invoked by assertive individuals who verbally create and place themselves above others by heightening their filiation—real or fictitious—with ideal forms of personhood and moral and social virtues and values. This is why *pakruok* is sometimes translated into English as "virtue boasting." David Parkin refers to this process of *pakruok* when describing the social dynamics of Luo Union meetings in Nairobi in the 1960s. He writes:

> At these meetings, whatever the manifest issue under discussion, the underlying assumptions of socio-economic status are expressed as initially lavish displays of prestige competition through cash donations known variously as *gisungore* (literally "they are being proud or boasting") or *gichamo nyadhi* ("they are eating *nyadhi*"...) or *pakruok* ("praising," usually by giving money to a traditional lyre-player who sings songs in praise of the donor's family, lineage or sub-tribe). This kind of pot-latching ... is nevertheless channeled through the "traditional" units of "sub-tribe" and lineage, for it is in the name of such units that the generous donor makes his contribution. (1978: 213)

The relation of *pakruok* to Luo assertions of self-worth makes it simultaneously a process of social integration and fission. Through *pakruok,* individuals define themselves as members of lineage groups, but *pakruok* also sets them apart from such groups in order to form or join new ones defined on the basis of either friendship or similarity to others in terms of esteemed social and personal values and achievements; through this interaction, Luo thus create sets of "emic dualisms" in their relations (Parkin 1978: 215). It is in this respect that both Amuka and Parkin depict *pakruok* as reflective of shifting parameters in Luo senses of social position and identity of individuals in a communal setting. *Pakruok,* then, is a genre of Luo speech events, a sort of public display of the features of individualism, such as artistry of speech, strength in wrestling, virility, and even other, more "modern" features that are manifested in socio-economic achievements and positions in society. *Pakruok* and *ngero* are part of the Luo sociology of knowledge (Blount 1975).

This Luo sociology of knowledge is historically and ethnically extended to the northern Luo-speaking Acoli people of Uganda in Odoch Pido's essay. Like Amuka, he too analyzes the everyday sayings, proverbs, and metaphors through which forms of social criticism and the knowledge of values are transmitted. This is not surprising, as the Ugandan Acoli and Kenyan Luo belong to the same cultural and language families. The influence of Okot p'Bitek's well-known satiric poetry (see, for example, p'Bitek 1966, 1967) is powerfully present in Odoch Pido's depiction of the impact of the growing urban lifestyles and values on the serenity of the traditional world. Like p'Bitek and several other critics of colonialism, Odoch Pido strongly argues that the colonial period brought a number of far-reaching social and cultural transformations in the Acoli communities of Gulu and Kitgum, including many changes in the very fabric of Acoli identity itself.

Of central concern to Acoli expression of crisis are the effects of crisis on the way in which Acoli are perceived in public. According to Odoch Pido, urban life has turned social interaction, especially that between men and women, into commercial transaction, producing a sex industry that is rife with disease and treated with scorn in the song he examines. But this scorn is not only a cultural satire against new values; it is also a cultural statement whose aim is to educate all those people who are exposed to the dangers of permissive urban life. These dangers, Odoch Pido tells us the Acoli people have concluded, deny people the opportunity to develop their personhood (*bedo dano*). The moral ontology of personhood, in Acoli, is constituted of a collection of culturally defined physical, social, moral, and spiritual capacities of an individual to influence and control his world. Loss of these capacities reduces an individual to the level of animality (*doko gwok*).

The emphasis here on creativity and use of language as key indicators of meaning and personhood is at the forefront of Corinne Kratz's essay on Okiek marriage negotiations. She states that among the Okiek, important matters such as marriage negotiations must be conducted in a controlled, elaborate, and reasoned manner. Not only does this requirement lead to the recognition of different capacities of individuals and groups to produce diverse effects on their surroundings, it is also used to justify the uneven but patterned distribution of roles in society. Yet this patterned linguistic economy of cultural production easily escapes the strictures of structuralism as stated in Pierre Bourdieu's theory of the logic of practice (Bourdieu 1977, 1990; Kratz 1994) or as inflated by Henri Maurier (1976 [1985]; also Masolo 1995). Kratz's observation here is that collective agency cannot be considered separately from the individual capacities and agency which make it possible. Likewise, the privileged capacities identified with the male gender are always preceded, at least in the actions and decisions that relate and lead to marriage, by the leading roles of the female members of family and community. In other words, collective and individual agencies, societies, and individual persons are complementary and interactive categories in the understanding of how culture is produced (Taylor 1985). This theme relates Kratz's essay to those of Parkin and Shaw.

The ambivalence described by Kratz as being characteristic of Okiek marital roles and relations is not unique. The advice or address which the bride receives at marriage is key also to the Luba conduct of marriage ceremonies in the Democratic Republic of the Congo and is part of a "master charter" which, according to Mudimbe (1991: 139ff.), "specifies and individualizes her major duties toward her spouse and his family and in so doing maintains the configuration of a patrilineal tradition." The bride becomes subjected to the interests of the patrilineal lineage, a means to its self-realization and fulfillment. But it is also through this instrumentality that the bride hopes to fulfill her own personhood, agency, and influence upon the dialectic of patrilineality. This too is shared by the Baluba in Mudimbe's text (1991: 142–43; and Theuws 1983). Gendered personhood subjugates, but it also liberates—and vice versa—actors related through different roles in the tangled game of the cultural ideology of everyday practice.

From a critical point of view, what this means for the victims of ideological oppression is "that those subject to oppression experience *even now* hopes and desires which could only be realistically fulfilled by a transformation of their [gendered] conditions" (Eagleton 1991: xiv). Kratz's position here is that the ideological reality of groups' interests is related to the phenomenal reality of social and economic roles through a linguistic reality—itself an unevenly distributed resource of meanings and significations—by which the other two are proposed, negotiated, and even canonized as referential tradition for future generations. Language thus becomes a form of social action, "*excluding* rival forms of thought, perhaps by some unspoken but systematic logic; and *obscuring* social reality in ways convenient to itself. Such 'mystification,' as it is commonly known, frequently takes the form of creating or suppressing social conflicts, from which arises the conception of ideology as an imaginary resolution of real contradictions" (Eagleton 1991: 5–6). But mystification through manipulation of language also "suggest[s] that ideology is a matter of 'discourse' rather than 'language.' It concerns the actual uses of language between particular human subjects for the production of specific effects" (Eagleton 1991: 9).

Every community has its own lineage idioms and other linguistic techniques of containing the random element of internal discord or the individual desire to escape the ambivalence of collective norm versus perceived personal fate (Parkin 1978: 214–42, especially 228–37).

The authors in this section present an epistemologically interesting view: that meanings, together with their criteria, are intersubjectively created in the course of cultural performance. They argue that meanings are created and reworked in communal settings by people who share and use linguistic tools for defining and communicating these meanings to others. But what happens if those meanings are not easily conveyed, when the pattern of circulation and the context of reception exhibit radical differences from the context of production? This issue is discussed in Part 3, "African Discourses on Development."

REFERENCES

Blount, Ben G. 1975. "Agreeing to Agree on Genealogy: A Luo Sociology of Knowledge." In Mary Sanches and Ben G. Blount, eds., *Sociocultural Dimensions of Language Use*. New York: Academic Press.

Bourdieu, Pierre F. 1977. *Outline of a Theory of Practice*. Translated by Richard Nice. Cambridge: Cambridge University Press.

———. 1990. *The Logic of Practice*. Translated by Richard Nice. Stanford, Calif.: Stanford University Press.

Eagleton, Terry. 1991. *Ideology: An Introduction*. London: Verso Books.

Kratz, Corinne A. 1994. *Affecting Performance: Meaning, Movement, and Experience in Okiek Women's Initiation*. Washington, D.C.: Smithsonian Institution Press.

Masolo, Dismas A. 1995. *New Perspectives in African Philosophy: Henri Maurier and Julius K. Nyerere*. Rome: Pontificiae Universitatis Gregorianae.

Maurier, Henri. 1976. *Philosophie de l'Afrique noire*. Bonn: Verlag St. Augustine, Anthropos Institute. 2nd ed., 1985.

Mudimbe, V. Y. 1991. *Parables and Fables: Exegesis, Textuality, and Politics in Central Africa*. Madison: University of Wisconsin Press.

Parkin, David. 1978. *The Cultural Definition of Political Response: Lineal Destiny among the Luo*. London: Academic Press.

p'Bitek, Okot. 1966. *Song of Lawino*. Oxford: Heinemann. Combined ed., *Song of Lawino and Song of Ocol*, African History Series. Oxford: Heinemann, 1984.

———. 1967. *Song of Ocol*. Oxford: Heinemann. Combined ed., *Song of Lawino and Song of Ocol*, African History Series. Oxford: Heinemann, 1984.

Taylor, Charles. 1985. *Human Agency and Language: Philosophical Papers 1*. Cambridge: Cambridge University Press.

Theuws, Théodore. 1983. *Word and World: Luba Thought and Literature*. Bonn: Verlag St. Augustin, Anthropos Institute.

4. The Play of Deconstruction in the Speech of Africa: The Role of *Pakruok* and *Ngero* in Telling Culture in Dholuo

Peter S. O. Amuka

"I AM THE CROCODILE'S EYEBALL"

There are times when there is no more to a name than the words. But not always. "I am the crocodile's eyeball" (*an tong wan'g nyan'g*): so a friend signed a recent letter to me.[1] I began to laugh but realized I was alone. Only the insane laugh to themselves. This signature was a dramatic statement whose impact could be felt only in a group, through dialogue. Had the letter's author been present, I would have henceforth called him by his last name, adding to it *Tong Wan'g Nyan'g* (the crocodile's eyeball). It would then have become a praise-name by which others could address him. Such a name becomes one's best-known identity in Luoland.

IS THERE A GENRE IN THIS TEXT?

I want to tell you about naming, about praise-naming and parody, about the living and the dead, about a man named Isak Ogoma, about storytelling and songs, about jousting, politics, and other hidden allusions—in short, about

Earlier versions of this essay were presented at the following: the "Translations of Africa" Conference (March 15–17, 1991); the Department of Anthropology, Rice University; Kenya Oral Literature Association Seminar at the University of Nairobi (1992); and at a Department of English Staff Seminar at Moi University (1992). My gratitude goes to Professor Michael J. Fischer, who hosted me as a Rockefeller Fellow at the Center for Cultural Studies at Rice University during the 1990–91 academic year. He suggested the shape that the essay finally took. The essay also benefited from comments by Professor E. S. Atieno-Odhiambo, George Marcus, and Anne Klein, all of Rice University. To them too I owe gratitude.

pakruok and *ngero* as complex genres of speech. Are they genres, these forms of speech which escape and undo classificatory logic?[2] Maybe they are better thought of as discursive tactics that dynamically put culture into play, that dramatize, that call for response, and that suggest always more stories: Let me give you yet another case, another example, a better story.

Pakruok, for instance, is a Luo noun. It is often translated as "praising one-self," "praise poetry," "praise-word-poetry," or "praise-word-game." But *pak-ruok* is closely associated with naming and in many respects is synonymous with naming; it is like a game with words. One is praised or praises oneself in order to provoke response, to initiate verbal drama. The layers of this drama are many more than are indicated by Ocholla-Ayayo's description of *pakruok* as "virtue-boasting" (Ocholla-Ayayo 1976: 45). Ocholla-Ayayo's translation reduces the genre to a static expression of moral values and standards. I have argued elsewhere that morality itself is an elusive ideal that is ceaselessly sought by society through the repeated and endless resolving of dramatic tensions between novel agencies of what come to be named virtue and vice (Amuka 1990). From the seemingly literal meanings, *pakruok* takes us ever deeper into translations as acts of interpretation of what the surface conceals. Meanings are inevitably created out of *pakruok:* they are meanings that one is led into by the nature of their surfaces and by the contexts in which they operate. *Pakruok* names entail deliberate manipulations of language by reducing stories to brief expressions of no more (in most cases) than five or six words. *Pakruok* is therefore a part of a larger and structured story whose parts pre-date and succeed it. To echo Jean-François Lyotard (1983), this act, praising and naming while concealing, forms a genre that is as much a story unto itself as it is part of a narrative tradition inherent in Luo culture. By employing *pakruok* as a mode of narration, my aims are to explore the Luo oral art of naming and to demonstrate how naming, in Luo oral texts, relates to the ontogenesis of the individual in communal settings.

The brevity of *pakruok* leaves us with many concealed meanings, with many leads and allusions to be explored. Brevity creates curiosity and desire for that which is not revealed or given. Curiosity leads to inquiry and inquiry to explication. At the end, a narrative merges which pieces out the concealing knot of *pakruok* into as many threads as will make sense, as if to testify to the verity of the popular metaphor that storytelling is a weaving process (Ong 1982; Bishop 1989). If we then reverse the process, the threads will be rolled back into a ball, the equivalent of the terse expression. The undone knot obviously gives the impression of artistic "disorder" and formlessness, thus displacing the easy-to-grasp monodirectional linearity. Ultimately only *pakruok*'s typical texts can delineate its directions and boundaries.

Ngero (plural, *ngeche*) is no more definable than *pakruok,* although proverbs and riddles are among its exemplary short forms. Like *pakruok, ngero* is usually brief, pithy, only allusive of the illusive meaning, often no more than three or four words. Brevity and allusion go together. Because conversation is the location at which forms of *ngero* are contracted into their varying shapes, it is sweetest and most elegant when it is indirect. All these features of *ngero* explain why it is a prominent tool of diplomacy and negotiation, because indirect language keeps people together and talking. Learning the art of conversation and negotiation involves learning *ngero.*

Ngero, like *pakruok,* is a contraction, abbreviation, or verbal knot that can be pieced out into many threads. *Ngero* signals more than you can hear: it is a proverb which unpacks into a folktale or narrative; more generally, it is allusive talk and therefore characterized by indirection and so also verbosity, circumlocution, and procrastination. Allusive talk is *ngero,* but *ngero* is especially talk in which some listeners are kept ignorant of the meanings being imparted, especially when the meanings involve them. Generally, the concealing power of *ngero* resides in the indirect verbal utterances which do not name their subjects directly. Any information, news, or report that takes long to narrate may be dismissed as *ngero* (or its close synonym, *sigana*), as being too circumlocutory rather than blunt and direct. A promise or visit that takes too long may likewise be dismissed as *ngero* or *sigana,* meaning that the undue duration might be an allusion to what is not apparent. Any complex matter that is difficult to explain, especially if it is riddled with mystery, is called *ngero* or *ngero matut* (a profound and loaded matter). When an adult complains that an issue is too complex to resolve, he says it is like a riddle that defeats a child.

People too, like riddles with their hidden meanings, can be *ngero.* Nowadays, especially in the South Nyanza region of Luoland, riddles are often called by the Kiswahili term *kitenda wili,* adapted into South Nyanza Luo as *kitanda wili.* The Luo of other regions use the word *mnaye* for riddles. But *kitanda wili* also refers to "night runners" (*jojuogi*). Night runners are also regarded as mysterious, like riddles, because their deeds are enacted in the secrecy of the night. People who keep two beds in their houses although they are single occupants are thought to be night runners: they must need two to jump from one bed to another at night; why else would they have two beds? Naked, they run about at night, kicking open people's doors, tossing some dirt or farting by the door or window, and then running away, laughing at those who complain at being awakened. (See J. C. Onyango Abuje's novella *Fire and Vengeance* for an imaginative re-creation of *jajuok*'s world.)

In the next section I present knots of *ngero* and *pakruok* and show briefly how these knots may be untied. I begin with praise-naming *pakruok,* as oral technique through which Luo people invent themselves as persons in relation to others.

CLODS AND HYENAS: *PAKRUOK* AS PART OF A TRINOMIAL

Friends address one another as *ondiek marach,* the terrible hyena. The allusion may be to some romantic, economic, or political exploits or achievement(s) by one or more of the individuals. At times friends may refer to one another as *liech,* elephant, as a code either for some big deed, real or imagined, or merely as a reference to one's bulky physical build. Such codes may conceal the nature of their interactions from the public. One politician from South Nyanza calls himself *Gogni* (clods of earth). The obvious reference is to his wealth, because he bribes (soaks) his constituents with money in order to win votes. The phrase "clods of earth" stands for the idea that like clods of earth that are full of weight, this politician is heavy with sacks full of money that his dusty opponent did not have. In full, he actually praises himself as *gogni owadgi Akinyi kamba nyiri:* "I am clods of earth and Akinyi's brother, I am the belt women tie around their waists"—i.e., "women will die for me." Like the other Nilotic groups of the Sudan and northern Uganda, who are culturally and historically related to them, the Luo of Kenya also once endowed their cattle with human praise-names. That style of praise-naming is increasingly turning away from cattle, the original symbol of wealth, to money, and it is indicative of a gradual shift from pastoral to predominantly cash-related symbolization of power and social status. The rich men with banknotes have become the bulls.

Praise-names make up the third set of names that an individual receives. The first and second sets of naming come at birth and at the ritual inheritance of an ancestor's name, respectively. At birth, Luo are given names in relation to the position of the sun in the sky or according to the time of the night or the state of the weather and numerous other natural phenomena. Major communal activities, such as weeding and harvesting, are also sources of names. Naming may be related to major historical events such as floods, famines, locust invasions, wars, and droughts. Or a baby's name may be related to the location of birth. Shortly after birth, Luo receive also a *juok* (spirit) name, the name of an ancestor. Babies cry until the parents dream of an ancestor, and when that ancestor's name is mentioned in telling the dream, the baby stops crying. Ancestors are believed to reproduce their identities in newborns in more ways than just the name, or *juok.* Newborns are believed to reproduce the moral and social qualities of the ancestors after which they are named. Sometimes newborns are also believed to bear the birthmarks of the ancestors who they reproduce in name and character. According to the Luo, social life is a process by which the past is reenacted and reshaped by new subjects, who nonetheless remain linked to those who have passed. It is, however, the third set of names in which I am interested here; I will call this set of names *pakruok*. While the Luo trinomial system might be analyzed as a classificatory system in the manner of Lévi-Strauss (1976) or Geertz (1973), I am interested here only in the stories that *pakruok* names abbreviate.

SPEAKING THROUGH *PAKRUOK:* ISAK OGOMA

His first name would have remained Ogoma but for the arrival of the Seventh-Day Adventist Church missionaries a few years before the outbreak of the World War I. He was baptized Isak after a few lessons from the Bible at the Lala Seventh-Day Adventist Church in Kanyada. This new colonial name was sold as being "more civilized" and polite. From then on, Isak became his praise-name, the name by which he was identified and addressed. He was variously referred to as *jasomo*, a person who could read, and *jananga*, a person who wore clothes.[3] His uncle also chose to join the Seventh-Day Adventist Church at Lala. His first name was Ochuti. He became Jakobo *jananga* and *jasomo*. Jacobo Ochuti and Isak Ogoma were among the first Seventh-Day Adventist adherents in Kanyada, and after them, it became fashionable to acquire names from the church and to wear shorts and stockings. Church names became terms of endearment, *pakruok*.

Jacobo died in 1973 and was buried with honor by the church. According to Isak, he was buried as an enlightened man, and as more "Seventh-Day Adventist" than most, because he died a monogamist. Isak hailed him as *nyawan'g achiel*, the one who was mono-eyed, because he had only one wife. The explanation is that having one wife if like having one eye: lose the one and you have nothing left. Isak himself died in December 1987, having married over twenty wives. Although polygamy was outlawed by his Seventh-Day Adventist Church, this church still participated in his burial. After all, he paid tithes throughout his life and even built a church for his clan community. The people of Kanyada were assumed to venerate him for having "more than one eye." Unlike Jacobo, Isak had no brothers. An only son to Wanga, he had many wives to bear for him as many children as possible. As he put it, his sons would double as his brothers (daughters are affiliated to the clans of their husbands) to compensate for the solitude of his own childhood. Through sons, his seeds would be firmly planted in Kanyada; his name and power would spread. Indeed, having fathered many sons and acquired many parcels of land, he capped his fame with a colonial chiefship at the beginning of World War II.

Neither Isak nor Jacobo could read or write, yet, ironically and as *ngero*, they were addressed as *josomo*—men of letters—because they worshipped every Saturday and carried a Bible. Neither of them could recall the year they were baptized: they could only remember what events preceded or succeeded their "enlightenment." Their six lower teeth had been extracted some time before baptism. Baptismal certificates had long been lost. I was interviewing Ogoma about *ngero* in Kanyada when he casually noted that he had not been told the significance of the certificates. Paper inscriptions did not seem to matter: it was quite adequate that he was identified with the history of the Seventh-Day Adventist Church, literacy, and European dressing and that he was praise-named Ogoma *Misungu*, Ogoma the European. And he was satisfied that the Luo method of recording events by means of *pakruok* greatly surpassed the passiveness of paper records.

Ogoma was also popularly known as *ragwel*, the bowlegged, a mark of beauty in Luo aesthetics. Ogoma recalled that Ochuti was short and small, like *apwoyo* or *Ogila*, the hare. He also fondly remembered him as Ochuti *jakwal wouth ka paka* (Ochuti walks stealthily and gingerly like a cat). The code name of *Ochuti Ogila* was an allusion to the praises of the hare as *ogila nyarondo*, a reference to the instinctual cunning and wit of the little animal. Like *ogila nyarondo* of Luo mythical legends, these qualities endeared Ochuti to all who encountered him. Ochuti was a tough and invincible physical and verbal wrestler. Although he was less than five feet tall by Ogoma's account, Ochuti wrestled the giant Ogoma to the ground many times. Ochuti was also good with words and won many women's admiration and love, but he died without marrying more than one wife. Hence, the suspicion and the nickname: like the cunning and witty *ogila nyarondo*, Ochuti probably lived a life of secret polygamy, preferring (and succeeding in doing so) to reveal to the public the character that he knew the church would see as exemplary.

Ochuti, said Ogoma, was *apuoyo tin to goyo rude* (Ochuti, the tiny hare that defies or compensates for the insignificance of size by begetting twins). He had fathered a giant of a son, who rose to become a renowned medical assistant in South Nyanza District, of which Kanyada is a part. The son, known simply as Samwel Oraw, was as good as twins or more children because of his physical prominence and professional fame. From him Ochuti earned more *pakruok*. And in Oraw's body, Ogoma read Ochuti's history.

According to Ogoma, no human being may claim existence without a name. And Luo names always pre-date the bearer. Nobody can have been born before rain, river, grass, sun, and the animals and objects of the wild from which Luo derive names. Also, genealogically, children come after the ancestors whom they reproduce and after whom they are named. A normal Luo baby cries for days on end, says Ogoma, until one night, one of the parents talks to an ancestor in a dream. The following morning the baby stops crying as soon as the dreamer declares and names the baby after the ancestor. The baby's ultimate character and social status are a re-creation of the oneiric dialogue with the dead.

Pakruok, on the other hand, involves communication with both the dead and the living. Lack of social interaction between one person and his friends and relatives in real life may lead to a cold or dormant relationship when any one of them dies. Their spirits are unlikely to be friendly enough to surface in dreams for social reproduction through naming. To paraphrase J. S. Mbiti, the individual's death may reach immediate completion because his relation with his kin is permanently severed. *Pakruok* is one way to keep human spirits happy and warm on earth and beyond. As with the Yoruba *oriki orile, pakruok* of Joluo helps show pride in ancestry and solidarity with one's kin and friends. Having acquired a name through this expressive process, one must keep one's social connections alive in the same way.

A person must have a repertoire large enough to sustain *pakruok.* For instance, a man should not perform the mock battle, *tero buru,* with a spear and heavy *kuot* (a shield of buffalo hide) until he can perform *pakruok.* To perform *tero buru* without a *kuot* signifies that one is a coward, one who cannot have fought and killed a buffalo. Not to have a *kuot* means that one is not descended from the brave, or else one would have inherited one. Such a man lacks names worthy of *pakruok.* He is teased and challenged to name his sisters-in-law, but they disown him because they resent association with a bare-handed coward. This man has nobody to name, and if named by others, he is named in derision. His social being is punctured, which in turn deprives him of positive attributes to sustain himself (Atieno-Odhiambo 1992).

CONTEMPORARY MUSICIANS AND INTELLECTUALS

In loading Ochuti with so many terms of appreciation, Ogoma tells of the many "persons" he visualized in him. In dance parties, barroom drama, and festivals during which *pakruok* arises, individuals create or appropriate praise-names, put a price on them, and retain the copyright until they are outdone by rivals with more money.

Henry Ochien'g has, for example, appropriated the name Kabaselleh. Easily one of the best musicians in Kenya, Ochien'g has come now to be known as Kabaselleh. The original Kabaselleh, now deceased, was the master of modern Zairian music in the 1950s and 1960s. For Luo fans, the name Kabaselleh is associated with excellence in vocals, instruments, and content: Ochien'g Kabaselleh's lyrics thrill when he sings love songs. Through sheer artistic achievement, Ochien'g has made the name Kabaselleh his sole property. One day, and in keeping with Luo oral art, another artist will deem himself as good, if not better, and will then appropriate the name and probably put his money on it.

Owino Misiani has been described as a leading popular intellectual and the most famous Luo musician. Owino praises himself in a song as *Owino Gari Ochayo Thim* (Owino the train defies the most dangerous forest). While the literal meaning remains that trains always negotiate some dangerous physical terrain in parts of Kenya, patrons have always been struck by the way Owino weaves his songs through very sensitive political patches. When in one song he remarked that the cat had turned against the chickens with which he was sharing accommodations and actually smashed their skulls, Owino was alluding to Idi Amin's state terrorism in Uganda, and Amin was only symbolic of other such deeds elsewhere in Africa. The images of the train and forest and cat then begin to expand like the Xhosa *ntsomi* (Scheub 1972). It is not only Owino talking or performing; it is the politicians. In between the lines, we begin to read of atrocities committed in Bokassa's Central African Republic and in Equatorial Guinea and of the stories of mysterious deaths of public personalities all over Africa. Only the "train that tears its way through the forest" can inspire such reading with the support of animal imagery. Animal tales offer some of the most precise but indirect social criticism in Luo oral art (Onyango-Ogutu and Roscoe 1974). Thus, to dub a politician a cat is to exploit the power of language in order to evade the possibility of incrimination. Owino does not name names of real people: he presents these real people only as cats or leopards. Relation to the real social world is left to the interpretive skills of the listener. Owino is unique because of his skills in language and because of the accompanying music, which adds intensity and power through rhythmic repetition. His language and music are simultaneously his audience's and his own because they are based on the familiar oral art of encoding concealed meanings in familiar symbols.

Obudo is a pub performer in the town of Homa Bay. Balding, he glorifies his receding hairline and attributes it to the art of *dodo,* beer-drinking songs, in which he excels: his body is a figure that, like his voice, takes on collective representation. This is achieved through his use of a chorus; the chorus, for instance, claims that it too is balding. He calls himself Obudo *nam,* the lake, because of his inexhaustible capacity for beer drinking, and Obudo *kom kamolo* (Obudo, the Kamolo chair), after the chair on which Kamolo people recline for comfort, leadership, and commentary. His songs are performed with a collective "I," and the chorus identifies with practically every character Obudo mentions. He encounters quite a few people along the road from Kisumu to Homa Bay and from Homa Bay to Magunga. Each character enjoys special behavior and mannerisms. The policemen are prone to waylaying would-be lawbreakers and receive words of applause; Asman is a renowned cyclist who narrowly misses Obudo as he lies across the road dead drunk; Margaret is brown like an Arab; Osoga is at once a kind and harsh doctor who saves Obudo from a gonorrhea infection. Obudo's songs constitute an "identity parade" (Cohen and Atieno-Odhiambo 1989: 27). By the end, Obudo brings all these identities and their differences together; through the singing, he has engaged in a continuous dialogue with them as a community. Through the chorus, the community has talked to itself. The "dialogism" here becomes, in Holquist's words, "a necessary multiplicity in human perception" (Holquist 1989), and in the final analysis, the song becomes a communal medium in which everything, including the elements of *pakruok*, is attributable to the community rather than the individual. Original as Obudo's compositions sound, his voice—his body—is an embodiment of other bodies, his self is other selves. A traveler traversing all the roads of Luoland, Obudo's lines name the people along the way and treat them to all manner of *pakruok*. Obudo praises his balding head for being simultaneously attractive and repulsive; he exalts all (including the policemen) who plunge into illicit beer like scavengers; he heaps praise on the bus transport system that facilitates his encounter with various towns and the accompanying experiences. He sings for himself, his chorus, his likes and dislikes, the people he meets and lives with, and all the places he visits. In all this, he teases, satirizes, parodies, critiques, historicizes, and shows off teasingly (*nyadhi*). *Nyadhi* is the practice of displaying one's worth, which can comprise possessions, moral qualities, intellectual abilities, or some coveted social or professional role. What is displayed need not be actually possessed, for it is sometimes enough that a person only identifies with such publicly coveted qualities and achievements as a way of playfully enhancing and displaying his perception of publicly recognized values. Thus, a person may sometimes make claims for him/herself which both the person and his or her audience know to be false in real life. In these senses, *nyadhi* and *pakruok* come close to each other as playful social forms. Showing off the bald head is a kind of *nyadhi*: Obudo's head is special because the hair has been shorn off by many years of *dodo* performance. Yet the same *nyadhi* may be classified as *ngero*.

PROVERBIAL TAGS AND RIDDLING NAMES: "I AM GRANDMOTHER'S LOVER"

Beer-drinking pubs sometimes employ resident musicians whose performances are often interrupted, for a fee, by one patron at a time. The patron then plunges into a praise-naming game. Another patron is likely to respond at double the preceding fee, and this second patron will then claim monopoly of the praise-names his predecessor had uttered. Claims and counter-claims continue until no more challenges come from the floor (often as a result of the high level of the fee). The laughter provoked by praise-naming is often aimed at a specific person; this laughter challenges him to respond, in turn causing even more laughter. Embedded in the *pakruok* and laughter lie many hidden truths. Those who do not wish for some truths about them to be revealed may use all the money they have for the evening to silence those who provoke them.

A young man in his twenties declares *an chot pim* (I am *pim*'s lover). *Pim* is an old lady, usually a grandmother, who has officially retired from active sexual life. Supposedly well past menopause, she must not share a bed with a man any more (including her own husband). She is allocated a special abode, *siwindhe*, in which she imparts social ethics to young girls before marriage. For a young man to say he is in love with a grandmother seems abominable, but what he may really be saying is that "warm memories of *pim* are understood not only as sources of earlier practices of nurturing and socialization but as stern critiques of the present nature of family and schooling" (Cohen and Atieno-Odhiambo 1989: 130). This is a hard critique of the *nanga*, modernity, from which Ogoma and Ochuti had derived so much pride. In this critique lies the recognition in local wisdom that every moment carries its contradictions: there are good and bad sides to everything, and success, the prize of the wise, resides in the attainment of the mean. When a young man says he is a lover of *pim*, he is in reality expressing a desire for the wisdom of the elders, who have withdrawn from the distractions of youth. He desires the good yet distant serenity of the grandmother. A similar ironic (Cohen and Atieno-Odhiambo 1992) critique may lodge in the use of the *pakruok* expression *afuong'o jang'u-ono* (in a skirt abides generosity).[4] New values have taken over; premarital sex has overthrown the prized virginity, and girls become pregnant out of wedlock. The laughter that accompanies such lines is not a sign of fun. Rather, it constitutes a ritual act, a catharsis related to the tensions of changing values.

An bwoch mor ka dhok tho (I am the impotent man who rejoices in the death of cattle): Perhaps no conversation is more painful than one in which an impotent man (*bwoch*) is alluded to as being filled with the joy or Schadenfreude when an epidemic hits livestock. Dowry is paid in cattle; the impotent man need not pay dowry because no sane woman would knowingly agree to marry him. Condemned to live alone, he will not be remembered after death. Tall stories are told, to the accompaniment of applause and laughter, about impotent men who died from pleasure upon learning that the last cows in their village had died. Whoever uses such allusions in conversation is sure of his manhood. The indirection heightens the pain of the impotent man, but the laughter engendered is not celebratory. Rather, it is a mere showing of teeth. It is not laughter as an emotive act. The Luo say of such occasions that *lak chogo* (teeth are bones): teeth are unfeeling items capable of flashing with seeming joy, even if the occasion warrants solemnity.

Tragedy, it is said, can only be softened and appeased by a sense of humor, because teeth are but bones laughing at nature's wrath. The laughter, then, can cut both ways; it can be aggressively hurtful to the impotent but also sympathetically philosophical: laughter is but bones staring at nature.

Rech ki siane guok (Fish cannot be hunted by a dog): Onyango-Ogutu and Roscoe (1974) consistently refers to Odingo Hawi by this *pakruok*. Not only are the gentlemen the best of friends, they meet practically every evening at one or the other of the restaurants near the University of Nairobi. The expression is meant to create laughter and joy among Hawi's other friends and to set him talking. The phrase indicates that certain things cannot be done: dogs do not fish (well), and yet dogs continue to plunge into the waters of desire. Another *pakruok* also indicates the way remarkable behavior patterns become formalized: *an janam ong'iyo gi olund wadgi* (I am as used to viewing my neighbor's anus as are lakeshore residents). Fishermen tend to fish naked on four-person dugout canoes. Unavoidably they see each other's nakedness so often that it is no longer strange.

Ngero operates similarly and often can be introduced into conversation by a single word, such as *Arujo* (the name of a river), *Oyundi* (the name of a bird), or *simsim* (the name for sesame, a delectable seed).

Arujo—Rivers that murder: The brief, pithy words of *ngero* often are allusions to songs, and song lyrics, as we discussed above, may in turn allude to political issues that cannot be talked about either openly or in plain language. One such song is a lament about the river *Arujo*, which for years had provided for the water needs of the communities and their livestock but which was then turned against its users at the order of a buffalo. The song is about a politician who was suspected of involvement in the murder of a rival whose body was dumped in the Ngong Hills to be eaten by hyenas—but the hyenas did not keep their appointment. It is a song about a political system that takes away its people's lives. The musician who composed this song was arrested and taken to court, but the court acquitted him, for when the song was literally translated in court it proved to be only about buffaloes and a murderous river. The government then claimed that the musician was really a Tanzanian and tried to deport him. Although the court could not convict the composer, people continued to speak of the murder by reciting the lyrics of the song or by simply mentioning the single word *Arujo*.

Oyundi—Bird: There is a little brown bird, the *oyundi*, that eats a tremendous amount in relation to its diminutive size. Small and fastidious, it notoriously eats only that grain that has been harvested and spread out to dry. It avoids unharvested grain for fear of ruffling its pretty feathers. Its enormous appetite is alluded to by the phrase *sese sese,* the onomatopoeic sound of the bird's slide into the grains. But when it is chased to go search for its own food or when it is sent to cultivate the land, it begins to limp, to weep, and to whine, and then it sings ever so sweetly that others are lulled to sleep, forgetting the work that needs to be done. In pity, it is left to feed a little more on the grain. The human *oyundi* is jolted out of his parasitism by the *sese sese* song. The mimic imitates the sliding and limping of the bird as it is grabbing and munching on imaginary food. The crowd laughs and jeers, driving home the humiliation. But the culprit is never mentioned by name. His name is shrouded in the reference to *oyundi.*

Simsim (sesame seed)—Stupid: There is a story about the herdsmen of Wasio country, who were duped by rustlers with a gift of *simsim.* The story is never told in conversation. It is only alluded to with the words *simsim* or *ja-Wasio* (a man from Wasio). Either expression is used to ridicule those who, like a *ja-Wasio,* have their attention easily drawn away with edible gifts or who are distractible with a gift of *simsim.* The story tells of unarmed cattle rustlers who walked up to the young men of Wasio with bags of *simsim,* tiny seeds that can be held only by cupping the fingers of one or both hands tightly together. *Simsim* are very sweet and a much-desired delicacy. The rustlers offered the *simsim* to the herdsmen on the condition that they wrapped their arms around tree trunks. The herdsmen's dilemma was how to unwrap their arms without losing the sweet and rare *simsim.* Some tried in vain to reach the *simsim* with their tongues. Others squeezed each hand more tightly together to ensure that no gap opened between the fingers and then tried to release themselves gradually from the trees they were embracing. At last, by the time they gave up and turned back to their cattle, the cattle were long gone. A variant of the story holds that the rustlers tied the herdsmen's hands together rather than wrapping them around trees, the better to form the cupped palms to hold the *simsim.* It is a proverbial tale of stupidity, of being led astray by greed.

Simsim—Love: *Simsim* can also allude to the pleasure of sexual gratification, as it does in the following tale of Nombi, a Kanyada elder who died without utilizing the last opportunity to make love to his youngest wife. As a respected elder, all the people wanted to bid him goodbye before his death. It is believed that elders know when they will die and are thus able to announce it to their kin in good time. As a result, there was a long queue to bid Nombi farewell, so every time he tried to have intercourse with his wife for the last time, he was interrupted by a well-wisher. This would-have-been-lovemaking is called "eating *simsim*." It is the *simsim* Nombi never ate.

The *pakruok Wendo Juogi* (the guest/stranger is a spirit) is normally applied to one who mistreats guests. Again, a proverbial story lies behind the proverb. According to the famous legend, an old and poor fisherman, Nyamgondho, went fishing one morning, but instead of fish, he caught a ragged, muddy woman in his nets. He took her home and reluctantly took her for a wife. She brought Nyamgondho great fortune and filled his home with wealth. Nyamgondho stopped fishing and took to drinking and a reckless life. One night he returned home late and found the gate to their home locked. He shouted to his wife in vain to let him in. In anger and frustration he shouted at the woman, telling her how she was only a "horror" that he had rescued from the lake, and therefore she had no right to decline him access to his own home. In anger and protest at Nyamgondho's violent behavior, the old woman left and walked back into the river. At that point, all the cattle and other wealth that she had brought with her into Nyamgondho's home and life followed her back into the depths of the lake. When Nyamgondho woke up from his drunkenness, he found himself back to his old poor self again. According to the story's teaching, those who disrespect strangers and guests only need be reminded of the story of Nyamgondho.

Udiya (You are squeezing me) or *Kanyada noyako udiya* (Kanyada people grabbed "you-are-squeezing me"): Encoded in this *pakruok* and *ngero* is the history of World War I and the appearance of the accordion. The Germans attacked Asego (now Homa Bay) in Kanyada. The British were routed, leaving the Indian shopkeepers undefended. The shopkeepers fled with the Britons, abandoning their stocks to the looters. An accordion was found. When the people pulled its sides, it wailed like a virgin experiencing the pains of her first sexual intercourse. When the sides were pushed inwards, it "cried" that it was being squeezed, hence the name "you are squeezing me" (*udiya*). Surprised at its capacity to produce sounds at a mere squeeze without visible chords, people thought that the accordion must have a hidden spirit that responded musically to the squeeze of human fingers.

While *udiya* encodes material representations of recent history as experienced by the Luo of Kanyada, the story of the bead and spear encodes an explanation of Luo social fragmentations and structures, and schismatic dispersions move away from each other. It underscores the role of strife as a dynamic of social mobility and reproduction. Boro and Nyada were brothers. Boro borrowed Nyada's spear and used it to attack an elephant, which bolted into the forest. Nyada demanded the spear back and would have nothing in its place but the original spear. Boro went through many ordeals and nearly died before he was able to recover the spear. But soon there was a new tension between the brothers. Nyada's daughter accidentally swallowed one of Boro's prized beads. In retaliation for his many trials in recovering his brother's spear, Boro demanded that Nyada give him back the very same bead swallowed by his baby daughter. Nyada had to split open his daughter's belly to recover the bead, killing the baby in the process. Embittered, Nyada moved away from his brother to form his own subgroup. The story is not only used to explain jealousies and feuds among brothers and divisions and splits among the lineages and clans of the Luo community; when a man wants to absolve himself from blame, he may swear he has neither swallowed the accuser's bead nor lost his spear.

CAN YOU NAME THIS SPEECH?

I am unable to treat either *pakruok* or *ngero* as exclusive genres because of their persistent connections with everyday reality and with other forms of speech. They resist reduction to easy definition. There is no ultimate text, and what I have used as examples to propel my narrative is not exceptional. The stringing together of allusive references of this type constitutes the processes of *ngero* and *pakruok*. *Pakruok* and *ngero* unpack into narratives, myths, anecdotes, and historical texts; they are complementary fragments of an open-ended literary tradition. They are contractions and abbreviations of open cultural weavings that are endlessly creative and unbounded. Once one tries to define them, *pakruok* and *ngero* generate more questions.

While appearing to praise, for instance, one also engages in parodying. The case of Isak Ogoma provides a good example of how meanings and social texts like names are constantly transformed into new meanings and given new social roles through *pakruok* play and invention of oral artistry. Ogoma's conversion is in the mind of the missionary rather than in external reality. This enables Ogoma to twist its significance, its meanings, to his own locally located convenience, where he, rather than the church or the missionary, becomes the center, as in *pakruok*. He wins praise for what he is not, which is to say that the art of *pakruok* may state the truth by seeming to contradict it.

NOTES

1. This comes from a letter from a friend who later confessed (in person) that every normal Luo must own a praise-name and that even what are regarded as ordinary and normal names are, in fact, praise-names.

2. This is an allusion to Stanley Fish's well-known book entitled *Is There a Text in This Class?* (1980).

3. For a detailed analysis of nakedness and dressing among the Luo, see E. S. Atieno-Odhiambo's "From Warriors to *Jonanga:* The Struggle over Nakedness in Western Kenya," in *Sokomoko,* pp. 11–26.

4. The expression is quoted from D. W. Cohen and E. S. Atieno-Adhiambo, *Siaya: The Historical Anthropology of an African Landscape,* p. 97 (1989). I have also been reliably informed that the expression is a favorite praise-name of a Luo academician, Professor Otieno Malo.

REFERENCES

Amuka, P. 1980. "*Ngero* as a Social Object." Master's thesis, University of Nairobi.

———. 1990. "Oral Literature and Fiction." In W. R. Ochieng', ed., *Themes in Kenyan History.* Nairobi: Kenya Literature Bureau.

Atieno-Odhimabo, E. S. 1992. "From Warriors to Jonanga: The Struggle over Nakedness in Western Kenya." In Werner Graebner, ed., *Sokomoko Popular Culture in East Africa.* Atlanta: Editions Rodopi, pp. 11–26.

Barber, K. 1984. "Yoruba *Oriki* and Deconstructive Criticism." *Research in African Literatures* 15, no. 4: 497–518.

Bishop, R. 1989. "Weaving and Woven: Metaphors for Understanding in Oral and Literate Cultures." *Intercultural Studies in Literature* 14: 117–43.

Cohen, D. W., and E. S. Atieno-Odhiambo. 1989. *Siaya: The Historical Anthropology of an African Landscape.* Athens: Ohio University Press.

———. 1992. *Burying SM: The Politics of Knowledge and the Sociology of Power in Africa.* Portsmouth, N.H.: Heinemann, and London: James Currey.

Culler, J. 1982. *On Deconstruction: Theory and Criticism after Structuralism.* Ithaca, N.Y.: Cornell University Press.

Derrida, J. 1977. *Of Grammatology.* Baltimore, Md.: Johns Hopkins University Press.

———. 1978. *Writing and Difference.* Chicago: University of Chicago Press.

Fish, S. 1980. *Is There a Text in This Class?* Cambridge, Mass.: Harvard University Press.

Geertz, C. 1973. *The Interpretation of Culture.* New York: Basic Books.

———. 1976. "From the Natives' Point of View: On the Nature of Anthropological Understanding." In Keith H. Basso and Henry A. Selby, eds., *Meaning in Anthropology.* Albuquerque: University of New Mexico Press.

Holquist, M. 1989. "Introduction." In *The Dialogic Imagination: Four Essays by M. M. Bakhtin.* Austin: University of Texas Press.

Lévi-Strauss, C. 1976. *Structural Anthropology.* New York: Basic Books.

Lyotard, J.-F. 1983. *Le Differend.* Paris: Éditions de Minuit. English translation, *The Differend: Phrases in Dispute.* Trans. G. Van Den Abbeele. Minneapolis: University of Minnesota Press, 1988.

Lyotard, J.-F., and J.-L. Thebaud. 1985. *Just Gaming.* Minneapolis: University of Minnesota Press.

Ocholla-Ayayo, A. B. C. 1976. *Tradition, Ideology and Ethics among the Southern Luo.* Uppsala: The Scandinavian Institute of African Studies.

Ong, W. 1982. *Orality and Literacy: The Technologizing of the Word.* New York: Methuen.

Onyango-Abuje, J. C. 1975. *Fire and Vengeance.* Nairobi: East African Publishing House.

Onyango-Ogutu, B., and A. A. Roscoe. 1975. *Keep My Words: Luo Oral Literature.* Nairobi: East African Publishing House.

p'Bitek, O. 1973. *Africa's Cultural Revolution.* Nairobi: Macmillan Books for Africa.

Scheub, H. 1972. "The Art of Nongenile Mazithathu Zenani, a Gcaleka Ntsomi Performer." In *African Folklore.* Bloomington: Indiana University Press, pp. 115–42.

5. Personhood and Art: Social Change and Commentary among the Acoli

J. P. Odoch Pido

This essay explores aspects of Acoli[1] concepts of the person through the song *Carama, Tere Obedo Abuny* (A Divorcée's Buttocks Are Dangerous Slopes). I chose this particular song for two reasons. First, it demonstrates that expressive culture in general and song in particular can provide privileged means for understanding dilemmas of personhood. Secondly, I hope to show that this song means a great deal to the people who sing it, that it is an attempt by Acoli people to deal with the spread of sexually transmitted diseases. Though exploring Acoli concepts of personhood through the analysis of one song is the primary objective, an overview of the Acoli as a people, the place of songs in their culture, and their general perception of personhood are important backdrops for this analysis.

THE PEOPLE AND THEIR SONGS

The Acoli are a people of northern Uganda who live across the border from the southern Sudan and who are culturally related to the following Sudanese peoples: Lukoro, Oboo, Parajok, and Kajokaji. Together with the peoples of Lango, Alur, Kumam, LabworOmor, Nam, CooPe, and Adhola in Uganda, the Acoli comprise the Jo pa Lwo (the people of Lwo), Nilotic peoples of Uganda and the Sudan who are culturally allied with the JoPaDhola in Uganda and the JoLuo in Kenya (Girling 1960: 12).

Acoliland is full of songs that express opinions on people, plants, animals, insects, and birds. These songs paint Acoli pictures of experiences with the physical ambient and social environments; Acoli songs could be equated to the schools of art, including Naturalism, Realism, and Impressionism (Janson 1969: 489). Acoli songs are artistic expressions, reflections on the self, and they constitute a major form for thinking about society and history.

The song that this essay examines is accompanied by a *nangaa,* a seven-stringed trough zither (Trowell and Wachsmann 1953: 410) that is similar in shape to a dulcimer. Songs accompanied by *nangaa* have, for at least a century, provided a medium for expressing views of everyday life and adverse opinions on political leadership. Moreover, the more recent history of Uganda has provided ideal political conditions for *nangaa* music to thrive, as such music has provided the only way to speak out in a repressive regime. In Uganda during the last three decades, the Acoli people have been subject to severe repression—during the Amin regime—or have been considered disproportionately influential in national affairs—under the two Obote regimes. In politically bad times, the Acoli have been forced to disguise their feelings, opinions, ideas, and discourses. In addition to being a means for hidden political criticism, *nangaa* music is also a general and popular vehicle for Acoli expressive culture (p'Bitek 1974: 11–13).

PERSONHOOD DEFINED IN ACOLI TERMS

The phrase *bedo dano* is fundamental to understanding and defining Acoli personhood; *bedo* is "to be, state of being," to become or the state of becoming, while *dano,* whose singular version is *ngat,* means persons or people. A close examination of the phrase shows that *bedo dano* can be translated as "a person who lives among people," or "to become a person who lives in society." The plural sense of *dano* used in this phrase might cause confusion. To be a person, in this context, more often concerns the physical, social, age-related, productive, emotional, and spiritual connotations. To be a person is to behave and do according to the "rules" of life and in relation to other persons. Hence, to be a person is never a singular activity. Anybody whose behavior is out of step with the codes of conduct is often said to be *pe dano* (a no person); such a non-person is involved as the subject of songs such as *Carama, Tere Obedo Abuny,* a form of non-concrete art whose content is an aspect of the Acoli sense of personhood.

PHYSICAL FEATURES, BIRTH, AND PERSONHOOD

The physical features of the individual are significant for the Acoli concept of the person. They distinguish humans from animals and other creatures; features such as the head, limbs, and trunk have physical properties which are characteristic of humans and which are different from those of animals or other creatures. Once a fetus has these features, it is recognized as a person. Abortions and stillbirths receive full burial rites, because a formed fetus is considered to be a person. A baby who is born with all the human features fully developed is a person. To be *langolo* (a physically deformed person) after birth does not deter one from being a person. However, a baby who is born breech or with physically abnormal features is called *latin jok* or *jok* (a child of supernatural powers or a supernatural power). It is believed that children born with supernatural powers retain their powers when they become adults. As children and adults, these individuals are *jogi* (plural for *jok*), the core of religion and of objects of ritual action (p'Bitek 1979: 72).

The supernatural powers of a baby born *jok*, however, should not be confused with those of one who was born *lajok*—having evil supernatural powers such as *yir*, evil powers in the eyes (Crazzolara 1955: 423). Some Acoli regard a baby with extreme deformity (absence of limbs and eyes) as *jok* but would not describe someone as *jok* who has enough physical features to be a person. In the former case, the baby is discreetly drowned; life is terminated on humanitarian grounds using a method which is seen as returning supernatural powers to the water, where they belong.

Soon after birth, the umbilical cord is cut (Girling 1960: 22). Cutting the cord physically frees the baby and gives it a symbolic independence from the mother. This independence is short-lived, however, and is symbolic only because severing the cord simply begins the next process, culturally and emotionally binding (socialization) the newly born person to its community.

Wino (the afterbirth) is placed in a pot and buried. The structural and surface designs of the pot depend on whether the birth is ordinary or *jok*. Following an ordinary birth, the afterbirth is placed in a broken pot in order to avoid competition with supernatural powers. In the case of twins, the afterbirth is placed in a new pot with two mouths that is painted reddish and fitted with a hole on the side; the two mouths signify the birth of twins, the red coloring represents supernatural powers, and the hole allows the powers to breathe or move in and out of the pot freely. Apart from having only one mouth, the design and rationale for choosing the pot used for the afterbirth of a breech delivery are the same as the ones used in the case of twins. The afterbirth is placed in a pot so that moving it from place to place and at different times is easy. The pot and its contents are buried in the ground to avoid witchcraft; it is said that if a witch gets his hands on the afterbirth, he can turn a fertile woman permanently infertile—a terrible fate. An infertile woman is "as worthless as a roadside pond of water which anybody and anything can consume" (she is socially insignificant). Burying the afterbirth within the home connects the baby to the people who are identified with the household.

The location at which the afterbirth is buried depends on the sex of the baby and on whether the birth is special or ordinary. As Girling witnessed in the 1950s, the afterbirth of a baby girl may be buried under the *simsim* (sesame seed) granary, because the *simsim* granary symbolizes a typical Acoli dish of *simsim* paste, which is associated with cooking and women. The afterbirth of a baby boy is buried under the millet granary. Millet stands for a hard-working man who cultivates many big fields of millet to ensure an annual harvest which fills many large granaries. Burying the afterbirth underneath granaries was changed to burial under the left or right doors of houses when thieves started stealing from the granaries. Theft is said to interfere with the healthy growth of babies and the fertility of their mothers. The afterbirth of a baby may be buried under a tree and in the bush when several children who preceded the particular baby have died. Burying the afterbirth under a tree is said to ensure the survival of such a baby. It disguises the baby so that death does not see it and take the baby away.

The mother and her baby are secluded for three or four days, depending on the baby's sex. Seclusion is a period of incubation intended to protect both the mother and baby from the rigors and dangers of everyday life—the time to rest after the hard work of giving birth, quietly soaking up the joy of having a child, of proving one's social worth—in short, living in an extraordinary world. On the third day for girls or the fourth day for boys, the baby and its mother come out of seclusion, a sign that they are resuming everyday life. This is when the baby is given a name, an identity that is a poetic expression of an opinion about life or a reference to an historical event.

The day the child is named is also the day it is clothed. Though clothing may be as scanty as a single line of beads around the waist, it ends nakedness and has a humanizing effect on the baby; subsequent body covers, perfumes, decorations, or adornments should be seen as an attempt to determine the emotions and appearance of the individual concerned. Either three or four days after birth, the baby gets a taste of saltless *simsim* sauce through the ritual of "touching the mouth of the child with cooked food"; the ritual introduces the baby to food and to the world of a people who are also known by their food. All of the above and additional birth rituals introduce and morally permit the baby into Acoli society (Girling 1960: 24); children without birth rituals are called *lurok* (strangers or foreigners); they are not members of the community.

EDUCATION AND PERSONHOOD

The expression *odoko dano* (has become a person) signals the onset of puberty, when adolescents are capable of having children. Infants, infertile adults, and the dead are not called persons "because they are incapable of having children." Acknowledging that children became teenagers once they reached the age of thirteen came with the introduction of Western modes of education. In traditional Acoli practice, puberty begins with voice changes, pimples, and when the testicles move lower in the scrotum or when the breasts ripen and menstruation begins. The boy is said to *ocot* (to have snapped), meaning that the testicles have descended lower in the scrotum, while a girl is said to *otur* (to have broken), meaning that blood has erupted to announce the beginning of menstruation.

At puberty, non-classroom-based education begins to train children to become adults. The children are now deemed old enough to take responsibilities and to contribute to the economic and social welfare of their community. Knowing who their relatives are and learning to speak are essential lessons for beginners; teaching is practical, gentle, piecemeal, indirect, and full of rewards, such as food and praise. Examples include the taking of verbal messages to or retrieving properties that are either left with or borrowed by relatives or friends in nearby villages. Taking messages to relatives helps the child to fit into a system of the extended family; prepares him to be responsible, accountable, and productive; and enables him to develop the capacity to listen, understand, remember, and transmit details. The extended family, responsibility, accountability, productive work, and oral communication are important aspects of culture.

The education which begins at the onset of puberty does more than prepare the learners for responsibility, productive work, and communication; it also means that one "must leave foolish behavior to little children" (p'Bitek 1966: 14). One such typical behavior is that little children play in dust and ash until they are dirty: this is the reason they are called *lukuce iburu* (those who roll about in ash). Adults dust themselves with soil only on special occasions, such as dances; they dust themselves with ash when celebrating the birth of twins and with hot ash when performing a serious act of *kir* (curse). Educating children to leave foolish behaviors (to grow up) takes place through folklore, words of wisdom, participation in discussions, and through the asking of questions.

Apart from education for beginners and the imparting of wisdom, there is a form of education which is similar to that of the Western school. In this program, the young men are taken to an *awi* (a camp), while the girls stay around the home. At home, elderly women teach girls how to be women who know how to persevere despite hardships, how to support other women and men, how to raise children, how to establish homes far away from where they were born, and how to tolerate other people as well as the ways of coping with bad and good husbands. Girls learn to avoid or deal with natural disasters, to cure ailments using herbs' supernatural powers, and to make food from a wide variety of plants and for a number of circumstances and personalities; all in all, girls learn to live in their physical and cultural settings.

Boys, on the other hand, attend a school called *awi*, where they receive training from a few selected male and, very occasionally, female elders. In the school (one without chalkboards and bells to change lessons) boys learn to hunt wild animals, to gather honey, to fish, methods of defense and offense, and how to survive under extremely difficult conditions. One of the school's fundamental philosophies is living for all; it teaches its pupils to enjoy communal life with their age-mates and it molds them into a society based on age grades.

When teenagers are ready, they graduate to become adults and they prepare to marry. Preparation for marriage includes going on raids, killing the enemy to earn *nying moi* (p'Bitek 1974: 176–98), and fetching cattle for bridewealth; *nying moi* is a name that one earns through a brave act, and it may be equated to a military medal. In defense of the home or livestock, a young man could also kill one of the attackers and earn this "medal." Killing a wild beast such as a lion is the third way a young man earns a bravery medal, which entitles him to marry. After acquiring the qualifications, a young man looks for a spouse, marries, has children, and begins adulthood.

ACHIEVEMENTS AND PERSONHOOD

In the preceding sections, I attempted to illustrate how birth defines personhood and how age, bravery, marriage, and other achievements "make" the person. Activeness, skill, wisdom, and wealth are the other areas of performance and achievement which critically determine the society's judgment of an individual as either a person or "something else."

To be active is a sign that one is full of organic and spiritual life, limitlessly generous, and able to be depended upon. The overall expectation is that one must be busy and work hard in the fields or in building construction, as it is only after such work that other people would say *man aye dano ada* (this one is a person for real). Mere energy and work are not sufficient; also required are skill and achievement in some aspects of work, such as weaving baskets, thatching roofs, or making pots. For a married man, the litmus test of his energy and skill is when he performs for and to the satisfaction of his mother-in-law; his mother-in-law is the root of his family and represents a person who has a quick temper and is difficult to please. Through the choice and preparation of materials, the skill and speed of weaving, or the erecting and thatching of a *simsim* granary for a mother-in-law, a man hopes to appease the female spirit and to have a happy, healthy, and productive family. While the man must please his mother-in-law, a married woman must please her father-in-law, because this is the way to ensure that her children are blessed with luck and will live happy and successful lives.

Apart from physical and skilled work, there is also the sense that a person develops wisdom over time; this wisdom is manifested in a combination of physical growth, intelligence, experience, upbringing, performance, and age. One who does clever things, such as resolving disputes and problems that other people have failed to resolve, is said to be a person. Wise persons often find themselves mediating and settling family and clan disputes; they are important participants in the negotiation of loans and repayment of loans and in negotiating bridewealth. These responsibilities are often the domain of elders, who have the experience and the wisdom required to handle these activities.

To possess wealth—to be wealthy—is one of the most common and greatest of human ambitions. The more traditional (and obviously understood) form of wealth is livestock; one who has many heads of cattle, goats, or sheep is wealthy. One who has many children (five or more) is also indirectly wealthy for three reasons. One, girls are the source of bridewealth and are considered as wealth in light of the heads of cattle that they bring to parents. Two, boys are the source of labor required to work and produce food, itself a form of wealth; young men also provide defense and security as well as peace. Security and peace are the third form of wealth. Thus, anybody who controls and benefits from the services of other people is also wealthy; wisdom, entertainment, medicine to ensure health, and skills to perform special acts are forms of wealth. Being poor—that is, having little wealth—is hated because it has a dehumanizing effect on the person.

AESTHETICS AND PERSONHOOD

In discussing any aspect of Acoli aesthetics, it is necessary to note that a hazy line of physical and behavioral qualities is drawn to divide beautiful from ugly. It is also necessary to observe that good appearance comes from an intellectually dynamic and delicate balance of extremes, as may be seen in the case of an individual who is tall but not too tall, short but not too short, or neither too fat nor too thin. In addition to inherited proportion and complexion, one needs to add characteristic makeup, hair, and clothing (especially during dances) styles and prescribed ways of doing things and of belonging. A person has a classically good appearance when he or she has all the said physical attributes. Classic beauty is admired when it is the attribute of another person but is ambivalently felt when it is an attribute of the self; as it relates to the self, classic beauty is bothersome because it attracts the evil eye (Fernea 1973: 24) and frightening because it rivals absolute beauty, the beauty of *Jok* (God), and is described as *ber ma rac* (so good that it is bad/ugly). The socially approved appearance is human, not overly extreme, and is what I refer to as "good," as opposed to classic, appearance. Good appearance is attractive, likeable, and beautiful; it influences in a positive fashion the relationships among the individual who bears this appearance and the people around him; consequently, it makes the person comfortable and secure, especially around people he or she is well acquainted with.

This Acoli view on the aesthetic of the body may appear contradictory, but I believe that this appearance is quickly resolved when the view is considered against the experiences of discomfort and insecurity that fame often brings to those who have it. While good and desirable in itself, fame is often a source of focused public gaze, obsession, and even envy and hate toward those who have it. Similarly, the Acoli view of beauty addresses this paradox about the desirability and non-desirability of physical beauty. As their southern cultural allies, the JoLuo of Kenya, say, "jaber jahula" (even the best has its downside); beauty comes with a price. Like their other cultural allies, the Acoli believe that extremely beautiful people usually have serious shortcomings; either they will not be quite as industrious as is expected of them or they will be infertile, probably the result of witchcraft practiced on them by those who envy them. Also, the Acoli believe, extremely beautiful people usually have behaviors which mismatch their beauty. These views express the Acoli belief in the human lack of perfection, a quality reserved only for the *jok*. Humans cannot be perfect in all characteristics.

In order to know how to behave, one needs the sort of training that comes from trial, experience, error, and instruction. Like good appearance, good behavior is moderate (not extreme), magnetic, and worthwhile; in general, a person is said to behave well when he or she is humble, tolerant, kind, considerate, and morally right. Good behavior and appearance make a truly beautiful person.

MORALITY AND PERSONHOOD

Morality takes center stage in Acoli life; as a consequence, *dano* is one who conducts himself according to the norms of society. Acoli refer to anyone whose moral conduct is out of step with the expectations of the society as *pe dano* (a non-person or a bad person). A bad person insults, despises, and does not help other people; he talks too much, roams about aimlessly, and in general does what makes other people dislike him. Anybody who is of loose moral conduct is also a bad person, such as someone who makes love in exchange for money (a commercial sex worker). However, the negative attitude toward commercial sex work is undergoing change; Acoli are beginning to see commercial sex workers as persons. The change in attitude and opinions is due to many factors, the key one being that the cash economy is taking over an economy that was based on the exchange of cattle and other domestic animals.

TEMPORARY LOSS OF THE SENSE OF PERSONHOOD

Early in this essay, the temporary loss of the sense of personhood was discussed in relation to birth, especially to the period of seclusion, when a mother and her baby live an extraordinary and superhuman life. The second instance during which one experiences a temporary loss of the sense of personhood has to do with the expression *adoko gwok* (I have become a dog). The expression applies whenever one eats little or bad food or when he eats it in a style or place which is unfit for human consumption, at which point he is seen as descending to a level as low as that of a dog. *Adoko gwok* graphically illustrates the close relationship between food and the sense of personhood; the amount and quality of food as well as how and where it is eaten determine whether or not the individual is a person. The same expression is also used whenever one is emotionally or physically distressed, when death has occurred, when wealth is lost or when mistreatment is taking place, or when someone has become disabled. In these instances, the individual concerned may say, "I have become a dog," meaning that her or his suffering is beyond description.

The subordinate and unfair relationship between the dog and its Acoli owner is the key to understanding the expression "I have become a dog." The relationship is unfair because a dog hunts for the owner rather than for itself. After a successful hunt, the owner enjoys the meat while the dog eats bones. To protect its owner, a dog sleeps outside, in the cold and without any visible reward; a starving dog turns into a scavenger and is severely punished when it snatches any chicken which may be roaming the compound. The life of a dog appears to be one of thankless service, yet a dog is important to its master, who protects his dog. Nobody kills a dog unless it does wrong, for it is believed that the dog's spirit haunts the killer as much as or more than the spirit of a person who is killed for no good cause. In this example, the dog is placed on par with, and may be even greater than, a person. "To become a dog" is similar to experiencing a demotion from a senior to a junior job position. It is to take a place one step below that of a person, and the effect of moving to that step is dehumanizing; it makes one feel terrible, less of a person but not enough to be a plant or another animal.

Sooner or later, one dies; the human sense of personhood ends while the spiritual sense of personhood begins. The end of life and personhood signifies the end of one who was born; one who has grown up spiritually, mentally, and physically and who has lived the life of a person. Death is mourned/celebrated through wailing, songs, dance, and other rituals; burial rituals are indications that death is the process by which life changes from the physical to the spiritual, but they maintain the identity of the one who has died.

THE SONG: CARAMA, TERE OBEDO ABUNY

1. *Tin angiyo ada*   Today I observe
    Aneno carama   I see a divorcée
    Ce mine gengo ngeye   Once her mother covers her back
    Oweko wi carama   The reason a divorcée's head
    Odoko tek lang   Is really hard like granite

2. *Labangcata*   One who does not walk straight
    Ka odok cen   When she returns to base
    Ce wone cwako   Once her father agrees with her
    Carama bene   Divorcée also
    Odoko lagero   Becomes wild and aggressive

3. *Labangcata ni*   One who does not walk straight
    Ka odok cen   When she returns to base
    Ce wone geno   And her father trusts her
    Carama ineno   You find a divorcée
    Lak ata   Roaming aimlessly

4. *Awobi*   Young man
    Kadi icunu   Though you seduce her
    Ni dako leng   Because the woman is pretty
    Meno mukora   That one is fishy
    Baa   Watch out
    Carama   A divorcée
    Tere obedo anang   Her buttocks are flat

5. *Kadi icunu*   Though you seduce her
    Ni dako ber   Because the woman is attractive
    Meno malaya   That one is a prostitute
    Baa   Watch out
    Oriyo wiye   She only plaited her hair
    Wici obutu agong   With thread lying in style

6.   *Onongo ilwongo*   Though you christen her
     Ni lato ada   Death do us part
     Meno mukora   That one is fishy
     Baa   Watch out
     Oriyo wiye   She only plaited her hair
     Wici obutu agong   With thread lying in style
     Wiye otal manok   Her head is a little bold

7.   *Jal*   My friend
     Inino dwe angwen   On day four of the month
     Wayi   Let me tell you
     Awoto wot ming   I went on a hopeless adventure
     Awoto   I went on
     Wot alii   A journey nobody expected

8.   *Oo ka mara*   On reaching my mother-in-law's place
     Anongo carama   I found a divorcée
     Tye ka dino bel   Busy thrashing millet
     Tek tin apenyo   As soon as I address her
     Ni min onyur   As mother of a baby
     Kong igam doga ba   Please talk to me
     Anongo   To my surprise
     Carama mere   A divorcée simply
     Ogama ki jwic   Responds with jeers

9.   *An awaco ni*   I thought she is
     Lato   Death do us part
     Kara   What a surprise
     Megu malaya   That one is a prostitute
     Odyedo ngwinye   She displays her arse
     Tere abedo anang   Her buttocks are dangerous slopes

10.   *Oyono ngute*   Though she sports a neck
     Calo ngut ojwiny   Like the neck of the *ojwiny* bird
     Kara   Surprise
     Korokoro   She is a rusty tin can
     Kara ducu ada baa   All of it and throughout

11.   *Oweko*   What makes
     Abedo ki lworo   Me live in fear is
     Anongo carama   I find a divorcée

Ka obutu piny	Lying down
Ikom pyen gongo	On a big cowhide
Butu ni	That lying down is shocking
Aneno butu ajut	I see and I am petrified like a stump

12. | *Jal anongo* | My friend I find |
|---|---|
| *Carama ka obutu piny* | A divorcée lying down |
| *Ikom pyen* | On a cowhide |
| *Maracu* | She looks bad |
| *Butu nu* | Lying down in that way |
| *Meno butu ajut* | That lying down stuns |
| *Butu obanga* | Lying down like a fool |

13. | *Pol jii tamo ni* | Most people think |
|---|---|
| *Gwok ogamo* | Perhaps she has received |
| *Kara mukora* | That is all wrong |
| *Ineno carama* | When you see a divorcée |
| *Ki wangi* | She is a pitiful sight |

14. | *Wa maa bene* | Even my mother thinks |
|---|---|
| *Tamo ni* | Thinks that |
| *Gwok ogamo* | Maybe she has conceived |
| *Kara meno agobi aye* | Yet that is venereal disease |
| *Two ni* | That sickness of hers |
| *Meno two ajut* | Is the kind which stuns |

15. | *Aneno remo mogo* | I see a little blood |
|---|---|
| *Jwico ki teng pene* | Trickling from the side of her vagina |
| *Meno slim aye* | She is suffering from slim |
| *Two ni* | That disease |
| *Two ajut* | Petrifies one to stump |
| *Two ka ayom* | It emanates from monkeys |

16. | *Awobi* | Young man |
|---|---|
| *Kadi icunu* | Though you seduce her |
| *Ni dako leng* | Because she is beautiful |
| *Kong inong ka gin ni* | Find out the truth of the matter |
| *Ilubu kor lim* | Don't pursue the bridewealth |
| *Ka wegi aye* | Once the owners abandon it |

17. | *Iweko* | The reason |
|---|---|
| *Abedo ki tam* | I entertain lots of thought |

	Aneno awobe	Is I see young men
	Cunu wa lumyen	Seduce even divorcées
	Meno cuna obanga	That affair is hopeless
	Meno cuna ming	The affair is foolish
	Cuna ajut	It is stunning
	Cuna lamat arege	An affair for drunkards
	Kadi iwaco	Though you think
	Ni lato	That she is sweetheart
	Kong itam wii bua	Just think in your head
18.	*Ka inyomo lalur ni*	If you marry the infertile one
	Ineko gang wu	You ruin your home
	Kong itam wii	Just think in your head
	Ibalo gang ka woru	You have ruined your lineage
19.	*Oweko yam*	As once upon a time
	Atingo lalur	I married an infertile woman
	Calo wanga pe	As if my eyes were absent
	Kun an manyomo	Yet I married her myself
	Akelo wa gang waa	I brought her up to our home
20.	*Jal anyomo*	My friend I married
	Layat ni	The wicked one
	Calo wanga pe	As if I had no eyes
	Kun an manongo	Yet I found her myself
	Ada do	That is for a fact
21.	*Oweko onongo angeyo*	This is how I know
	Aneno ni dako leng	Though I see a woman is pretty
	Meno mukora baa	That is false, all right
	Carama	A divorcée
	Tere obedo anang	Her buttocks are flat
	Iye oleng manok	Her belly swollen a bit
22.	*Kadi iwaco*	Though you say
	Ni dako ber	That a woman is beautiful
	Meno mukora ada	She is truly a loose woman
	Ineno	Do you see
	Carama	A divorcée
	Tere obedo abuny	Her buttocks are dangerous slopes
23.	*Kadi ibedo bot*	You may be a bachelor
	Kono baa	All the same

Meno bedo ajut	That is living foolishly
Bedo muyici	A hopeless life
Ka dingo kongo	When filtering alcohol
Bedo ka labot	The way a bachelor sits
Bedo wa ikom	She sits even on a chair
Kadingo kongo	When she filters alcohol

ANALYSIS OF THE SONG

Before I begin the analysis, I will describe the position of a divorcée in Acoli society. Ideally, an Acoli girl marries between the ages of twenty and twenty-five. If she turns thirty before marrying, she is usually an unmarried mother. If she is a divorcée, she becomes *carama;* "divorcée" is the appropriate translation for *carama* because the third verse mentions that she returns to her parents' home. Among the Acoli, marriages promise continuity, while a divorce is disappointing and condemned because it fails marriage and frustrates continuity. However, a divorce is sometimes condoned when one member of the couple is a night runner, a witch, or is ill or violent. Any divorce which takes place without acceptable excuses makes the social position of the divorcée difficult, because she is believed to have "let down" the community; she is punished, becomes the subject of songs, is deprived of friendship, finds it difficult to remarry, and so on. The return of a divorcée to her parents' home makes her look like a little child; it belittles her and is perceived as a form of punishment.

THE ODD THINGS IN SOCIETY

1.	*Tin angiyo ada*	Today I observe
	Aneno carama	I see a divorcée
	Ce mine gengo ngeye	As long as her mother covers her back
	Oweko wi carama	The reason a divorcée's head
	Odoko tek lang	Is really hard like granite
2.	*Labangcata*	One who does not walk straight
	Ka odok cen	When she returns to base
	Ce wone cwako	As long as her father agrees with her
	Carama bene	Divorcée also
	Odoko lagero	Becomes wild and aggressive
3.	*Labangcata ni*	One who does not walk straight
	Ka odok cen	When she returns to base
	Ce wone geno	And her father trusts her

Carama ineno	You find a divorcée
Lak ata	Roaming aimlessly

Observing the society as well as noting and stating the strange events in this society are the themes of these three verses. It is strange that parents cover the back of (socially support) their divorced daughter; yet the divorcée is badly behaved in that she is bold and aggressive and roams about aimlessly. The parents of the divorcée are acting strangely because the normal practice is that a divorcée does not get any support from her parents or relatives; by divorcing, she lets them down and should be given the cold shoulder. The divorcée should behave politely, timidly, meekly, like a wrongdoer, because she broke the rules (divorced) and hurt the feelings of her community.

The divorcée is also out of step with traditional codes of conduct; in general, an Acoli conducts himself with restraint, respects other people's space and opinions, and is polite. On the contrary, the divorcée is perceived as hardheaded and aggressive; she is seen to roam aimlessly and to violate the norm of hard work.

To be hardheaded is to behave as if one owns the world, which is abrasive, offensive, and morally wrong. The Acoli say that only the highest spiritual power, no man, owns this world; anybody who claims that he owns the world contradicts common sense and is a liar and a shame. On the other hand, aggressiveness is frightening because it symbolizes the strength of a superhuman power and the possession of possible means of physical destruction. One who is aggressive shows the strongest and most destructive force, which frightens a lot of people; he or she is pretentious, for one conviction of the Acoli is that only God possesses the superior strength required to cause massive destruction; man's physical capability is modest.

The divorcée's failure to behave as expected is the reason why she is seen as *labangcata* (one who does not walk straight), as senseless—as behaving in an overly foolish way (p'Bitek 1986: 27). To tell someone that he is *labangcata* is to insult the person concerned; an insult threatens its subject by giving messages that contradict and disappoint the belief of the subject. The divorcée is also considered to roam about aimlessly, which is equivalent to saying she loiters; loitering is symbolic of loose sexual conduct, of being a rumormonger, and of dissatisfaction with oneself, all of which are seen as bad behavior.

WARNINGS AND ADVICE FOR YOUNG MEN

4.	*Awobi*	Young man
	Kadi icunu	Though you seduce her
	Ni dako leng	Because the woman is pretty

Meno mukora	That one is fishy
Baa	Watch out
Carama	A divorcée
Tere obedo anang	Her buttocks are flat

5. | | |
| -------------- | ----------------------------- |
| *Kadi icunu* | Though you seduce her |
| *Ni dako ber* | Because the woman is attractive |
| *Meno malaya* | That one is a prostitute |
| *Baa* | Watch out |
| *Oriyo wiye* | She only plaited her hair |
| *Wici obutu agong* | With thread lying in style |

Awobi (young man) in verse 4 is one way to address a male of equal social status, an age-mate or an intimate friend; *anyaka* may be used instead of *awobi* when the addressee is a female. The social relation among equals, friends, or age-mates is often sincere; there is nothing to hide or fear. By intimately addressing the audience of the song, the performer emphasizes the honest nature of his message. He is boldly telling the truth: young man, don't marry a divorcée, however pretty she may be, because she is crooked and ugly—because her buttocks are flat. The phrase "her buttocks are flat" conveys a number of aesthetic meanings. As applied to the divorcée, it means the divorcée is sexually worthless in the same way a flat beer is worthless because it has no alcoholic taste and strength to satisfy anybody. The same phrase may also mean that the divorcée is ugly because she does not conform to Acoli norms of beauty. The overall effort in verse 4 is to discourage any young man from developing a love affair with a divorcée because she is not the right (socially approved) kind of person—that is, she is a person whose surface beauty is marred by a hidden flaw.

A man seduces and marries a female primarily because life is produced by mating pairs of gendered opposites; life without courtship and an unmarried life are signs that something is wrong with the unmarried people. The beginning of courtship is characterized by random approaches: chance meetings in marketplaces, expected meetings at teenage dances, and pursuit of attractive people. As courtship advances, the process of choosing a spouse for life takes place. The choice favors a good heart, behavior, beauty, personal hygiene, making-up, upbringing, and home. However, in verse number 5, the warning is that a prostitute seriously pollutes her own goodness and ruins her marriage potential. The essence of the verse is similar to the message of the proverb *laber ume ngwe* (the beautiful one has a smelly nose), meaning that something is wrong with the beautiful one (p'Bitek 1985: 30). By warning individuals against having relations with ugly people and being satisfied with the false qualities of life, the proverb more or less encourages people to behave in a proper way.

The words *mukora* and *malaya* are borrowed from Swahili; the two words entered the Acoli language most probably through the Acoli who served in the military or worked in the urban centers and who had to use Kiswahili in their places of work. After their employment ended, they returned to Acoliland but continued speaking some Kiswahili, as doing so was a sign of affluence or upward social mobility. It is from these returning Acoli that those who remained in the village learned about *mukora* (to be fishy or crooked) and *malaya* (to have a reckless sexual appetite).

A WAY OF EXPRESSING LOVE AND DISAPPOINTMENT

6. | *Onongo ilwongo* | Though you christen her |
Ni lato ada	Death do us part
Meno mukora	That one is fishy
Baa	Watch out
Oriyo wiye	She only plaited her hair
Wici obutu agong	With thread lying in style
Wiye otal manok	Her head is a little bold

Christening or giving someone a love name is an expression of "deep-hearted" love and is characteristic of young love. As would occur in the case of giving Christian names, one may choose from a pool of names, such as *meya* (my lover/love), *latona* (my forever one), *cega* (my concubine), *labal wiya* (one who spoils my head), and *labal cwinya* (heartbreaker). The opinion in the verse of the song is that one should not have and express deep love for one whose conduct is out of tune with that of society—that Acoli cannot tolerate bad conduct.

So far, the divorcée has been called many names (an idiot, a loiterer, a prostitute) and has been described as someone who has flat buttocks and who is slippery, crooked, without a sense of direction, and bald-headed; in short, she has been abused. In general, hurling abuses is aggressive; to be aggressive is a virtue in a culture of warriors, hunters, pastoralists, and makers of kings as well as empires (Onyango ku Odongo and Webster 1976: 177–87). Though an aspect of hurling abuses is seen as *oree* (play and theater), hurling abuses is also used to demoralize offenders. Demoralizing offenders serves two purposes. First, it educates and corrects those people who step over moral, humility, or performance boundaries, because the morals of the society must be maintained. Second, it levels and brings into the fold those who indulge in excesses, because the society is seen as a mosaic of "equal" people; the society ruthlessly trims anybody who does not conform to the mosaic effect.

DISAPPOINTING DISCOVERIES AND REGRETS

7.	*Jal*	My friend
	Inino dwe angwen	On day four of the month
	Wayi	Let me tell you
	Awoto wot ming	I went on a hopeless adventure
	Awoto	I went on
	Wot alii	A journey nobody expected
8.	*Oo ka mara*	On reaching my mother in-law's place
	Anongo carama	I found a divorcée
	Tye ka dino bel	Busy thrashing millet
	Tek tin apenyo	As soon as I address her
	Ni min onyur	As mother of a baby
	Kong igam doga ba	Please talk to me
	Anongo	To my surprise
	Carama mere	A divorcée simply
	Ogama ki jwic	Responds with jeers
9.	*An awaco ni*	I thought she is
	Lato	Death do us part
	Kara	What a surprise
	Megu malaya	That one is a prostitute
	Odyedo ngwinye	She displays her arse
	Tere abedo anang	Her buttocks are dangerous slopes
10.	*Oyono ngute*	Though she sports a neck
	Calo ngut ojwiny	Like the neck of the *ojwiny* bird
	Kara	Surprise
	Korokoro	She is a rusty tin can
	Kara ducu ada baa	All of it and throughout

To understand verses 7 to 9, a short social background in courtship is necessary. Acoli social organization is such that people who live in one village are close relatives; they have a few relatives in adjacent villages and virtually no relatives in distant villages. To court and eventually marry, a man travels to distant villages, where most of the potential partners are not his relatives. Marriage does not take place between relatives for fear of *gwok* (incest), which is one of the most severe forms of taboo. Courtship depends on chance meetings in public places such as markets, on meetings at expected occasions, such as dances, or on meetings that occur when young men go looking for girls in homes; taking an afternoon trip to look for girls is the method described in the verses.

When a young man takes a short trip in the afternoon, a trip which appears to be aimless, the understanding is that he is looking for girls to befriend and court. His chance of succeeding is enhanced by the daily pattern of life of unmarried females. The average afternoon program for an unmarried female finds her thrashing millet in the compound, grinding grains in the veranda of the house, and fetching water from the river. While she is at home, her parents and other adults are working far away from home. The absence of parents and other adults of the home frees courtship from interference. It is a silent permission for courtship to take place in that home—a way in which parents respect the rights of their children and a way of making courtship easier for shy females. On the whole, the average daily pattern of work is designed to enhance a more cordial meeting and courtship between young people.

The beginning of every courtship appears to be unpleasant; it is full of rough words and actions because everyone involved wants to know the character of the potential spouse (is he or she tolerant, serious, wise, charming with words, and so on). The rough words are indicative of vigorous bargaining to establish common ground before continuing with the sexual component of the relationship. In this bargain, a male tries to show a female that he is the more important partner in the proposed relationship, while she keeps bringing him down, cutting him to size, and making him feel small. There are many opposing moves at the beginning of courtship: a male advances, speaks, proposes, and asks, while a female withdraws, keeps quiet, opposes, and answers. It is the opposing moves which establish which of the two individuals has a final say in family matters when a marriage takes place.

As was explained in verse 7, the young man finds the divorcée thrashing millet, and he addresses her as *min onyur* (mama). Addressing a single female as such is degrading, presumptuous, and very rude. To be polite, the young man should have either stood at the edge of the compound, a sign which means he wants to talk to the divorcée, or addressed her as *anyaka* (lady). She, of course, responds by jeering at him, which is as rude as saying "mama." A woman does not jeer at a man, especially the one who courts her, for the rule is that every woman needs a man and vice versa. The approved courtship protocol is that she places a cowhide on the floor of her mother's house and invites him in. He enters the house crawling, sits on the cowhide with his legs crossed, and remains seated until she dismisses him; crawling into the house and sitting with legs crossed are signs of respect and of the man's willingness to forfeit his pride for the lady he wishes to marry.

After the bad experiences described in verses 7 and 8, verse 9 expresses regret and "sour grapes." The young man began to call the divorcée a prostitute (she displays her arse), and he says she is ugly (her buttocks are dangerous slopes, too flat). Women like men with flat buttocks, because they promise big sex organs and abrasive sexual intercourse, while men like buttocks that are big and "dance" as the owner walks, because they are symbolic of juicy and sweet sexual experiences. The buttocks represent sex organs; to display the arse is as immoral as displaying the vagina in public—it is a great curse—and it frustrates sexual practice, because the success and enjoyment of sex largely depend on the sense of feeling and touch, not on sight. To maximize feeling and touch, Acoli prefer sex in the dark of night and in private, not in the light of day or in public.

In verse 10, the young man is sorry for mistaking the divorcée to be as beautiful as the *ojwiny* bird, since she is really useless and ugly. The Acoli sense of beauty is derived from birds, especially those that inhabit environments around rivers and lakes, where *jogi* (the spirits) live. Acoli classical beauty is found in the characteristic blue and white as well as in the long tail of the *ojwiny* bird and the long and elegant neck of the crested crane. The *ojwiny* bird is not only beautiful, it also has a religious meaning, since it is termed as *gin paco* (a thing of the home), which means the spirit which lives around the home. The bird builds its nest in the grass-thatched roofs and lives around homes; it is neither killed nor eaten. Therefore, to say that a woman sports the neck of the *ojwiny* bird is to combine classical and religious aesthetics; her beauty is classical, as pure as the Holy Spirit and beyond words.

However, no man should fall in love with and marry a divorcée, since she is as worthless as a rusty tin can; *apado* (a broken calabash) is the original and equivalent Acoli word for a rusty tin can. A broken calabash is said to be worthless because adults find it useless; however, children use a broken calabash in toy making and in playing. The phrase "the divorcée is as worthless as a rusty tin can" implies that she is empty, infertile, or unable to conceive and produce a child; she is useless in creating life, which is the most important goal in life. Among Acoli, the fear of permanent death (extinction) makes creation and continuity the principal hopes in and reasons for life, *korokoro*. A rusty tin can contradicts the hopes and reasons for life.

ADDITIONAL VISITS REALIZE GREATER DISAPPOINTMENTS

11. *Oweko* What makes
    Abedo ki lworo Me live in fear is
    Anongo carama I find a divorcée

Ka obutu piny	Lying down
Ikom pyen gongo	On a big cowhide
Butu ni	That lying down is shocking
Aneno butu ajut	I see and I am petrified like a stump

12.
Jal anongo	My friend I find
Carama ka obutu piny	A divorcée lying down
Ikom pyen	On a cowhide
Maracu	She looks bad
Butu nu	Lying down in that way
Meno butu ajut	That lying down stuns
Butu obanga	Lying down like a fool

13.
Pol jii tamo ni	Most people think
Gwok ogamo	Perhaps she has received
Kara mukora	That is all wrong
Ineno carama	When you see a divorcée
Ki wangi	She is a pitiful sight

14.
Wa maa bene	Even my mother thinks
Tamo ni	Thinks that
Gwok ogamo	Maybe she has conceived
Kara meno agobi aye	Yet that is venereal disease
Two ni	That sickness of hers
Meno two ajut	Is the kind which stuns

15.
Aneno remo mogo	I see a little blood
Jwico ki teng pene	Trickling from the side of her vagina
Meno slim aye	She is suffering from slim
Two ni	That disease
Two ajut	Petrifies one to a stump
Two ka ayom	It emanates from monkeys

Let us assume that verses 11 to 15 concern additional visits. During one of the visits the young man finds the divorcée lying in a cowhide bed. On seeing her in bed, he is surprised and many ideas occupy his mind. First, he imagines she is lazy, staying in bed on account of laziness, a very foolish act (verse 12) in a society in which hard work is an integral part of the culture. Second, in verse 13, he thinks she has received a stomach (is pregnant); pregnancy is suspected whenever a female remains in bed, as early pregnancy often makes a woman sickly and forces her to stay in bed. A woman discusses her pregnancy only with close female friends or the father of the expected baby, because pregnancy is a private and female affair. Staying in bed and an unwillingness to discuss what keeps the individual in bed are recognized as an unspoken announcement of pregnancy. Third, the young man is afraid and shocked to think that the divorcée is suffering from a venereal disease. Obviously, disease threatens life and frustrates the making of a family and clan. To suffer venereal disease is a most petrifying occasion. European Christian missionaries taught Acoli that venereal diseases are for sinners, and sinners are not people. From the British who were the administrators of the Uganda Protectorate, the Acoli also learned that venereal disease is for people who are morally dirty and worthless, such as prostitutes. Fourth, in verse 15, upon seeing blood, the young man begins to imagine that the divorcée must be suffering from "slim," another name for AIDS; he is stunned or petrified like a stump. Blood is most probably a way to dramatize the imagined experiences of the song. Not surprisingly, the Acoli find slim a horrifying and dehumanizing epidemic.

A WORD OF ADVICE AGAINST LOVE AFFAIRS WITH MARRIED WOMEN

16. *Awobi* — Young man
    Kadi icunu — Though you seduce her
    Ni dako leng — Because she is beautiful
    Kong inong ka gin ni — Find out the truth of the matter
    Ilubu kor lim — Don't pursue the bridewealth
    Ka wegi aye — Once the owner abandons it

In the above verse, the song turns to warning young people against indulging in a love affair with a married woman and one who is suffering from "slim." It suggests that it is important to establish the true health conditions of a spouse before undertaking a "love" relationship. To love in this cultural context includes and often refers to sexual lovemaking. At the beginning of the song's analysis, I explained that *carama* also indicates someone who was once married, a divorcée. Acoli marriages entail bridewealth, which is returned to the former husband after a divorce. Before the bridewealth is returned, the marriage remains legal and in force. If the divorcée has a love affair during separation, she is said to "pursue the bridewealth of another man." Making love to a married woman is a serious offense in Acoli customary law and an unwise undertaking, because it can lead to a legal suit in a court of elders and severe punishments when the man is proven guilty.

The customary law that bars making love to married women is based on several convictions. One of them is that marriage is a fulfillment of the "obvious" and a solemn promise. In the minds of the Acoli, to get married is as obvious as growing up, becoming an adult, getting old, and dying. As I said earlier, marriage is the ritual by which one becomes an adult and by which one makes a promise never to return to *tino* (childhood); love affairs with more than one person are for children, and they signify the breaking of the promise to remain adults. This conviction and its law are oftentimes compounded by the paradox of misunderstanding/understanding associated with *lim keny* (bridewealth), *cul* (payment, compensation, or token of appreciation), and *gira* (my thing or person).

A RIGHT BEGINNING MAKES A RIGHT END

17. *Iweko*   The reason
    Abedo ki tam   I entertain lots of thought
    Aneno awobe   Is I see young men
    Cunu wa lumyen   Seduce even divorcées
    Meno cuna obanga   That affair is hopeless
    Meno cuna ming   The affair is foolish
    Cuna ajut   It is stunning
    Cuna lamat arege   An affair for drunkards
    Kadi iwaco   Though you think
    Ni lato   That she is sweetheart
    Kong itam wii baa   Just think in your head

18. *Ka inyomo lalur ni*   If you marry the infertile one
    Ineko gang wu   You ruin your home
    Kong itam wii   Just think in your head
    Ibalo gang ka woru   You have ruined your lineage

19. *Oweko yam*   As once upon a time
    Atingo lalur   I married an infertile woman
    Calo wanga pe   As if my eyes were absent
    Kun an manyomo   Yet I married her myself
    Akelo wa gang waa   I brought her up to our home

20. *Jal anyomo*   My friend I married
    Layat ni   The wicked one
    Calo wanga pe   As if I had no eyes
    Kun an manongo   Yet I found her myself
    Ada do   That is for a fact

"A right beginning makes a right end (a good beginning makes a good end)" is the essence of verses 17 through 20. The opinion in verse 17 is that seducing a divorcée and "drunk courtship" are not the right ways to begin a marriage; this illustrates the consequences of beginning on the wrong foot. A divorcée's social position was already explained at the beginning of this analysis. The social position of a divorcée is clearly written in the phrase "a divorcée is like firewood on the roadside; a young man never takes it." The ordinary practice is that someone who is physically strong is expected to deal with the more difficult task of getting firewood from the bush, far away from the road. Firewood that is near the road is left for the old and physically weaker members of society. Nobody picks firewood that is left on the side of the road, because either it belongs to someone else or something is wrong with it. To say that a divorcée is like firewood on the roadside means that she is unfit for a young man and a wrong beginning for a marriage.

"A courtship for drinking *arege*" is full of lies, since it takes place between drunkards and is also a wrong way to start marriage. Alcohol made its mark on and eventually influenced the course of courtship in the 1970s; "drunk courtship" was the name of a courtship style. "Drunk courtship" was greatly supported by the mushrooming of alcohol markets in almost all corners of Acoliland, the lessons taken from domestic tourists. The tourists, Acoli soldiers, and civilians who came home for holidays found markets and market days to be the places and days to display their modern (Western) fashions and manners of consuming alcohol. The villagers, convinced that Western lifestyles were better than their own Acoli lifestyle, began consuming alcohol in the markets and participating in courtship while under the influence of alcohol.

In the marketplace, alcohol was sold by unmarried females who found the drunken men very easy to "defeat" and outwit in the game of courtship, in which one tries to gain a psychological advantage. Without knowing that they were helping drunk courtship to mature, alcohol saleswomen enjoyed themselves a great deal.

Drunk courtship is characterized by *abil* (let me taste). What happens is that a potential customer positions himself near the pot of *kwete* (a beer made from millet, sorghum, and, later, maize). The saleslady offers a little calabash of the brew for him to taste. He has a free drink and gets the opportunity to meet and talk to her. Men who have no money get drunk on free booze, socialize, and get the courage to tell lies in courtship. As a whole, alcohol-adulterated courtship is perceived as an insincere and socially meaningless love affair.

In verse 18, seducing a divorcée is likened to marrying an infertile woman. *Lur* (inability to conceive) spoils one of the meanings of marriage in that it prevents one from "getting" children. The fear of marrying a female who is infertile, and thereby of getting oneself into a childless marriage, is one of the primary reasons for sex before marriage, the absence of virgins, and polygamy. The song centers on a female divorcée, but for a woman to marry an impotent man is even worse, because having children that are born outside of marriage is more difficult for them. Knowing that society does not approve of having children outside of marriage, women tend to be very intolerant toward impotent men, and they usually describe them as saltless vegetables, which is similar to saying that they are good-for-nothing men.

Verse 20 illustrates further the dilemma of courting a divorcée. The spotlight of the verse is on *layat* (one who has/uses poison to kill other people). The performer of the song advises the young man not to do the bad thing he once did: he married a woman who poisons other people, a killer who nobody should have married. *Layat* is a wicked, hated member of society. However, a *layat* is appreciated when he or she frees the same society of its deviants, wizards, night runners, witches, arrogant people, thieves, and people who are suicidal.

FINAL LAMENTATION AND DILEMMA

21. *Oweko onongo angeyo*   This is how I know
    Aneno ni dako leng   Though I see a woman is pretty
    Meno mukora baa   That is false, all right
    Carama   A divorcée
    Tere obedo anang   Her buttocks are flat
    Iye oleng manok   Her belly swollen a bit

22. *Kadi iwaco*   Though you say
    Ni dako ber   That a woman is beautiful
    Meno mukora ada   She is truly a loose woman
    Ineno   Do you see
    Carama   A divorcée
    Tere obedo abuny   Her buttocks are dangerous slopes

23. *Kadi ibedo bot*   You may be a bachelor
    Kono baa   All the same
    Meno bedo ajut   That is living foolishly
    Bedo muyici   A hopeless life
    Ka dingo kongo   When filtering alcohol
    Bedo ka labot   The way a bachelor sits
    Bedo wa ikom   She sits even on a chair
    Kadingo kongo   When she filters alcohol

These three verses repeat and emphasize the verses that preceded them. The last two lines of verse 21 (Her buttocks are flat/Her belly swollen a bit) are, in fact, lamentations of shame entailed by courting a divorcée. The last line of verse 22 (Her buttocks are dangerous slopes) gave this essay its title. It could be understood both in the ordinary and aesthetic senses: the slopes of her buttocks are too steep and that makes her an ugly person. The phrase could also be seen and understood to be abusive, a way of demoralizing the person of the divorcée. Finally, "buttock" is an oblique reference to vagina; it is a discreet and respectful way of stating physical facts. "Her buttocks are dangerous slopes" also means that making love to a divorcée is dangerous because she has AIDS.

The divorcée is discredited from verses 1 through 22. Verse 23 expresses the dilemma of bachelorhood, of life without the divorcée, who may be the only available choice. The unmarried life of a bachelor/spinster is seen as insulting to God—it is a lifestyle that breaks the law of life because it is incomplete. Marriage fulfills the law of mating pairs, while bachelorhood does not. Bachelorhood is also seen as a waste of the time and human energy required to make love and to produce children while one is still young and strong enough to look after his or her children. The word *muyici,* used to illustrate the lack of sense in bachelorhood, has its origin in the political history of Uganda and is most likely a combination of Kiswahili words that mean thief or crook.

When the Uganda Liberation Army, backed by Tanzania's Armed Forces, overpowered Idi Amin Dada in 1979, a new lifestyle surfaced. The life of a *muyai* (*munyici* in the song) is the new lifestyle which apparently took over from its predecessor, *mafuta mingi* (there is lots of oil, meaning there is lots of money). A *muyai* is often a bachelor who has a lot of money and lives a rich but crooked life. Often he makes dirty money, does not have an office or home, conducts his business from his briefcase, and is referred to as a "briefcase business executive."

A *muyai* is a contemporary person, and his idea of romance is modern: sitting close to and squeezing girlfriends on chairs. Acoli see the life of a *muyai* as different from their own—as foolish and immoderate. The life is foolish because it persuades one to become blind to fact, irrational, and to consume sex without control. An Acoli person is supposed to go into sex with open eyes so that when something is wrong, the process of making love is terminated. Romance in the sense of surveying and caressing the body is seen as extremely strange; the people who choose this style of romance are also seen as strange. Add to this the fact that Acoli women do not sit on chairs when they are filtering alcohol made from *kwete* (explained in the section on how alcohol influenced the courtship in Acoliland). In the end, one may understand why it is awkward to find a divorcée, who has now become an unmarried girl, sitting on a chair while she is filtering *kwete*.

A normal woman's regular posture while she is filtering alcohol is as follows: she stoops to a position where she can easily reach two pots, one containing unfiltered alcohol and the other one containing filtered alcohol. Using a calabash, she scoops the unfiltered alcohol and pours it into an *adinga* (a filter which is a bag of finely woven palm leaves). She squeezes the filter containing the alcohol in such a way that alcohol filters into another pot. Stooping in this position puts a strain on and often tires the waist of the body. Any woman who filters alcohol while sitting on a chair instead of while standing on her feet is seen as old, sick, or awkward. This is why the singer finds the divorcée's actions awkward: she sits on a chair while filtering alcohol.

The aim of this essay was to explore everyday Acoli concepts of personhood through the study of one song, *Carama, Tere Obedo Abuny* (A Divorcée's Buttocks Are Dangerous Slopes). In general, the phrase *bedo dano* (to be a person) is fundamental to understanding personhood; it is the process of forming and becoming a person through time and in space, place, and culture. In the beginning of life, personhood refers to the features which are characteristic of and distinguish humans from animals and other creatures. Features such as the head, limbs, trunk, and other body parts have physical properties that are characteristic of humans and that are different from those of animals or other creatures.

A baby who is born with all his human features fully developed is a person; physical disabilities, such as those that may impair the child's ability, do not change the baby's status as a person. To be born with some absent, extra, or abnormal features makes one *jok* (a person with supernatural power). One who is born a twin, born breech, or born after twins or a breech birth is also *jok*, while *lajok* is someone who is born with evil supernatural powers. Given a choice, few people would choose children with supernatural powers, because they are spiritually delicate, temperamental, and generally difficult to handle.

Soon after birth, the ritual process of making a person out of a baby begins. To start with, the umbilical cord is cut to physically and symbolically free the baby from its mother. The afterbirth is buried in the soil, because it is believed that doing so protects the baby and preserves the fertility of the mother. Burying the afterbirth in the soil also begins the cultural root of the newborn and establishes the newborn's sense of belonging, place, and people.

Three or four days after birth, several activities take place. The child comes out of seclusion and makes contact, for the first time, with the world. The baby is given a name; the process of individual identification begins. The name the baby receives may determine the way she handles her relations with other people in the community. She is clothed and tastes food; clothing and food are some of the procedures involved in "making" a person. On the whole, the baby and its mother undergo *kwer*, a ritual through which the baby becomes an Acoli.

The other concept of *bedo dano* also concerns education, which intensifies at the age of puberty. Before puberty, children go through a theoretical program involving folklore and being a messenger. At this stage, the child is trained to develop the capacity to listen, understand, remember, and orally transmit details. In this and any other community in which oral communication dominates other means of transmitting information, the significance of training—so as to sharpen the child's ability to listen, understand, remember, and transmit verbal messages—seems obvious. The child is also expected to know close and distant relatives; this expectation is an attempt to fit the child into the system of extended family. It is in the extended family that one finds security and the best place to live a life.

From the onset of puberty, teenagers must leave foolish behavior to little children and they must *odok dano* (turn into persons). To do this, teenagers receive both intensive and extensive theoretical and practical education to prepare them to live the life of adults. Girls are also taught to persevere through hardships, to support other women and men, to raise children, to establish homes far away from where they were born, to tolerate other people, and to learn ways of coping with bad and good husbands. They learn how to avoid natural disasters and what to do when the disasters are at hand. They learn about ailments and how to cure them; all in all, they learn to live in physical and cultural settings. Boys attend a school called *awi*, where they receive training from a few selected male elders. They learn survival skills, how to raise resources from scanty sources, how to communicate, how to handle offense and defense, how to manage community life, how to tolerate hard times, how to be good husbands, and how to remain human in the face of provocation (temptations to turn into animals). This form of education, which was for all and by all, has given way to and is being replaced by classroom education.

The struggle for the wife or husband could also be seen as an effort toward becoming a person at another level. Marriage is a promise to live after death, and the child is the fulfillment of the promise, an assurance that the individual continues his or her life after death. Nonetheless, this important achievement is often inadequate. One must be industrious and work hard at farming or construction, as it is only after doing so that other people would say *man aye dano adada* (this one is a person for real or a person indeed). Raw energy and work are, again, often inadequate. It would be better if one were also skilled in some aspects of work, such as weaving of baskets, thatching of roofs, or making of pots. A mother-in-law almost always sets the final test, is the examiner, awards the "certificate" of thanks and blessing to all candidates who pass the tests, and empowers them to continue their good work.

Apart from performance, Acoli culture also involves aesthetic evaluations of the person. For an Acoli to be pretty entails more than that the individual possess the right proportions and everything which contributes to good appearance. It also entails that the individual displays intelligence, advancement or progress, cleanliness, good upbringing, and family origin; it has to do with hairdos and styles of dancing and walking. Eventually, a sense of aesthetics has to do with satisfaction through meaningful work, for Acoli believe that one who does not engage in meaningful work is like a dog.

The expression "Doko gwok" (to become a dog) goes beyond the idea of meaningful work. It is common to find one who is deep in death and sorrow, material and financial deprivation, or any other extreme hardship uttering *adoko gwok* (I have become a dog). What, how, and where one eats influences the way people see an individual—either as a person or as a dog. In recent times, many Acoli find themselves eating outside their homes and outside the prescribed situations, because modern developments require one to travel to and work in places far away from home. While traveling or at work, life is so hard that one accepts food and eats in places that are deemed unsuitable for people; *adoko gwok* is the name given to such eating places and the foods served therein. In a way, the expression *adoko gwok* is a protest against and testimony to social and cultural changes.

A song, especially one accompanied by the *nangaa* musical instrument, can be a discourse on such aspects of everyday life as personhood. The song *Carama, Tere Obedo Abuny* is a part of *nangaa* music and serves as an oblique discourse on personhood; its messages and teachings are disguised in the person of a divorcée. Disguising the lessons of the song in the person of the divorcée is a teaching technique which requires finding and using an example to highlight points of emphasis, interest, and education and to make the lessons credible and relevant. Besides, the choice and use of the divorcée is a part of the injustices and ill practices in life, in which a majority and minority are established and in which the majority dictates its will at the expense of the minority. In other words, choosing a divorcée as an example to illustrate the teachings of the song is seen as socially expedient, because the divorcée is socially insignificant.

Notwithstanding the reasons for choosing and using the divorcée as an example, one message of the song is that "to be a person you ought to behave like one." The message is intended to generate good behaviors based on the belief that "good behavior makes a person and it is good to be a person." The other message of the song is that "to be a person you ought to be healthy." This message aims at producing good sexual behavior, with the intention of avoiding AIDS. The method of teaching the lessons is that of threat; the song threatens one with becoming a divorcée, prostitute, bachelor, infertile person, and someone who is *pe dano* (bad enough not to be a person).

NOTE

1. In this work I have chosen to use "Acoli" as the spelling for a word whose alternatives are "Acholi" and "Acooli." This is the spelling used by Okot p'Bitek in most of his earlier works and is also the one used by Margaret Trowell and Klaus Wachsmann in their *Tribal Crafts of Uganda*. The alternative spelling is "Acholi," adopted by Frank Girling. "Acooli" was the spelling used by Father Crazzolara in his *A Study of the Acooli Language: Grammar and Vocabulary*. Girling's spelling is the more official one and makes Acoli easier to pronounce for most English-speaking people. "Acoli" is phonetically correct and is preferred by many Acoli writers themselves.

The word Acoli refers to the people, land, and language, a fact that may confuse many readers. This work uses Acoliland and LebAcoli to refer to the land and language, respectively. "Acoli" refers to the people, and in some cases, this term is used as an adjective. Acoliland is a part of Uganda that borders southern Sudan, although Jo-Parajok and Oboo of South Sudan are also known as Acoli of Sudan. Together with the peoples of Lango, Alur, Kumam, LabworOmor, Nam, and CooPe, Acoli are part of a broader set of language and ethnic groups which consider themselves to be Jo-Lwo. The word "Jo-Lwo" is a short form of "Jo pa Lwo," meaning the people of Lwo, which is the same as "JoLuo" in Kenya (Girling 1960: 12). These peoples constitute a large part of the Nilotic-speaking peoples of East Africa.

During Amin's regime, from 1971 to 1979, Acoliland was divided into the Kitgum and Gulu districts, with Kitgum and Gulu as respective district headquarters. Kitgum District comprises the original Lamwo County, Cwa County, Agago County, and part of Omoro County (a county is the equivalent of a subdistrict). Palabek, mentioned in this work, occupies the northwestern part of Lamwo County and borders South Sudan.

REFERENCES

Almagor, U. 1978. *Pastoral Partners: Affinity and Bond Partnerships among the Dassanetch of Southwest Ethiopia*. Manchester: Manchester University Press.

Crazzolara, J. P. 1955. *A Study of the Acooli Language: Grammar and Vocabulary*. New York: Oxford University Press. Italian original, Verona: Verona Fathers Publications, 1938.

Dyson-Hudson, N. 1966. *Karimojong Politics*. Oxford: Clarendon Press.

Evans-Pritchard, E. E. 1940. *The Nuer: A Description of the Modes of Livelihood and Political Institutions of a Nilotic People.* New York: Oxford University Press.

Fernea, Robert A. 1973. *Nubians in Egypt: Peaceful People.* Austin: University of Texas Press.

Girling, F. K. 1960. *The Acholi of Uganda.* London: H. M. Stationery Office.

Janson, Horst W., with Dora Jane Janson. 1969. *History of Art: A Survey of the Major Visual Arts from the Dawn of History to the Present Day.* Englewood Cliffs, N.J.: Prentice-Hall.

Karp, I. 1978. *Fields of Change among the Iteso of Kenya.* London: Routledge and Kegan Paul.

Onyango ku Odongo, J. M., and J. B. Webster. 1976. *The Central Lwo during the Aconya.* Nairobi: East African Literature Bureau.

p'Bitek, O. 1966. *Song of Lawino: A Lament.* Nairobi: East African Publishing House.

———. 1971. *Religion of the Central Luo.* Nairobi: Kenya Literature Bureau.

———. 1974. *The Horn of My Love.* London: Heinemann.

———. 1979. *African Religions in Western Scholarship.* Nairobi: Kenya Literature Bureau.

———. 1985. *Acholi Proverbs.* Nairobi: Heinemann Kenya.

———. 1986. *Artist, the Ruler: Essays on Art, Culture, and Values.* Nairobi: East African Educational Publishers.

———. 1989. *White Teeth.* Nairobi: Heinemann Kenya.

Trowell, M., and K. P. Wachsmann. 1953. *Tribal Crafts of Uganda.* New York: Oxford University Press.

6. Forging Unions and Negotiating Ambivalence: Personhood and Complex Agency in Okiek Marriage Arrangement

Corinne A. Kratz

> Mainte inka tarei kaaito kityo.
> —*Laato enole Leboo,* March 9, 1989

"No one finishes marriage arrangement alone," my co-wife Laato once told me, aptly condensing and drawing attention to the complex negotiations and social relations involved when Okiek in Kenya arrange marriages. Indeed, many people do take part on both sides, but their involvements are not all the same. Okiek descriptions of marriage arrangement recognize this. They represent some participants as more active and influential, though others may play decisive roles. Notions of personhood and agency are critical both in defining the various relations and involvements of marriage arrangement and in shaping representations of the process. These notions are also central to consequential shifts in identity and social relations that the start of a marriage entails for all concerned. Okiek marriage arrangement, however, takes place under an aura of uncertainty and indeterminacy; these diverse involvements, representations, and shifts together comprise a space of disagreement, negotiation, and persuasion—a conjunction of different perspectives and interests. Marriage arrangement thus provides an illuminating arena in which to consider how Okiek differentiate, recreate, and challenge definitions of personhood and agency.

This essay had many early versions, parts of which were presented at the Sixth International Conference on Hunting and Gathering Societies, the 1990 meetings of the American Anthropological Association, the Institute for Advanced Study and Research in the African Humanities, Emory University, and the African Centre for Technology Studies in Nairobi. Thanks to all at these venues for comments. Special thanks to Ivan Karp for many critical readings and animated discussions.

While theoretical emphasis these days often falls on "agency"—at times wrongly taking it as a simple sign of autonomy (Karp 1995)—ideas about personhood and agency are always intimately entwined. Different kinds of persons are culturally defined, in part, by the various rights, abilities, and responsibilities associated with them, including the right to undertake certain kinds of action and responsibility for their effects. "Problems of identity and person" (Fortes 1983) also arise through questions of action and agency—e.g., when someone presumptuously does something that they have the capacity but not the right to do or when it is unclear that actions have the consequences they are supposed to. Agency includes not only one's own effects on the world but also the extent to which one controls others' actions and effects as well.

Okiek marriage arrangement is a process that occurs through a series of meetings, discussions, and negotiations between and within families. Okiek often describe it in terms of three key activities: seeking, giving, and agreeing. Notions of personhood and agency are joined and embedded in these idioms; each action assumes certain kinds of actors and certain capabilities. Aspects of personhood, agency, and social relations are also defined through the way negotiations proceed and as topics of explicit discussion during marriage meetings. In these ways, personhood and agency become linked with and defined through differences in power and authority, thereby creating distinctions based on gender and age.

With its multiple participants, temporal extension, and episodic nature, Okiek marriage arrangement offers a fruitful entry into the situational intricacies of what Hobart (drawing on Collingwood) calls complex agency, where "decisions and responsibility for action involve more than one party in deliberation and action" and where "a person may be more or less willingly part agent, part instrument, part patient in relationships, and at different times" (1990: 96). Hobart outlines a welcome route beyond the Scylla and Charybdis of methodological individualism and methodological collectivism—treating all agents as individual humans or treating all agents as collectivities—by emphasizing the polythetic nature of classification and the fluctuating, temporally unfolding nature of social situations.

The notion of complex agency, however, bears closer examination: wherein lies the complexity? Theories of agency usually include at least three sets of considerations, those related to actors, actions, and consequences. Hobart concentrates on variable, changing, and simultaneous definitions of actors; what of the complexities of action and consequence? This essay will explore the analytical distinctions contained in the notion of complex agency by looking in turn at the complexities that cluster around the actions, actors, and consequences involved in Okiek marriage arrangement. Though clearly inseparable in social life, these analytical shifts bring out different dimensions of the ways in which Okiek constitute and negotiate personhood and agency in social action.

This essay focuses on Kalenjin-speaking Kaplelach and Kipchornwonek Okiek in Narok District, Kenya, the southernmost Okiek groups on the western Mau Escarpment.[1] Living in forested Kenyan highlands, these Okiek once supported themselves chiefly through hunting game, collecting honey, and trading with Maasai and Kipsigis neighbors. At present, most also cultivate maize and herd domestic animals, and many engage in small-scale trade. Okiek regard marriage as an agreement between two patrilineages, although smaller extended family groups and close matrilateral relatives are most intimately involved. This understanding of marriage as a lineage matter points to a central problematic of individual and collective personhood in marriage arrangement, an issue that will be thematic in the discussion that follows.

Each lineage is internally differentiated, made up of individuals, but lineages are also represented as collective agents with well-defined roles and positions. Marriage meetings are simultaneously a forum in which knowledge of family relations, history, and rhetorical skill are demonstrated, produced, debated, and recreated through discourse. Both the collectivity and its decisions are constituted through marriage meetings and discussions. The multiple participants in marriage arrangement thus engage in a complicated dynamic defining both the individual and collective agents involved. More than one kind of union is forged through marriage arrangement.

The "collective person" of the lineage emerges out of individual differences, their unity of decision forged in discussion. Yet individuals are not equal; the scope of agency associated with some actors widens at the expense of others. Senior relatives act on and for their juniors, subsuming their agency as individuals.[2] These differences are associated with different points in the developmental trajectory of personhood, a subject that will be my second thematic concern in this essay.

Marriage arrangement inevitably foregrounds developmental aspects of personhood and agency, i.e., the ways in which their definitions might change over the life course. For Okiek, marriage continues a process of social maturation whose major divide is marked by initiation into adulthood. It thus highlights notions of agency as manifest in a critical transformation of personhood. Gendered notions of adult personhood are central to the efficacy of initiation ceremonies (Kratz 1994), but the ceremonial boundary is both an endpoint and a beginning.

Ceremonially constituted conceptions of Okiek adulthood become personal, specific, and problematic in particular ways as the new adults experience life after initiation. Adults enjoy greater control over their own actions and decisions and over those of certain others. As agents, however, their decisions inevitably affect others. Adult control and agency entail consideration of those effects, but young adults beginning married life have yet to appreciate fully what that means personally, in practice. Their experience and the scope of their influence and effects as adults develop together, and they develop differentially by gender.

Adult responsibilities are part and parcel of the rights achieved through initiation. Many of those responsibilities are shaped, embodied, and created through marriage, though they may be accepted with ambivalence. Yet ambivalence at marriage is not the bride's and groom's alone. The bride's family must relinquish their child, while the groom's family accepts a stranger into their home. Neither is easy or unproblematic. While forging unions in marriage arrangements, then, those involved also negotiate various kinds of ambivalence that can arise in a situation defined through competing values and perspectives (Shore 1995: Ch. 12).

Such ambivalence is part of the indeterminacy that surrounds Okiek marriage arrangement, a condition that stems in part from uncertainties related to the shifts of personhood involved and from the dynamics of individual and collective agents. The distinction between person and individual, which Fortes developed from Mauss's contrast of *la personne morale* and *moi*, is helpful here. Fortes pointed to possible discrepancies between social definitions of persons (person) and how particular individuals come to know, accept, and experience themselves as the persons so defined (individual).[3] Okiek marriage arrangement, for instance, is based on definitions of the young couple as adults who will cooperate and behave as they should. Whether they will indeed do so, however, remains uncertain, even after the wedding. This uncertainty is articulated during marriage talks in terms of personhood—the couple might still act like children rather than the adults they have become. From another perspective, though, this might also represent different understandings of the capacities of choice that adulthood brings. Because marriage is a moment of change from the perspective of both person and individual, arranging marriage retains this ambiguity of explanation, an ambiguity that is socially useful at times.

In addition to questions about the young couple's eventual agreement, the multi-faceted involvements of those arranging the marriage also surround the process with indeterminacy. While joint lineage action is constituted through marriage discussions, any participant might break from that collective sense. For instance, one of the girl's fathers could refuse to proceed and could insist that she be given to another suitor family. The ongoing negotiations of individual and collective agency and influence make marriage arrangement a process that is full of uncertainty.

Before beginning my analysis, let me recapitulate the structure and foci of the essay. In order to explore the various complexities encompassed in the notion of complex agency, each of the next three sections will focus on one aspect of Okiek marriage arrangement, emphasizing in turn the complexities of action, of actors, and of consequences. In addition, two themes central to any consideration of Okiek marriage arrangement will thread through each of these sections (though foregrounded differentially): developmental aspects of Okiek personhood and the dynamics of individual and collective personhood. The concluding section will summarize and synthesize these analyses.

In Okiek marriage arrangement, concepts of personhood and agency are constituted, enacted, and challenged, in good measure, through discourse.[4] The central material for my analysis will be two kinds of such discourse. The next two sections of the essay deal mainly with the way Okiek describe and talk about marriage arrangement. In considering these Okiek representations of the process, I pay particular attention to how key verbal idioms and patterns of participation illuminate Okiek notions of personhood and agency. These sections also provide a background outline of the events, participants, and general procedures of marriage arrangement. The following section turns to a particular situation, looking at advice given to a bride and groom in 1983.

When the decision jointly forged in arranging a marriage is finally enacted at a wedding, the consequences of marriage arrangement begin to be felt, and certain individuals within collective agents become key to its realization. Those gathered exhort the newlyweds to comportment that is appropriate to their new status and simultaneously recognize the ambivalence each might feel at the change. The ambivalence addressed arises in part from discrepancies between person and individual; exhortations rely in part on the dynamics of complex agency and on tensions between individual and collective personhood. Comparing the idioms used in wedding advice and in describing marriage arrangement will also illuminate gendered and developmental aspects of Okiek personhood and agency.

SEEKING, GIVING, AGREEING: DEPICTING ACTIONS AND ACTORS

As Okiek describe it, successful marriage arrangements are completed in a series of four (or more) visits to the bride's family. The first visit, *esiretit* (<-*sir*, to engage, to reserve; cf. Maa), simply serves as a declaration of interest and intent to pursue marriage. The future husband's parents (sometimes only the women of his family) bring a chain, honey, and/or liquor to the girl's home.[5] There are no extensive discussions; the visitors are simply told "We've seen you," i.e., we recognize your interest.

On subsequent visits, called *enkiroretit* (cf. Maa),[6] several elders from the groom's family (usually including his father) and his mother (or other senior kinswomen) bring liquor to the girl's home. Some senior men in her family have also gathered. With liquor and elders, discussions begin in earnest. This visit could be the last if the girl has already been promised. If visits continue, the groom's family may eventually be told that they "have been given the child/ house," discussion will turn to bridewealth, and they will be told to "go and prepare" (i.e., to find the required property). Ideally, arrangements are finalized during the bride's initiation seclusion. Soon after that, groom and family come for the final marriage visit, ending with the couple's wedding. Only then does the bride's participation become necessary; it is often the groom's first official visit as well.

This description presents marriage arrangement as a broad dialogue between families, glossing visits and extended discussions with summary messages: "We've seen you," "We've given you the girl," "Go and prepare." Okiek also describe marriage arrangement in a yet more general outline. Arranging marriage is then presented as a distinctive set of actor–action associations. The husband and his family "seek a child." The bride's family "gives them a child" (or refuses to). Though part of their respective families, bride and groom also constitute a separate, shared position in the process. Their role is "to agree" (or not) to what their families arrange, though they show acceptance at different points in the process.

These three key verbs characterizing the actions, roles, and relations of marriage arrangement also clarify connections between Okiek definitions of persons and their agency. Abilities, capabilities, and properties that define aspects of personhood are often known and shown through the actions and effects of agents, whether individual or collective. This section will examine the complexities of these three constitutive actions of marriage arrangement and their implications for Okiek notions of personhood and agency.

Seeking (*ceeng'ei*), giving (*kaaci*), and agreeing (*yanei*)[7]—each key verb carries different implications for the definition and agency of those involved, placing different emphases on collective and individual persons and containing important distinctions related to gender and age. For instance, the abstracted triad of agent–action associations emphasizes the collective agents involved in giving and seeking, clearly defining their positions in relation to one another. At the same time, however, arranging marriage involves reaching accord within as well as between families; the acts and wishes of individuals and the lineage agent they collectively constitute must generally coincide for the marriage to proceed.[8] Individual lineage members can also be said to seek and give.

The groom and bride, by contrast, stand as individuals who by agreement can join and reinforce these collective and individual wishes. Refusal brings them into confrontation both with individual relatives and with their collective lineage force. The groom's refusal, however, has different repercussions than the bride's, pointing to gendered notions of personhood that will be considered below. His refusal terminates the process, while hers need not.

It is worth noting a grammatical difference in this regard: the verb "to agree" (*-yan*) differs in valency from the other two. It is a one-place, intransitive verb (i.e., only the subject who agrees must be specified; it takes no object, though of course it can be elaborated with other phrases). On the other hand, "to seek" (*-ceeng'*) and "to give" (*-kaaci*) are both two- to three-place, transitive verbs.[9] While the powers of different actors cannot be read directly from such limited grammatical forms, the difference is suggestive of situational definitions that are relevant to differences of personhood and agency.

In marriage arrangement, the key actors who agree are both individuals that have been singled out within their lineages and individuals that are junior; both features are relevant. Agreeing involves active will, with groom and bride originating their acts of agreement. But it does *not* involve creating a new state of affairs. Rather, agreeing entails *refraining* from creating one by *not* disrupting the still-delicate alliance the families are forging. To fulfill their expected part, bride and groom must limit their range of action and effect, ceding them to their lineage seniors. The intransitive *-yan* (to agree) here shows that groom and bride, both adults, actively affect the process by their compliance, but their sphere of action remains unspecified and vague. Seeking and giving, on the other hand, always specify the magnified scope of action of the others that are acting on and on behalf of bride and groom.

Seeking and giving encompass the dialogic exchanges prominent in the first description above; families seek and give through discussion. But the degree and ease of accord within giving and seeking families differ in ways that the dialogic portrayal captures by attributing statements to the bride's family alone. The seekers' message is constant throughout: We're looking for a bride. The premise that sets the process in motion, it is unspoken but understood in the description. Progressive statements attributed to the wife-givers, on the other hand, show a more gradual persuasion and decision, created in good part during the marriage meetings.

Representations of marriage arrangement also point to situational constraints on individuals and lineages. These constraints on their abilities and capacities are related to their positions as wife-givers and wife-seekers. The key verbs foreground certain facets of the multiple identities that people bring to the arrangements and the conditions under which these facets are most relevant and significant. For instance, in other circumstances, the senior men might all be equally qualified to direct ceremonies or legal proceedings. In arranging marriage, however, wife-seekers have less capacity to dictate the outcome, though their comportment can certainly influence it. Their intervention sets the process in motion, but much of the initiative and control of the actual meetings then passes to the wife-givers. These are situational and relational differences between the elders of the two families, not intrinsic ones. Those who seek a wife today will give a wife tomorrow. Differential capacities defined by gender and age are as fundamental to marriage meetings as they are in other contexts, but the situation also introduces other agency-defining parameters for individuals within such categories, particularly as they represent and embody collective actors.

The cultural associations that the verbs seeking, giving, and agreeing call forth also illuminate the actions and agents concerned. They cast lineages into strongly gendered positions, though other gender dynamics occur within and between lineages. The husband's family, seeking a child (*ceeng'ei laakweet*) or going for marriage (*peenti kaaita*), is depicted as active but uncertain of the outcome. Going and seeking are also the primary verbs used to describe men's forest work; they go to the forest and seek honey and/or animals. Marriage discussions are peppered with metaphors and proverbs that relate arranging marriage to trapping animals and hunting for bees, thus emphasizing the wife-seekers' perspective. These analogies also stress the role of fate and destiny in marriage, simultaneously portraying both lineages as absorbed in a process that they do not, ultimately, control. Lineage agency and responsibility in the process are simultaneously asserted and denied, which is perhaps indicative of the fragility of collective agreement as well. Should the girl be refused to those seeking her, this accent on fate is also evoked to help deflect anger and animosity between families.

In another strongly gendered euphemistic usage, the verb seeking refers to a man trying to gain sexual access to a woman, who is said either to "give" or to "agree" if she concurs (Kratz 1991). The woman clearly controls her own body in this sense, though having an adulterous liaison with a married woman is called "stealing" her (*coorei*) or "stealing one another" (*coorkee*). The collective agency of the bride's family in arranging marriage is based on the claim that she is *theirs* to give, in this case, including sexual, reproductive, and productive rights alike. Similarly, the quest of the groom's family assumes that the family acts on his behalf. (Of course, these claims about bride and groom are not quite the same.[10])

In relation to one another, then, each lineage takes the gender position of the individual they represent. In relation to groom and bride, however, lineages are constituted as agents *for* the two, acting on their behalf. The young people themselves are in part agents *of* their lineages, the ones who will finally produce the collectively desired result. Karp identifies paradoxes of agency in Iteso marriage that are associated with the distinction between acting as agent of and agent for, paradoxes related to gender (1987: 148–49). Relations of seniority are most prominent in forming these Okiek relations of agency, much as they are in other associations that link the verb "to agree" to initiation ceremonies.

During their ceremonies, initiates are exhorted to agree to ritual trials, to follow the footsteps of their older relatives. In seclusion, they are urged to agree to ritual teachings, to respect their seniors. Agreement in these contexts demonstrates their maturity, self-control, and readiness for initiation. Yet the capacities and possibilities they gain in initiation are those of junior adults; the hierarchy of age is particularly foregrounded and reproduced during seclusion (Kratz 1994). First marriage is the critical next step in the development of adult personhood and agency for both men and women.[11] Agreement continues to be the accepted way for them to demonstrate continuing maturation and to develop a realm in which they can practice their growing influence and potential. The different timing of agreement for bride and groom at marriage, however, points to gendered distinctions within their shared place as junior participants, distinctions that were also part of seclusion teachings (Kratz 1990).[12]

I cannot delve into the history of Okiek marriage arrangement in this essay, though much has transformed over the past fifty years.[13] One facet of this history, however, sheds particular light on gendered notions of personhood and agency and the uncertainty of marriage arrangement. Alternative marriages, initiated by the children themselves, have always been part of Okiek life, although they are not mentioned in general accounts and descriptions and are downplayed after the fact.[14] The form and idiom of these alternatives, however, have changed over time in ways that suggest shifts in gender roles and their representation, shifts with implications for Okiek understandings of personhood and agency.

In the past, a young woman who yearned for a particular man and/or was unhappy with her chosen future husband would simply go reside with the man of her choice, "coming out for him" (*mang'teci*). Stories of women (now in their forties and fifties) who "came out" for a man sometimes relate escapes on the very day these women were to be given to another husband, dramatic arrivals, and arguments between suitors. The man picked by the young woman sometimes did become her husband. In other cases, the favored fellow rejected the offer or the girl's relatives came and took her back home.

Regardless of outcome, the action and idiom underline the young woman's choice, independent will, and ability to try to decide her own fate. Perhaps she conspired with the man in question, but *she* is portrayed as the most active participant in the decision. Very few women have "come out" for men in recent years. Instead, elopement has become the main alternative marriage initiative.[15] Elopement is represented quite differently: a young woman is "stolen" by her boyfriend, like a cow. As before, such marriages might later be approved and legitimated by the families involved, but some young women are tracked down and brought home again. Young women must agree to elope, but their portrayal is more passive, closer to that of "official" arrangements, i.e., to agree and follow a chosen husband.

To be sure, the difference between "coming out" for a man and "being stolen" is not simply in the naming. An eloping couple might go to town, where the young man arranges accommodation or seeks temporary employment. In any case, he devises their escape plan, which takes them out of the immediate area. A woman coming out for a man, on the other hand, went to his home; in some cases they then went off to the forest until the ensuing furor died down. The two require different ranges of experience that underline the gendered nature of personhood and Okiek understandings of men and women.

Okiek capture the contrast neatly when they refer to women and children together as *eemeet aap kaa* (the home country) and to men as *piik aap saang'* (people of outside). Women travel far less than men and have a narrower experience of administrative, town, and formal situations. Men range more widely, visit towns far more often, attend political meetings, and used to leave home for days on end to hunt and collect honey (Kratz 1994: 84). The idiom of "stealing" the bride, then, underlines and confirms the limits that Okiek understand as appropriate to women, based on properties of female personhood. The female initiative and self-determination encoded in "coming out" for a man were possible in part because coming out took place within the realms of Okiek life that were open and familiar to women.

Okiek have become more integrated into regional and national concerns in the last twenty years.[16] Okiek are still seen as marginal, but women especially find themselves peripheralized in such matters, including issues with fundamental implications for their lives, their children, and their future, such as land rights. Their current situation is the outcome of decades of daily decisions and interactions based on Okiek understandings of male and female personhood, which have created divergent expectations and possibilities for men and women. In talking about alternative marriage initiatives, the switch of idioms is one indicator that women's possibilities and potential scope of agency may have actually diminished in this process. As the reach and framework of Okiek life expanded and transformed, Okiek men developed the requisite experience and networks of interaction to a far greater extent than did Okiek women.[17]

The kind of responsibility attributed to young women in marriage arrangement is of particular interest in light of changing marriage alternatives. If a bride agrees to follow her new husband, as she "ought" to, the successful arrangement is presented as the outcome of meetings and long discussions between families. If she refuses, however, she is blamed for obstructing the families' plan. As with a woman who "came out" for a man, the potential bride initiates independent action, and its disruptive effects are attributed to her. In other words, the only situation in which a young woman can be clearly recognized as using her ability to initiate consequential action is a subversive one (from the families' perspective).

This "negative agency" is the clearest recognition that the bride, the youngest person involved, also holds the capacity of adult decision, even as a woman. But the adverse effects—the negativity of her act—then become rhetorically central in efforts to persuade her to agree, efforts that can become coercive. The only response she can make is to insist, "Maaweenti. Maamace ciicaan" (I'm not going. I don't want that person). The situation allows no debate that can foreground her dilemmas, respect her self-determination, and distinguish "rightful, self-defensive protest from unwarranted disloyalty" (Beidelman 1986: 183).

Alternative marriage initiatives suggest both the complexities of "agreeing" and how gendered understandings of personhood and agency have figured in Okiek marriage arrangements. They also show that while young people are expected and counseled to relinquish marriage decisions to lineage seniors, that yielding has always been a negotiation over relative scopes of agency. These negotiations of agency and influence between junior and senior relatives are themselves part of the development of adult personhood. Positions and influence within and between families might be similarly contested, as the next section discusses.

Okiek parents are convinced that their children have become more rebellious over marriage decisions in recent years. This is probably a perennial claim, but their perception and the different idioms for marriage alternatives do point to the shifting circumstances in which young Okiek have developed adult personhood and agency in recent years. Socio-economic changes and the growing regional integration of Okiek life have opened new possibilities to young people and alternative means to establishing their status as mature adults. Able to develop a broader scope of influence at a younger age, young men might increasingly claim marriage decisions for themselves, in the process redefining the developmental trajectory of adult personhood and agency. Indeed, while many other demographic, economic, and educational factors intervened, by the mid-1990s, an increasing number of young Okiek were eloping, and few marriages were being contracted through the kind of arrangements here described.

Seeking, giving, and agreeing succinctly characterize the actions and positions of Okiek marriage arrangement, but each key action contains complex claims of influence, assumptions about personhood, negotiations of agency, and fundamental uncertainties. In arranging marriage, participants assert and reinforce their control of their daughter or their influence on their son by exercising it. They simultaneously predicate and create the marriage as a collective endeavor. The next section will consider more closely the complexities related to the actors involved in marriage arrangement. Examining who takes what part in the process will clarify the nature of the endeavor, the kinds of participation predicated for different kinds of actors, and how seeking and giving lineages emerge from their discussions.

ARRANGING MARRIAGE: PERSONHOOD, PARTICIPATION, AND PROCESS

The terms seeking, giving, and agreeing summarize the actions of Okiek marriage arrangements, but neither the actors nor the actions contained in that synopsis are simple. Each action emerges from complex interactions and elaborate discussions held during the marriage meetings, a process that can stretch over years. Discussions involve a number of people from both families. Together they represent their lineages, collective persons, yet each participant also speaks simultaneously from positions defined by his or her own identities and relations. Marriage meetings are expected to follow a particular protocol, but what that protocol entails may be far from clear and agreed upon. Marriage meetings are also debates about how discussions should proceed, about how to define and interpret conventions in particular situations (cf. Keenan 1975 on Malagasy marriage oratory).

In considering the complexity of actors involved in Okiek marriage arrangement, this section considers an important part of that protocol: who attends, who speaks, and in what order. Looking at patterns of participation in marriage arrangement takes us inside the collective actions of seeking, giving, and agreeing. It shows how Okiek definitions of personhood help shape the process and politics of marriage arrangement, establishing individual capacities to affect discussions. In this way, marriage arrangement becomes a field in which some actors assert and exercise authority over others, claiming and demonstrating their personhood and the extent of their agency. Of course, arrangements can also become an arena in which others resist and undermine those claims. All this subtle maneuvering becomes part of the dynamics of individual and collective personhood in Okiek marriage arrangement, one aspect of the complexities of complex agency.

The play of individual and collective identities begins from the first marriage visit (*esiretit*). The groom's parents initiate the process, acting as individuals, as parents, and on behalf of the lineage. Such a limited party can do no more than indicate interest, but their action will call into being lineage gatherings. Arrangements proceed only later, when both sides assemble sufficient and appropriate representatives who can act as and for the wider lineage collectivity.

During marriage talks, lineages are recognized and treated as collective persons in a variety of ways, simultaneously constituting the lineage through such recognition and action. First, the two sides use collective lineage names. People often refer to an upcoming visit, for instance, by saying, "Kap Meng'-ware [the Meng'ware lineage] will come for marriage talks tomorrow" rather than by identifying particular households or individuals. During discussions, the two sides address each other with collective names (Kap Leboo, Kap Meng'ware, etc.) as well. Lineage membership is also adjudicated at several points, which defines and delimits its boundaries. Before formal discussions begin, neighbors and hangers-on who just want to share the liquor are given a cup and asked to leave. Each side can request that certain people be allowed to stay, but those who stay are then are seen as advocates for that lineage.

For the bride's relatives, marriage visits are the impetus and occasion for joint discussion. The husband's family already debated at home; their visits, seeking the child, are the outcome. However, the bride's family breaks off during each visit to consult privately (*enkileepatait*), to air different opinions among themselves, to reach some consensus, and to plan discursive strategies. They send the wife-seekers out, using lineage names to identify sides and to again determine the affiliation (for that occasion) of people who have multiple connections.[18]

Just as participants in marriage discussions affirm and make explicit lineage membership and affiliation, thereby grounding and recreating the lineages, they also build bridges through time. Lineages certainly exist as an idea and identity throughout Okiek life, but lineages materialize in gatherings to act as collective persons on an occasional, intermittent basis. During marriage discussions, people create lineage continuity and identity through time in the short term by recapitulating and referring back to previous discussions of the same marriage. Longer-term links emerge in the central substance of discussions, when previous marriages, attempted marriages, and other relations between the lineages are recounted or invoked.

Lineage representation furnishes a topic of perpetual debate and a regular rhetorical device in marriage discussions. The entire lineage is never present, so just how many members, and which ones, are sufficient for discussions to proceed? Wife-givers can always claim that a particular absent brother or father is critical, thereby postponing discussions that they are reluctant to conclude. They may indeed want to avoid offending close relatives, but marriage talks sometimes do proceed without the ostensibly vital presence of these relatives. Wife-seekers might also be sent away because their own contingent is slight, lacking essential senior speakers. The ambiguities of individual and collective personhood thus become strategic resources in the negotiation of marriage as well as in other relations among those involved.[19]

I turn now to consider those who *are* considered necessary to marriage discussions and those who together *can* represent the lineage. This leads back to distinctions of gender and age that are prominent in Okiek definitions of personhood and agency. I discussed above the way in which age and seniority figure in "agreeing," the key action attributed to (and hoped for from) the bride and groom. Okiek do not make absolute distinctions of age among other participants in marriage arrangement, but relative seniority and generation certainly influence who leads discussions, when one speaks, and how often an individual speaks. Junior relatives rarely even accompany the groom's group. On the bride's side, young adult men might attend, but they usually contribute little to formal discussion. Newly married themselves, they are still developing capacities as adult men, increasing the scope of their influence and agency. Young women do not take part in arrangements on either side, joining only later to celebrate the wedding.

Mature men (*paaiik*) from both families are regarded as essential for marriage talks; no discussions can be held without them. Several social and jural concerns make them important, an extension of men's role in legal and political meetings. Men from the husband's family represent a guarantee of care for a married daughter, a warranty based on their influence and senior/supervisory relations with her husband. They form a joint judiciary with senior men of the bride's family if the marriage has difficulties. As elders describe it, the young woman is given to her husband's family by her own family. Responsibility for initial marital stability is thus somewhat removed from the couple; if either "child" misbehaves, the marriage will not dissolve until one proves incorrigible. If the marriage does founder, these men are witnesses to property transfers— a judiciary and guarantee then for the husband's family. "If the child [girl] then goes and runs away, they know what was said and they can repay things."[20]

These representations reinforce the sense that agency and responsibility expand with maturity. They enhance elders' responsibility and importance (as lineage representatives) and diminish that of the groom and, especially, of the bride. Yet the bride *is* an adult who has earned the right to choose. No marriage can be finalized until it is clear the bride will stay:

Go first and see [if] the child [will stay]. . . . We'll keep our ears open too, and you all watch the child. So when it has become true and clear that she will no longer go away and her heart becomes good, then go and try to find the things that are wanted. [21]

Such explicit allowances in marriage discussion underline the negotiation of responsibility and agency involved. Elders' control is far from assured or absolute. As discussed above, responsibility and blame seem to be allocated on a sliding scale, depending on the young couple's cooperation. If all goes well, elders congratulate themselves on the arrangement. If unresolvable problems arise, blame will fall on the young people for their obstinacy and immaturity.

Okiek also justify elders' role as marriage spokesmen in terms of their ability to speak calmly and reasonably during a delicate process. "Amu iceek inken kong'alaal. Naiye nee laakweet?" (Because they are the ones who know [how] to speak. What does a child know?) The explicit contrast drawn is the now-familiar developmental one between elders and youngsters. The unspoken contrast is between men and women, for women are considered unable to speak in a controlled, elaborate, and reasoned manner. The wife-seekers' demeanor should be discreetly modest, measured, and respectful, even when challenged. This is the kind of self-control that Okiek attribute especially to men.

These justifications rest on a set of associations that Okiek make between ways of speaking, emotional control, cognitive and organizational capacities, modes of authority, and jural roles. Together, this configuration establishes differences of personhood that are attributed to gender (Kratz 1994: 83–88, 95–98). Participation in marriage arrangement is an extension of and largely in concordance with these gendered definitions. Representations of men's participation in marriage talks epitomize what elders are thought to be like (though the way in which discussions actually proceed may belie those ideals). Women's participation, however, introduces a certain tension into these gendered notions of personhood.

Most participants in formal marriage discussions are men. All of the girl's fathers and adult brothers can participate; her sisters' husbands and matrilateral relatives might also be consulted. But men cannot finish things alone. Nor can they even start them. In some ways, the marriage process is led by women, though certainly it is not ruled by them.[22] The first *esiretit* honey, brought by the husband's mother, is for the girl's female relatives. Subsequent visits begin with women of both families sharing a calabash of wine. Women are important during the wedding as well.

In marriage, a child is requested and given; future reproduction is the union's essential goal and measure of fulfillment. These symbolic aspects of marriage arrangement recognize women's critical involvement in bearing and caring for children. Indeed, maternal care is one explanation for bridewealth: "We compensate for children. We repay the feeding/care of the mother. You feed the child and carry it in your stomach." That nurturance also supports the claim of the bride's family that she is theirs to give.

At the same time, the expansion of women's influence and agency is tied to the growth of their children and is modified in an immediate way by a daughter's marriage. Children's work contributes to their mother's household and is under her management to a fair extent. When a daughter marries, her mother relinquishes a certain measure of labor and influence in her own domestic sphere, even though she simultaneously broadens affinal links. Thus, the scope of men's agency as individuals systematically expands over the life course, diminishing only after their sons have matured and they themselves become grandfathers. Women's sphere of influence and management, however, both increases later (as discussed below) and fluctuates more explicitly when their daughters are given away.

From the lineage perspective, women's involvement in marriage arrangement presents a double paradox of agency (Karp 1987; Jackson and Karp 1990: 20–21). First, in the most fundamental sense, women's reproductive capacity is the means through which their husbands' lineages are perpetuated; they are critical to recreating collectivities of which they are not members. A woman's individual agency, then, helps create the collective agency of the lineage. Second, this primary paradox emerges in a particular form in marriage arrangement. Though they are not members, women have a say in lineage decisions about marriage. A girl's mothers, brothers' wives, and adult sisters can all attend and speak during family conferences.

This contrasts with other formal decision-making contexts, in particular judicial and political meetings, which exclude women. Yet women's active role and potential agency in marriage decisions is framed in a way that minimizes the immediate influence and effect of these women. Nor do men always treat women's voices as significant. Women's participation is both essential and anomalous, a tension that emerges from the conjunction of gendered definitions of personhood and the dynamics of individual and collective personhood.

Women are characterized as being unable to listen and follow reason, since they do not know how to deliberate and speak well. Yet women are essential to the lineage person and are deeply implicated in decisions about their children's marriages and their future success. The tension of this paradox emerges in a variety of ways, including the very procedures of marriage meetings. Their conventions reproduce certain aspects of men's meetings, so that women might feel constrained from voicing their views, or their opposition might be overridden.

(1) Men are the ones who talk first, and then you can ask mothers who is for and who against the family after men have said theirs.

(2) When she [the mother] has gotten to hear well and has the need, she speaks. Like when I have finished, so that she hears what I have said. Yes. So then she says hers while remembering that one that I said.

In other words, women are called to speak only after men have begun to shape the direction of consensus. Further, they speak after exchanges that might resemble in style men's eloquent and extended orations at political meetings, a style most women have little opportunity to master. To be sure, many women *do* speak their minds at marriage talks, but the situation is one that might seem daunting (cf. Lederman 1984).

The girl's biological mother is the key female participant; if any woman's opinion were to carry weight, one might think hers would. Yet the consideration given to her view and to those of other mothers varies considerably, another indication that their individual positions as women are hard to reconcile with their role in the collective person of the lineage. The following Okiek comments reflect this variation and the apparent incongruity of women's participation in such important decisions. The first two are men's views, the final two from Okiek women:

(1) She doesn't go if the mother doesn't want them. The mother can refuse . . . and say that person dislikes her and doesn't treat her like a person. She can refuse to put the fat on the day the girl would be taken.

(2) Then he doesn't get her if the mother doesn't agree. Even if all the others want him. Because the mother can curse her and she won't have children.

(3) Some will give her to them even if the mother says, "No." If the child refuses, she is beaten and the mother is quiet because she'll be beaten too. There are some that if the mother says "No," then she doesn't go to those people.

(4) They still give her [even if the mother refuses]. They insist. They give her forcibly. The mother is just annoyed until she is quiet, as she will be beaten along with her daughter. They will say "Is she hers to refuse?"

The bride's mother can try to derail a proposed marriage through other avenues, but then she acts as an individual spoiler, against the collectively authorized agreement, and reconfirms the idea that women lack self-control and do not listen. Note that the men above cite such possibilities (refusing the wedding anointing, cursing her daughter's fertility), not women's oratorical persuasion, to support their contention that she is heeded. Such threats, they suggest, compel them to listen. Other threats, the women seem to answer, compel them to silence.

These debates about mothers' influence, agency, and effect in marriage arrangement again emphasize—this time in relation to gender—situational constraints and definitions of the rights and capacities of personhood. This example, however, also shows the importance of cross-situational analysis for examining the multiple facets of personhood and the variable means and scope of agency. Deterred from thwarting a marriage during formal talks or the wedding, some mothers might still undermine it through subversive advice and support for their daughters. Situations outside of formal marriage talks are also important in returning now to the complexities of the final actors to be considered, the groom and bride, and of how "agreeing" is differentially constituted by gender.

Neither groom nor bride plays a prominent role in formal marriage arrangements; the lineages are acting on their behalf as collective agents. In the last section, I discussed the action expected of both of them—"agreeing"—in relation to the "giving" and "seeking" of their families. Compliance with others' actions rather than instigation of one's own action, "agreeing" encodes the hierarchy of age that structures Okiek marriage arrangement and the couple's position as individuals vis-à-vis lineage collectivities. There are further complexities, however, within lineage claims to act for young adults who "agree." These are related both to the transition from child to adult and to gendered definitions of personhood. Bride and groom are distinguished in both ways by the timing of their respective agreement, defining different capacities to influence the process. These differences also have ramifications within the scope of agency conferred by marriage, as seen in the wedding advice discussed in the next section.

The future husband's role in formal visits and discussions ordinarily is minimal.[23] He usually appears only on the final wedding visit. It is up to him, however, to visit potential in-laws between discussions, bringing small gifts, helping with work, or simply checking on their welfare. Moreover, marriage arrangement rarely proceeds if he tells his parents he refuses the girl they seek, though they may not seek the girl he prefers. As Sebaya's mother (K.S.; C.K. represents Corinne Kratz) said,

> K.S.: I won't go if he refuses and says he doesn't want a bride yet or he doesn't want that one. How can I go for marriage for someone that doesn't want her?
>
> C.K.: But then why go for Shololo if it's Saipeny'o that Sebaya wants?
>
> K.S.: I like Shololo myself because her mother is not a bad person. Yalaakweet has gone for marriage for Saipeny'o, and he and Sebaya are brothers, so we don't want to go there too.
>
> C.K.: Why don't you go for the girl of the Ning'u family then?

K.S.: It depends on what the young man wants. If he doesn't want someone, we don't go there.

The point for the future husband's agreement, then, is quite early in the process. He has an important veto power even if he does not represent himself in marriage discussions. Furthermore, his own demonstration of interest and assumption of preliminary affinal relations outside of formal meetings influence the success or failure of the arrangements. Kirutari (K.) explained this, expressing dissatisfaction with the young man who wanted to marry his daughter:[24]

K.: Basi, so [after saying he can have her] don't we staaaaaay? So I am also testing him so I can see his secrets. If I see that he has corners [i.e., faults], then when they bring honey wine later [for further discussion], I tell them, "We didn't get along together after all. You should go, you should go and look someplace else again—look for a child somewhere else." . . . He doesn't come to help me with this garden. Have you seen him yourself?

C.K.: No, I've yet to see it. I just see him the days they bring honey wine.

K.: Hoo! The day he brings honey wine! And if I clear [the garden] here, [and tell him] "Look at that tree I felled. Look here, clear it for me." And he refuses. That time I'm measuring him. Yes.

C.K.: So you tell him "Go. Because you didn't help"?

K.: "Go because you don't help me-e. And you don't help Nemboko's mother [the girl's mother] there-e. And you don't help me here-e." So what good is that? It's just useless.

As for the future bride, she may well be a child during early visits, excluded from adult proceedings. When negotiations are completed during later visits, she is in initiation seclusion and is thus removed from daily interaction with adult men. She might tell her mother, sisters, brothers, or even her father that she does not want the man they are considering, and they may listen.

We don't give her to someone she doesn't want. She won't go and do anything there if you do, she won't work or help them. Because she was given forcibly. If she goes there by force and is beaten and comes home, she'll tell you, "I told you I don't want them, and now see what he does to me?" And you end up taking her back and then that's another meeting [to return bridewealth].

In contrast to her future husband, who may be absent from formal proceedings but who nonetheless can influence the process along the way, the girl must depend on others to influence it for her. Her agreement becomes an issue only later, on her wedding day.

All arrangements are usually completed, then, before the bride becomes an adult woman. This timing sustains the founding premise that the young woman is "theirs" (the family's) to give, that the child will follow their wishes. Children are supposed to respect and obey adults. Of course, they are rarely the docile creatures this supposition would suggest, and adults are not always reasonable either (cf. Kratz 1991). Nonetheless, to give a bride immediately after initiation draws on her lingering childhood reactions to the adult men from whom she was secluded. It capitalizes on a tentativeness in her new adult role and on the immediacy of seclusion teachings about respect to parents, husband, and affines.

On her wedding day, the bride's position is analogous to that experienced during her first initiation ceremony. The patterns of performance in that ceremony focused a dramatic and rhetorical effect on her. She did not speak in any ritual event. When her fathers and brothers encouraged her in speeches, she could only respond through action, i.e., by braving initiation trials (Kratz 1994). Once again at her wedding, the young woman becomes part of a process that gives her no opportunity to speak. Once again, her relatives gather to talk to her, advising the new couple.[25] This time she is told to agree by following the husband to whom they have given her. Yet unlike initiation, she will not shame them in the same way if she refuses. In this case, she has had no clear part in the process leading up to this point. She is inserted into a virtual fait accompli, needing only their final blessings and requiring one more act of obedience and compliance from her, now as an adult.

The rhetoric of persuasion is similar in both situations, invoking personal ties and stressing responsibilities it is assumed that only she can fulfill. In initiation, the work and resources devoted to her ceremony created a responsibility to complete it; in marriage arrangement, an obligation develops from eating the food and property of the waiting affines. However, *she* (the bride) asked for and is made responsible for initiation, while *they* (her family) committed themselves to provide a bride. The fact that persuasion is part of wedding advice points to the uncertainties and tensions in Okiek marriage arrangement. The very moment at which childhood acquiescence properly and publicly becomes adult choice, the bride is enmeshed in the dynamics of individual and collective personhood. Her agreement will simultaneously avert problems for close relatives, confirm her own lineage loyalty and right to future support, and show her to be the respectful young woman that initiation idealized. The agency of adulthood is not autonomy.

By concentrating on the actors of marriage arrangement, this section examined another range of the intricacy contained in the notion of complex agency. Questions of personhood have proved central to this discussion, including the paradox presented by women's participation, the dynamics through which lineages emerge as collective persons in marriage meetings (and the ambiguities of definition associated with them), and the differentiated involvements and persuasions that lie behind the couple's seemingly shared position as absent but agreeing. The different possibilities encompassed by "agreeing" are related to the different points that bride and groom occupy in the developmental trajectories of adult personhood. However, those trajectories and the timing of their involvements are firmly grounded in gendered distinctions of personhood. Gender and age define uneven opportunities and abilities for bride and groom to influence arrangements.

The bride can still alter the ultimate outcome after the wedding, but only by offering continued resistance in her new home. That difficult, sometimes risky possibility also has repercussions for the relatives who would arbitrate repeated conflicts and ultimately repay her bridewealth. Nonetheless, some young women take that path. The groom, too, can nurture the new union or destroy it with neglect and mistreatment. The responsibilities and adjustments of married life are major topics for wedding advice to the couple, turning attention from collective lineage persons back to the individuals who will fulfill the joint decision. At this point, the consequences of marriage arrangement come particularly to the fore. The next section looks more specifically at how marriage advice incorporates and addresses the ambivalence felt by different participants at these consequences and how it both questions and constructs different kinds of agency and control for men and women.

WEDDING WORDS: ADVICE, AGENCY, AND AMBIVALENCE

Marriage arrangement has proved to be a rich topic for exploring different facets of complex agency and Okiek understandings of personhood and agency. In previous sections I focused on key actions in arranging marriage (seeking, giving, and agreeing) and on the definitions and dynamics of individual and collective actors involved. This section on wedding advice brings to the fore a third aspect of agency, the consequences of marriage arrangement. Centered most immediately in the lives of bride and groom, these consequences, too, have their own complexities. In completing marriage arrangement, wedding advice also brings further changes in terms of the dimensions of actions and actors already discussed.

Developmental aspects of personhood again figure prominently in the advice. The social maturation marked by marriage is associated with a range of new situations, of which the possibilities and constraints on agency are specifically addressed. For bride and groom especially, marriage entails changes in their daily lives and in the way they make choices and decisions. Other people experience simultaneous, related adjustments in the scope of their own influence and agency. Some of the complexity of marriage arrangement consequences also emerges in the ambivalence addressed in advice, ambivalence that is especially concentrated in the threshold moment of the wedding. Seen simultaneously from the perspectives of a young single man and woman and of a newly married woman and man, these changes and adjustments hold various attractions, burdens, and dilemmas. The bride and groom may not yet realize all these implications, but mature adults relate telling incidents from their own early marriage experiences and exhort them to behave properly. These retrospective narratives combine indirect advice, prospective suggestions, and warnings about situations the two might encounter.

In the wedding context, the distinction between lineages that dominated marriage meetings realigns along lines of age and experience, differentiating mature advisors and the couple that is advised. As the advice proceeds, it also becomes clear that the authority of age is applied to recreate gendered differences of agency, power, and authority within the new household. The collective force of the lineage actors remains important in finalizing and witnessing arrangements; it becomes a potent rhetorical source in encouraging the couple as well. At the same time, however, personal relations and a still more inclusive adult collectivity also come into play. Individual relations with bride and groom are invoked to induce them to heed wedding advice. Furthermore, the larger collectivity into which members from both lineages now merge—a collectivity more vague, without the corporate character of the lineages—also becomes the avatar of "tradition" (Kratz 1993), arrayed in contrast to two junior individuals.[26] United by shared interests in concluding the property/ resource/personnel transfers in which they are engaged, both sets of relatives join forces to encourage a lasting union between their children.

This time both bride and groom are part of the proceedings, along with the groom's "best man" (*enkiyeuit*[27]) and a child who joins the wedding procession. As the bride is being anointed and dressed, people begin to speak to the couple. They tell them what is expected of a husband or wife and advise them about the difficulties and responsibilities ahead. Marriage and parenthood are integral to the identity and social destiny of adult Okiek. Bride and groom both became adults through initiation, but marriage brings them to a new threshold. Adult personhood and agency are developed, fulfilled, and demonstrated through the relationships of marriage and parenthood, for men and women alike, although in different ways. The gathered company of relatives presents a united front of older, married adults who represent, attest to, and address the joys and difficulties of that process through their own experience.

In their own household, the new couple will be responsible for others as never before. Initially they care only for each other, but soon children will increase their joint adult responsibilities. Wedding advice emphasizes these responsibilities, which can no longer be denied, diverted, or ignored, at least not without consequences. Through initiation, the bride and groom secured the prerogatives and potential of adult agency. Through marriage, each learns the parameters and constraints within which these can be exercised, qualified, and expanded. Marriage gives both rights and duties concrete and personal form. These consequences come out in a number of themes and idioms.

Some of the verb-based idioms central in marriage meetings carry into wedding advice as well. Giving and agreeing are still prominent, but they are now used in ways that differentiate bride and groom. The groom is told that he has been given a wife, the bride that she has been given away. But only the bride is repeatedly counseled to agree, thus manifesting the differences discussed above in terms of what this means for bride and groom. The advice is also her public persuasion.

Work, mutual care, and consideration become central themes in wedding advice, explicated through particular examples, exhortations, and reminiscences:

A.O.: Do a garden, my sister's son.

M.: Do a garden, friend. . . . If it's [purchased] maize meal from Melilo that you cook with [all the time], what does that become? Won't this money of yours run short? . . . Ee. Make a garden, friend. Cultivate. Grab a panga. . . .

A.O.: So now I've told you, "There she is, Leng'eng'. You've been given a child. Go take care of the child." . . .

A.N.: Feed your husband.

M.: Feed him. We don't say go and feed yourself. . . . If it's a small *ugali*, cut it and share it together. Leave [him] a bit, and you eat a bit.

Care and consideration for the spouse is only part of a wider network of obligations that marriage creates for both husband and wife. Each is also admonished to help particular affines. The bride's new community of mutual responsibility is named; it includes her husband's mothers and sisters and his brothers' wives. The husband is told to remember his wife's family, especially his mother-in-law. These identifications both describe and prescribe their widening scopes of consequence. At the same time, they indicate that mutual realignments are necessary, adjustments that can become complications and stumbling blocks.

Two prominent verbs encapsulate the themes of work and consideration in wedding advice, idioms that also anticipate the parenting to come: "feed" (*-pay*) and "care for/protect" (*-riip*). Their antithesis is selfish disregard for the new spouse, evident in various ways that reveal lingering childish attitudes and behavior and a refusal of adult responsibilities.

(1) We don't want, once you have taken her, for you to go wandering around and throw away your home. You go and staaaaay and just feed yourself until you grow fat and you have a thick neck. And you don't think of home if you get something, you don't run to take it home to the children.[28]

(2) We don't tell you to just go if you think to help someone, and go wandering around here and there. When you hear that she is sick, go and tell your husband, "I'm going. I'll go and split firewood for her." You go and split that firewood, you put it down, and then come [home]. Don't go around then laughing. Do you hear? . . . You go and split firewood for her, but don't steal it for yourself, just thinking, "Let me go." You tell your husband, "I'm going."

Adult personhood is still a matter of pride for the young couple, still a status recently achieved. Relative autonomy and self-determination have been a sign and a privilege of growing maturity for them as individuals, but these are suddenly redefined. Marriage recasts excessive independence as selfishly immature, even childish, thereby capitalizing on attitudes associated with the major change of personhood that is marked by initiation. The developmental nature of adult personhood makes for shifting grounds of evaluation for young adults.

As "agreeing" was not the same for groom and bride, the implications of "feeding" and "caring" also differ for the two. Both are told to work hard and to care for one another and for their new kinsfolk, but their work differs, as do their relative positions in their new household and community. The gendered notions of adult personhood reinforced during initiation attribute different capacities to men and women, endowing them with different degrees and spheres of agency. This process continues during marriage, the differences further elaborated and specified in the context of the new household. Wedding advice spotlights these expectations and those situations in which they might become problematic.

Let me look first at images of adult men and the sense of male agency constructed in advice to the husband. Agency includes not only effects created through one's own actions and intentions but also the extent to which one controls one's actions and those of others, bringing in relative power and authority as well. "'Power' in the narrower, relational sense is a property of interaction, and may be defined as the capability to secure outcomes where the realization of these outcomes depends on the agency of others" (Giddens 1976: 111). This side of male agency is particularly significant in representations of marriage as a transfer not only of bridewealth property but also of control.

A bride's guarantee of protection comes from her male relatives, her "owners." Upon her marriage, her husband becomes her "owner" (*ne pa*). Advising him against extreme suspicion, one husband was told, "Don't be so very jealous that you become the first in jealousy. That's bad. . . . But don't leave jealousy alone either, because she has an owner." Men are portrayed as protectors, managers, organizers, and controllers, but they must have something to protect, manage, organize, and control. Beehives, hunting products, herds, gardens, and commerce may seed a young man's future prosperity, but his wife and family provide an essential part of his property and social status, an impetus for good management. His actions and decisions affect their well-being and future as well as his own. As the "organizer," he is vested with some control and with the right to decide about their actions as well.

Thus, advice to Seraset, the young woman addressed above, refers to her husband's right to know her movements and plans, her need to inform him and to request "permission" before going somewhere. Her husband holds a physical sanction if she fails to respect his rights and authority, flouting them continually. He is enjoined not to abuse this power, not to beat her mercilessly, regularly, or without reason.

> A.M.: We don't beat a child in drunkenness. Ever. I don't want drunkenness where someone is beaten.

> M.: Truly, we don't beat someone when drunk. . . . Beat her when you are not drunk.

Male agency is enhanced through dependents but tempered with responsibility. Fulfilling responsibilities, wisely managing productive possibilities, and recognizing the limits of control are part of the ideal image of a mature adult Okiek man.[29] Yet responsibilities also bind, breeding ambivalence and conflicts of interest as well as respect and social standing. As marriage begins, groom and bride might feel discrepancies between the social persons they have now become (a married man or woman) and the ones they leave behind but still identify with. These divergences between person and individual are one source of ambivalence.

A young man beginning marriage feels the bonds of responsibility before he enjoys all its fruits. An alternative view of marriage, from his immediate present vantage point, recognizes the restrictions it places on a young man's freedom. Of course, the groom cannot express hesitations during the wedding, but relatives address his possible ambivalence at these life changes, bringing this alternative image into marriage advice. The restraints are felt and summarized most importantly in restrictions on roaming, a particular freedom of single young men. Bachelorhood is pictured as a time of adventure, formerly for cattle raids and trips to hunt meat and honey. In the company of age-mates, young men visit one another, taste town life, and go looking for romance. Once married, however, such a young man will be considered irresponsible. What once was self-sufficient survival becomes selfishness:

> M.R.: You climb way up to the top of the treeeeeee . . . and first you eat the first runny honey, and when your stomach is full [others laugh]—

> A.M.: He thinks he'll eat [just] a little.

> M.R.: And when he has gone and eaten, [then] he goes and takes it [to the wife] and there is nothing left of the honey. She looks on that side and gets just a little bit down at the bottom. . . . Is that good?

Restrictions on roaming are also prescriptions about providing for wife and children, injunctions to work and to manage a household like a mature adult man.

Having a household and a family are steps toward becoming a mature adult (or "junior elder"). Yet initially, the pride and status of having one's own home, of being able to entertain friends, relatives, and age-mates, might be colored by anxieties raised by the very experiences a young husband is supposed to leave behind. Now the "owner" of a young woman, he has "owner's" rights to worry about as well. One of the bachelors only yesterday, he can hardly forget their amorous rendezvous with grown girls and flirtatious encounters with young married women. His wife was one of those girls just months ago. She may leave other boyfriends to follow her family's marriage decision only reluctantly. This double standard—wanting still to pursue other girls and young women yet wanting to monopolize one's own wife—is another ambivalence that emerges in wedding advice.

A young man may feel ambivalence at marriage, but he agreed to the choice of wife. The bride has yet to implicate herself in the process; the wedding is her moment of public agreement or refusal. The newest and youngest adult, her adult behavior is still unproven, her reaction to the first demands of adult life uncertain. This uncertainty is reflected in comments during marriage discussions and wedding, e.g., the family will have to see if she follows the husband and if she "stays well" (i.e., acts as a young wife should). Both young people are on trial initially, but the young woman is the greatest unknown. Her ambivalence may be greater than her husband's; her benefits from the union are less obvious and less immediate.

Furthermore, the bride must make a major adjustment that her husband is spared: leaving home and family. Her husband's family home might not be unknown to her. Nonetheless, she leaves the familiarity of her parents' home to take a junior role in another family. If she does not agree wholeheartedly to the match, the potential emotional and practical difficulties of relocation can be compounded. A reluctant bride was encouraged thus:

CORINNE A. KRATZ

Or.: All of these [women] sitting here [who stayed with their husbands]—do you think they didn't have family? Hee? So are you the one now that will change our customs? Isn't there anyone you listen to? Are you deaf to all? Hee? We elders come, and we think we're coming to bless and give away a child—and don't think it's enemies you're going to [live with]. It's your country, like this.

The bride, then, might confront ambivalence that arises from a variety of sources: leaving home and family versus the satisfaction of starting her own home and family, pleasing and helping her family by following their choice versus the wrench of leaving preferred boyfriends for an unwanted mate. In addition, like her husband, she also faces ambivalence that might arise from the tension between adult freedom of action versus responsibility. She experiences this in different ways, however—ways related to the female personhood and agency created through initiation and marriage.

As her husband expands his agency with the right to control some of her actions and decisions, the young woman must cede some supervisory power to him. She leaves what was a brief period of relative independence just prior to her initiation, when she could pick her own boyfriends and visit nearby friends fairly freely. If she occasionally ignored tasks, she was only a willful, disobedient child. A married woman's responsibilities entail restrictions on mobility, greater work, and at times reduce her control over household decisions, even as her husband's managerial role enhances his. In theory, her husband monopolizes her sexually too. Her interactions, demeanor, and even natural reactions should be brought into line (e.g., lest excessive laughter be taken as flirtatiousness rather than cheerfulness).

She, too, affects the family's fortune and fate. However, her agency and influence (toward good fortune, at least) are represented as an extension of her husband's, her effects subsumed. Once again, as in the bride's refusals discussed above, a wife's adverse actions and consequences are not likely to be claimed by or attributed to her husband. "Negative agency" of this sort can become further evidence for the nature of female personhood. A young bride who consistently embraces such actions might deliver herself from an unwanted marriage.

For the bride who stays, influence and authority will expand only later, within the domestic realm, when she has children. As the children grow, she helps manage their labor as her husband supposedly manages the household. Influence in other realms also comes in part through motherhood (e.g., as ritual leader). Sons become adults she can influence, married to young women whom she can advise. She can be influential in affinal relations for both sons and daughters.

162

Presented as the image of fulfilled adulthood, marriage is largely a matter of delayed and circumscribed returns for women. Initially a husband's property and work benefit his wife little more than did those of her father and brothers before marriage (cf. Collier and Rosaldo 1981: 283). Female agency is enhanced only gradually, through time, as offspring grow and as the wife becomes established in her husband's community. Her husband experiences delayed returns, too, yet he also enjoys immediate benefits as head of the independent household his wife's labor makes possible, and he has authority over his wife. Further, in contrast to his sanction for wifely failures, his wife's only resort is to call on her fathers and brothers by returning home. Her marital difficulties then become part of her male relatives' expanded arena of agency, drawing in senior women to a certain extent as well (the couple's mothers). The bride will never experience the more secure position and greater influence of a mature mother, however, unless she agrees to follow a husband.

Marriage propels bride and groom alike into wider arenas of personal relations and consequence, further developing the potentials of adult personhood. Each individual's distinctive trajectory of development emerges from the combined repercussions of his or her own decisions and acts (over time), the effects of others, and the particular circumstances within which he or she lives; historical patterns and life cycle patterns emerge from these particularities. Marriage links bride and groom, binding their individual potentials and weaving together their developmental paths. The simultaneous and highly gendered adjustments that this requires define one complex set of consequences arising from marriage arrangement. This binding also presents another facet of the dynamics of collective and individual agents, projecting the two young adults into a new household union. Although they feel it most forcefully and steadily, the bride and groom are not the only ones who must adjust to the new marriage—facing new situations, considerations, and constraints. The complex consequences of marriage arrangement simultaneously affect many other relationships as well.

The verbal idioms that become prominent in wedding advice—"feeding" and "taking care of"—predicate this new union, illustrate some of its implications and limits for groom and bride as individuals, and explore the varieties of ambivalence that these might produce. A second set of complexities consequent on marriage arrangement, such ambivalence stems at once from the couple's negotiation of individual and joint interests and needs, the adjustments these entail, and from the multiple perspectives that coexist in this transitional period. The aura of uncertainty and indeterminacy that surrounds Okiek marriage arrangements does not dissipate entirely with the wedding. The couple still faces the adjustments and ambivalence in a variety of concrete ways. While families expect the marriage to endure, the ultimate outcome and agreement is still in the making.

MULTIDIMENSIONAL COMPLEXITIES OF AGENCY AND PERSONHOOD

This essay has focused on how Okiek notions of personhood and agency are represented, recreated, and embodied through the discourse of marriage arrangement. Illustrating the multisided nature of language as social action, it ranged through verbal representations of marriage arrangements, topics and patterns of participation in marriage discussions, verbal idioms that differentiate participants, and the themes of wedding advice. A conjunction of young, old, male, female, individual, and collective, Okiek marriage arrangement has been an effective ethnographic focus for exploring the notion of complex agency and for attempting to specify the different kinds of complexity contained in the concept. Looking in turn at complexities centered on the actions identified in marriage arrangement, the actors who take part, and the consequences of marriage arrangement has underlined the close and varied linkages between personhood and agency, their contingent nature, and the dynamics of individual and collective agency. The right and ability to undertake certain kinds of action, the kinds of action one does undertake, and the consequences of action are all facets of agency and are all part of the way people know and show their social placements and personhood.

Integrally related to social maturation, Okiek marriage arrangement foregrounds developmental aspects of personhood and agency; young adults secure, elaborate, and particularize adult capacities through marriage.[30] The gendered nature of the paths for that development are manifest in the different ways bride and groom figure in marriage arrangement and afterwards in their new home. This gendered nature is also evident in the different roles of senior men and women. In marriage arrangement, individuals simultaneously draw on and redefine ideal types and relations of gender and age, inscribing particular politics of gender, age, responsibility, and power in the process. The differential distribution of influence and authority among men and women, mature and young, those seeking and those giving a child, and the children who agree is constituted in part through discourse. The very procedures and discussions of marriage arrangement are part of this discourse.

The development of personhood and agency does not involve simple, separate, individual trajectories but rather complex negotiations among individuals and between individual and collective persons. Male spheres of influence and agency are seen as expanding systematically over the life course, abating later in life, when grown sons reach full maturity. Female influence and agency also grow with age but include a reversal. At marriage, a bride is to cede a degree of self-determination to the authority and management of her husband, starting anew within his family. Such linked and fluctuating spheres of agency are not only a matter of gender, though women are expected to yield decisions and responsibility far more often than are men.

Both bride and groom make similar concessions of responsibility and agency to their lineages; these concessions are part of the dynamics of individual and collective personhood in marriage arrangement. Claiming lineage responsibility for the marriage (if the young people agree), senior members initially encompass and discount contrary actions of the new couple. The couple's accountability and adult agency are downplayed (though they may be privately reproached) while they adjust. By acting like responsible newlyweds, the two will claim and demonstrate their maturity, at once part of the development of adult personhood and part of the negotiation of responsibility between the couple and their seniors. The dynamics of individual and collective agents in marriage arrangement go beyond this as well, including situations in which people simultaneously act as individuals and as lineages and situations in which lineages and individuals combine as a body of mature adults to advise the couple.

Marriage transforms the couple's lives most forcefully and intimately, but its arrangement is a social arena for their parents and other relatives as well. Through marriage arrangement, these individuals continue to develop, contest, display, and comprehend their own relations, gendered adult personhood, and agency (and that of the lineage). Their authority and influence on the process are rights produced over time through their concern, care, and investment as they relate to the children marrying. For parents, marriage arrangement is part of the widening realm of agency and interaction that they have elaborated since their own wedding. The complex consequences of marriage arrangement ramify into many lives for many years.

Marriage arrangement contains two revealing anomalies of gender, contradictions in Okiek notions of personhood and agency. The first relates to the constitution of lineages as agents in marriage arrangement. Mothers and other senior women must be heard, and their opinions should be taken seriously. This is anomalous both because they are outsiders, not unequivocally members of the patrilineages responsible for the arrangement, and because they are women participating in consequential decisions. Divergent opinions on the actual attention given to women's views and on their capacity to influence the process point to the tension between these definitions.

The second anomaly centers on the bride. Her decision to follow or refuse her chosen husband has far-reaching effects; her wedding is a rare public moment of power for a young woman, the most junior participant in the process.[31] Her right of choice is a recognition of her adult agency, her ability to affect many others, and her responsibility for those effects. Yet the power is momentary and the choice constrained by concepts of a woman's social destiny, appropriate adult behavior for men and women, and the commitments of kinship relations. She reaches that choice point through no real power of her own. If she does not agree, she seems to usurp the family's right to dispose of her, and she might jeopardize their future protection. Here the anomaly combines gender and age. A context that unites senior men and women in collective lineage decisions creates a tension between the rights of adulthood and the young woman in whom they are vested at that moment.

The "negative agency" of young women is also related to this anomaly. Responsibility and effect are clearly assigned to a young woman who "comes out for" another man, thereby disrupting plans, or to a bride who acts badly in her new home. The agency and abilities of a young woman who follows her chosen husband or who "stays well," on the other hand, are claimed and incorporated by those who arrange the marriage, assimilated into continuing relations between families. Full recognition of adult capacity and responsibility is accorded to young women in marriage as blame, imputing to them the negative effects of their actions and decisions. Credit for the positive effects of young women's actions is shared with the families who arranged the match as well as with her husband.

This negotiation of responsibility continues in the bride's new household, as the bride helps widen her husband's influence and control, which are "appropriately" greater for an adult man. As they produce children, her status and the scope of her agency will grow as well. Her husband's behavior is similarly encompassed in the larger affinal context, but his own standing and influence are immediately enhanced through marriage. All these moderations and mediations of agency point to the uncertainties involved in Okiek marriage arrangement, in complex agency, and in understandings of personhood.[32] They also show the significance of situational influences and constraints on how personhood is relationally defined and on how relative scopes of agency are demarcated, claimed, and denied. "Agency and patiency are situational, overlapping, ironic and under-determined" (Hobart 1990: 96).

Okiek marriage arrangements are inherently and necessarily multivoiced. Each participant brings to the process different personal, social, and political perspectives. Terms such as voice and perspective draw attention to the multiple actors involved, emphasizing one aspect of complex agency in marriage arrangement. This essay suggests, however, that considering the actions and consequences involved can introduce other complexities as well. These analytical distinctions are useful in considering how some perspectives are expressed more clearly, accorded greater weight, and ultimately wield greater influence, while others are suppressed or overlooked at times. These distinctions also illuminate the complicated interrelations of individual and collective persons and agency.

In addressing the consequences of marriage arrangement, Okiek wedding advice provided an example of how alternative voices can emerge and be amplified in the same settings (though the ambivalence of bride and groom is expressed and addressed by others). Relatives reassure the couple and counsel them about future paths through the rights and responsibilities of adulthood. These relatives also hope to convince the bride and groom to act in ways that are defined as appropriate. Through agreement, the newlyweds continue to develop as adults and simultaneously reinforce and extend their relatives' own influence. Wedding advice might recognize problems and air other perspectives, but it does not suggest fundamental change in the arrangement of marriage or household relations; rather, it is about how to adapt within them.

Further, their relatives' advice does not and cannot resolve the uncertainties or reconcile the ambivalences of marriage at the wedding. As the procession leaves for the husband's home, the couple and their families likewise proceed toward the events, experiences, and decisions through which their marriage and relations will take particular shape, easing some reservations and alleviating certain qualms even as others arise. Ideal rights and responsibilities may be represented in initiation teachings and official marriage procedures, but they are lived and negotiated through the particular compromises, opportunities, demands, and accommodations of daily life and its diverse interactions.

NOTES

1. Above the level of the patrilineage, Okiek recognize named local groups (i.e., clusters of patrilineages which once held adjacent forest tracts). Kipchornwonek and Kaplelach are both local groups. My field research with Okiek began in 1974–75 and continued again from 1982 to 1990 and from 1993 to 1994. This essay describes Okiek marriage arrangement up to the mid-1980s; since that time, marriage patterns have changed extensively. Thanks to all who have supported the research: Anthropology Department, Wesleyan University; National Science Foundation; Social Science Research Council; Fulbright-Hayes program; Institute for Intercultural Studies; Wenner Gren Foundation; University of Texas at Austin; and Sigma Xi. I also thank the Sociology Department at the University of Nairobi for academic affiliation, the Office of the President of the Government of Kenya for permission to conduct research, and all the people with whom I lived and worked in Kenya.

2. Rosalind Shaw develops the notion of subsumed agency in her essay in this volume.

3. This phenomenon is captured, for instance, in the English phrase "going through the motions." One might show signs of a kind of socially recognized identity (person) while not fully embracing that definition as part of one's experience and definition of self (individual).

4. Diverse ways of speaking are part of arranging Okiek marriage, but abilities and opportunities to use different forms and styles of language are distributed unevenly, in ways that are socially patterned. Those patterns help define differences of personhood, agency, and power. For instance, protocols of speaking during marriage meetings (the definition and order of speakers, the metaphors used, the styles of speech) are one means by which age and gender differences are created. Part of a larger project on Okiek marriage arrangement (Kratz, in preparation), this essay only considers a few macro-level aspects of discourse. Detailed discourse analysis in progress looks more closely at micro-level aspects.

5. Spencer (1988) is a useful source for the vocabulary of marriage procedures in the Maa language. In this summary description, I collapse certain historical distinctions related to what was brought to the girl's home and by whom as well as distinctions between contemporary practice and verbal representations of the process. In some descriptions, for instance, there are three *esiretit* visits: to put a chain on the child, to bring honey, and lastly, to bring honey wine. This summary also leaves aside important details of such visits (e.g., ritual costume worn by visitors, symbolic conventions of arrival and leave-taking, formulaic openings and organization of discussions, etc.). However, these elisions parallel those in descriptions through which Okiek summarize the process.

6. According to Spencer (1988: 26–27), *esiret* refers to the "anointment," the name for the first small gift to open marriage negotiations. *En-kirotet,* he says, is the name of subsequent gifts, deriving from *ol-kirotet,* "the favorite." The Okiek terms refer to the visits and occasions as well as to the gifts.

7. Agreement can also be indicated by the verb "following" (*sipi*). All these verbs are given in the third-person durative form.

8. Intrafamilial departures from these collective actions and decisions are often raised and addressed during the extended discussions.

9. Adding the suffix *-ci* would make "to seek" (*-ceeng'*) into a three-place verb, taking an indirect object (i.e., to seek something for someone). The base root *-kaaci* ("to give") already includes this suffix; it is inherently a three-place verb. In other circumstances, *-ceeng'* can also be made intransitive by adding the suffix *-sa.* This is one indication that *-ceeng'* is a transitive verb root. The Okiek verb *-yan* (to agree), however, is already intransitive and does not take the detransitivizing suffix.

10. Cf. Collier (1988: 237): "[T]he assumption that women's kin can give them in marriage casts women and men as having different possibilities for achieving power and privilege."

11. These relations of age and seniority are most important in a first marriage; a man might arrange subsequent marriages himself, with little parental involvement. This is sometimes true for women, too, but families are involved in most cases involving women who remarry.

12. The allusions to marriage destiny can be seen in another way relative to these junior–senior negotiations of agency. In addition to glossing over responsibility for re-

fusing to give a bride to the wife-seekers, they can also cover difficulties of uncertain control. Elopements and refusals by bride or groom certainly create situations of high tension and emotion. Yet if they cannot be resolved, invoking marriage fate can again minimize the responsibility of the lineage and its members for its unruly youngsters.

13. These alterations in marriage arrangement include changes in the standards of bridewealth, the timing of visits, and the very modes of marriage arrangement in some places.

14. When such marriages proceed, they are regularized after the fact with inter-family discussions and bridewealth. Later indistinguishable from marriages organized "officially," their tempestuous beginnings live on in the memories of age-mates and parents.

15. Another alternative also opened to some Okiek girls in the 1980s, a choice beyond simply substituting a different husband—to postpone or reject marriage through education. Schoolgirls are "engaged by the government" and "rule themselves"; they are often withdrawn from marriage consideration if suitors come.

16. For Kipchornwonek Okiek, the late 1970s saw the opening of a school at So-goo, construction of a road, the establishment of the government post of assistant chief for the area, and rapid growth of a market center. This was quickly followed by more of the same. These developments also had implications for Kaplelach further to the east. Schools and shops in their immediate area began opening in the mid-1980s.

17. This situation is far from immutable, however. Okiek girls who opt for educa-tion as a way to postpone and control their choice of partner simultaneously subvert and diminish such differences.

18. For instance, someone might not belong to either lineage involved but might be related matrilaterally to both lineages.

19. Hobart also notes "the subtle shifts by which families, patrons and clients, local groups, courts and so on change themselves and their goals through unpretentious, if interminable, discussions, meetings, and activities. . . . [A]gency is far from confined to moments of dramatic public spectacle" (1990: 98).

20. Family pride is another facet of this guarantee: "This child has people who follow her." A man who "has people" will not be allowed to mistreat his young wife, supposedly, and others would care for her if he does. A woman who "has people" cannot be abused without retribution (i.e., without being taken back [kenam] for some time). "So if we hear that [he is troubling her], we'll take her because she has owners; her father and them are there." To speak of "having people," then, and to show them during marriage arrangements is simultaneously a boast, a guarantee, and a threat. The "people" referred to tend to be men.

21. Okiek quotes are drawn from transcriptions of tape-recorded events and inter-views or from verbatim quotes included in my field notes. Because linguistic form and discourse structure are not the focus of analysis in this essay, I use only translations here.

22. Cf. Karp's (1987) discussion of a similar "paradox of agency" in Iteso mar-riage ceremonies.

23. A man looking for a second wife, however, represents himself. His first wife plays the role his mother took in his first marriage.

24. I retain some of the expressive features of Kirutari's account here, using the following conventions: (1) basi, a word that means "ok," is also a narrative marker used to start new episodes or points; (2) elongation of a vowel, as in "staaaaay," indicates the

passage of time (i.e., continuing to stay over some time); (3) Okiek emphasize words and points by suffixing *-e* at the end of words and clauses. Kirutari's emphases near the end of this quotation show his exasperation with the young man.

25. If the wedding occurs soon after the bride's seclusion, it may indeed be her first encounter since initiation with more distant fathers and brothers.

26. Keenan (1975: 109) discusses similar rhetorical joining of families in Madagascar weddings.

27. Thereafter groom and best man call one another *enkiyeu*. Okiek also use this as a permanent term of mutual address between a husband and the child who takes part in the ceremony when he first eats food in his wife's house. The word means brisket fat in Maasai, though Maasai usage for ritual relations differs from that of the Okiek. For Matapato Maasai, *enkiyeu* is used as a term of address between age-mates who share this fat during the ceremony of *loolbaa,* a feast that elders should hold before their first child is initiated (Spencer 1988: 252–66). Maasai call the "best man" at a wedding *olcepulkerra. Enkiyeu* is part of a ceremony of friendship among Kisonko Maasai (Mol 1980: 66).

28. "Children" means both wife and/or children here.

29. Seraset's husband, Leng'eng', is also advised on managing money, garden, and other sources of food and on his relations with brothers, friends, and affines after marriage. Taking a wife means starting a household, and so makes Leng'eng' a potential host, one who provides for and influences others as well.

30. Resonances with ceremonies of initiation into adulthood also reinforce the momentum set up through arrangements (e.g., the idiom of "agreeing," expectations created in seclusion teachings, the parallel situations of bride and initiate before a gathering of senior relatives).

31. I have not considered in this essay distinctions and protests possible within a bride's "agreement" (e.g., to follow the husband gladly, to go with protest, to follow after being forced, etc.). For instance, Seraset had eloped and had been retrieved by her brothers, resulting in a hurried wedding to Leng'eng'. People commented on the lack of proper procedure that had been forced upon the family by the bride's willfulness and the uncertainty of their control over her. She did follow Leng'eng' (and remains with him today, with several children), but she registered her unhappiness and reluctance by refusing wedding ornaments and clothing, by throwing bracelets into the fire, and by thus going to his home "like a log."

32. "[I]n matters of complex agency . . . the outcome is always potentially fraught with risk of uncertainty" (Hobart 1990: 121).

REFERENCES

Beidelman, T. O. 1986. *The Moral Imagination in Kaguru Modes of Thought.* Bloomington: Indiana University Press.

Collier, Jane. 1988. *Marriage and Inequality in Classless Societies.* Stanford, Calif.: Stanford University Press.

Collier, Jane, and M. Rosaldo. 1981. "Politics and Gender in Simple Societies." In S. Ortner and H. Whitehead, eds., *Sexual Meanings.* Cambridge: Cambridge University Press.

Fortes, Meyer. 1973. "The Concept of the Person." In G. Dieterlen, ed., *La Notion de Personne en Afrique Noire.* Paris: Editions de Centre National de la Recherche Scientifique, pp. 283–319.

———. 1983. "Problems of Identity and Person." In A. Jacobson-Widding, *Identity: Personal and Sociocultural—A Symposium.* Uppsala: Humanities Press.

Giddens, Anthony. 1976. *New Rules of Sociological Method.* New York: Basic Books.

———. 1979. *Central Problems in Social Theory.* Berkeley: University of California Press.

Hobart, Mark. 1990. "The Patience of Plants: A Note on Agency in Bali." *Review of Indonesian and Malaysian Affairs* 24: 90–135.

Jackson, Michael, and Ivan Karp, eds. 1990. "Introduction." In *Personhood and Agency: The Experience of Self and Other in African Cultures.* Washington, D.C.: Smithsonian Institution Press.

Karp, Ivan. 1987. "Laughter at Marriage: Subversion in Performance." In D. Parkin and D. Nyamwaya, eds., *Transformations of African Marriage.* Manchester: Manchester University Press for International African Institute.

———. 1995. "Agency, Agency, Who's Got the Agency?" Paper presented at the meetings of the American Anthropological Association, Washington, D.C., November.

Keenan, Elinor. 1975. "A Sliding Sense of Obligatoriness: The Polystructure of Malagasy Oratory." In M. Bloch, ed., *Political Language and Oratory in Traditional Societies.* New York: Academic Press.

Kratz, Corinne A. 1990. "Sexual Solidarity and the Secrets of Sight and Sound: Shifting Gender Relations and Their Ceremonial Constitution." *American Ethnologist* 17, no. 3: 449–69.

———. 1991. "Amusement and Absolution: Transforming Narratives during Confession of Social Debts." *American Anthropologist* 93, no. 4: 826–51.

———. 1993. "'We've Always Done It Like This . . . Except for a Few Details': 'Tradition' and 'Innovation' in Okiek Ceremonies." *Comparative Studies in Society and History* 35, no. 1: 30–65.

———. 1994. *Affecting Performance: Meaning, Movement, and Experience in Okiek Women's Initiation.* Washington, D.C.: Smithsonian Institution Press.

———. In preparation. *Looking for the Hairless Cow: Arranging Okiek Marriage.*

Lederman, Rena. 1984. "Who Speaks Here? Formality and the Politics of Gender in Mendi, Highland Papua New Guinea." In D. Brenneis and F. Myers, eds., *Dangerous Words: Language and Politics in the Pacific.* New York: New York University Press.

Mol, Fr. Frans. 1980. *Maa: A Dictionary of the Maasai Language and Folklore.* Nairobi: Marketing and Publishing Limited.

Shore, Bradd. 1995. *Culture in Mind: Meaning Construction and Cultural Cognition.* Oxford: Oxford University Press.

Spencer, Paul. 1988. *Maasai of Matapato.* Bloomington: Indiana University Press.

Part 3.
AFRICAN DISCOURSES ON DEVELOPMENT

Introduction to Part 3

African Discourses on Development

"Development," in all its many senses and with its complex associations with ideas about progress, modernity, and rationality, is an underlying theme of virtually all of the literature on African philosophy. The question of African development and of the political, social, and cultural forms that it should take is often the subject matter of critical discourse in and about Africa. The essays in this section examine the meaning and impact of the global economic order as they relate to the evolution of African nations and their civil societies as well as the values associated with them, as the global order attempts to impose its ideology and order on the ways in which historical transformations are defined and managed.

In this order of things, Africans have been ambivalently drawn to both sides of the dominant and competing developmental ideologies and strategies. They have also tried to articulate an autonomy that is commensurate with ideas of nationalist freedom and perceptions of agency at the state level. This has all along been a subtext of African philosophy. The debates between collective and individual reason or between reason and culture produce antagonistic categories and ambivalences similar to those found in the Enlightenment period from which capitalist ideology derives its terms. The essays contained in this section of the volume critically address different facets of this ambivalence toward development and modernity as manifested in African discourses on development.

Wiredu's essay raises important questions about the idea of "development" from the perspective of analytical philosophy (and also within the limits of this philosophy). It critiques classical modernization theory by objecting to its polarizing and individualizing effects on society. To paraphrase Apter (1987: 15), the "analysis" of development remains crucial. Still, it is only one among several possible "languages," each of which is a mode of signifying and establishing meaning. No single language is powerful enough to monopolize so complex a subject. Thus, according to Wiredu's analytic view, modernization is not bad in and of itself, but ill-conceived programs of implementing modernization have been harmful to African societies. For Wiredu, the role of philosophers must complement that of sages—philosophical or otherwise—in articulating the nature, value, and direction of social needs and changes. Systematic thinking about the nature of African society must embrace idioms of Africans' senses of themselves, as expressed in the words of the sages as well as in the ethic of everyday life.

Bogumil Jewsiewicki's essay on the Congolese artist Chéri Samba examines how these very issues, as well as the themes developed in Part 2, play out in a visual medium whose products circulate not only at the national site of production but also internationally and for a rather different audience, one which does not fully share the same cultural and performative assumptions with the producers of the cultural object.

Fabien Eboussi-Boulaga's essay is a philosopher's account of the harmful consequences that Wiredu refers to in his chapter. He argues that the human flourishing or the development of the humane society, the *mos maiorum* in the ancient Greek civic republic, takes place within, and is at the same time a product of, the political good; it is simultaneously part of and produced by the civil society (*civilization*) as a social–political condition and space for action. Eboussi-Boulaga's essay is, in a very general sense, part of a recent and powerful genre of scholarship issuing from Cameroon (see, for example, Bayart 1979, 1981, 1986; Rowlands and Warner 1988; Mbembe 1989, 1992; Eboussi-Boulaga 1993; Bidima 1994; and Geschiere and Fisiy 1994), the main focus of which is the critical analysis and examination of the conditions required for the legitimacy of state and, specifically, the conditions under which the state in Cameroon (like patrimonial states throughout the continent) delegitimizes itself through practices (such as corruption, encouraging civil strife, and apathy to dehumanizing social conditions) which undermine social order. In the end, these states also undermine their own legitimacy, especially when the collapse of the Cold War deprived their regimes of international patrons who desired to use them to pursue geopolitical goals (Richards 1996).

For Eboussi-Boulaga, current transformations in Africa reveal a state of affairs that could hardly be described as symbolic of what Wiredu has called "human flourishing." Rather, these transformations reveal a disruptive change, a crisis in social order: economic crisis; state bankruptcy; human catastrophes resulting from wars, famines, and coercive, violent, and murderous regimes; extortions; and disregard for the law.

The collapse of the state in Africa, Eboussi-Boulaga argues, is due partly to the tendency to consider the state and its constituents, ethnic groups, in the context of a thesis–antithesis relationship. The obsessive focus on ethnicity in Africa and in accounts of African nations that are both in favor of its promotion or for its suppression—both dimensions of tribalism—undermines the legitimacy and authority of the state and places this legitimacy and authority in the fragmentary ethnic components of society. This focus creates the kind of state–society tensions—in the form of tribalism and corruption—which political writings have identified as characteristic of the crisis of the contemporary African state (Shafer 1955; Kohn 1967; Callaghy 1984; Young and Turner 1985; Ronen 1986; Chazan et al. 1988; Migdal 1988; Potholm 1988; Rothchild and Chazan 1988; Sitton 1989; Dubois 1991; Davidson 1992; Zartman 1995).

Yet the ideological structures that define ethnic groups as "tribes," that set up evolutionary schemes that place Africa at the bottom of a hierarchy, are neither new to postcolonial Africa nor located entirely in Africa. In his essay on Chéri Samba, Bogumil Jewsiewicki uses a comparison between the works of Paul Gauguin and Chéri Samba to analyze and appraise the paradoxes and ambivalences that underlie and define the categorical relations between "the modern" and "the primitive," "the Westerner" and "the non-Westerner," "the white" and "the black," and "the civilized" and "the savage" from colonial discourse to their disguised forms in development discourse in the postcolonial state. In Jewsiewicki's view, Samba's painting is an ambivalent critique of the categories underlying development discourse, as it is a discourse on the primitive and the modern themselves, if the two could even be separated. The relationship between these identity categories is organized as a paradoxical dialectic, in which difference is claimed through appropriation of the Other by both parties. But the logic of this appropriation does not work the same way in both directions. While the "modern" hunts for the "primitive" in order to appropriate its raw energy in order to invigorate itself, the "primitive"—represented by Jewsiewicki in the form of Chéri Samba's artistic work—searches for the "modern" in order to enhance itself by means of a reverse imitation, in which "the Western" (as a body of norms and values of judgment in ethics and aesthetics) becomes "the primitive" and an object of scorn. What we see in Chéri Samba's artistic and political expressions is almost a replay, in aesthetic terms, of what had taken place in Zaire (now the Democratic Republic of the Congo) three decades ago, when it briefly played a leading role in defining a new and cultural and political ideology—*authenticité*. Since then, the Zairian arts have become the only positive contribution that Zairian society has made to world culture, in the face of the collapse of state and society. Zairian music and painting were both influential internationally and were powerful instruments for social and political critique at home.

In Gauguin's works, the European search for and re-incorporation of the "primitive" serves to expose "modernism" as an ideological construct, one that pretended to be "'a unitary, revolutionary phenomenon' instead of the 'forward—*and* backward—looking' tendency it in fact was" (Hiller 1991: 87). In Chéri Samba's art, the representation of European desire for the black woman's body and the European woman's desire for Chéri Samba is a two-edged act of leveling difference(s), an act of scorn and contempt for that which poses itself as "superior," an act of conquest. Samba reduces the "superior" to the level of the ordinary, such that it is subject to natural and instinctive drives that are free of ideological bounds: *indifference*. Chéri Samba's art is a commentary on the vanity of the ideology of power, whether this is political, social, cultural, or racial. Samba dismantles the myth of "primitivism," just as Gauguin dismantles that of "modernity" while practicing his own form of cultural colonialism.

While those sections of Jewsiewicki's writing which discuss Chéri Samba are loaded with the idiom(s) of "locality"—emphasis on the local and particular, on Chéri Samba himself, and on Kinshasa—the image that this vernacular idiom creates also captures the entire and vast landscape of change in African cultures and histories. It invokes other artists and writers in other African countries who have also played significant roles as critics of state and society. The scenes that they evoke and critique are too familiar across the continent (Mbembe 1992): social and economic inequality; official indiscipline, which creates oppression, injustice, and corruption, even to the point of assuming to be ordinary, the preying on the nudity, dignity, and privacy of the powerless women and children by political "big men."

By contrast, E. S. Atieno-Odhiambo's essay on Samuel Ayany's cultural discourse shows that the idea of progress and, by implication, the idea of history, clearly indicate that the self-invention of a "new" subject takes place in the postcolonial period and discourse. In both his (litigious and confrontational) character and (universalist) ideology, Ayany loved to defy unjustified beliefs. His text, by suggestion, could have opened with an epigraph from this Cartesian dictum: *We ought never to allow ourselves to be persuaded of the truth of anything unless on the evidence of our reason.* He (Ayany) considered cultural traditions as one type of unjustified collective belief. "It is this accumulation of complacent, confident conviction, and its acceptance, which leads men into error. There must be another and a better way" (Gellner 1992a: 2). Ayany's text significantly reproduces the European Enlightenment rationality, which is predicated on the acceptance as knowledge of only those propositions which are rationally justifiable. He views local histories as the imperfect imitations (shadows) of the "real" history of the state. These local histories are doomed, he believed, to be like life in the Platonic cave, where people are "chained" to the powerful influence of the illusions of shadows (beliefs), unless an intervention is made by one of their own who has become enlightened and thus knows the difference between the imperfections of the cave and the realism of the universal. The enlightened intellectual has a mission: to liberate his folk from the damnation of the cave and from the misleading visions of their cultural historians. The text, translated and re-presented by Atieno-Odhiambo here, leaves little doubt that Ayany envisioned himself as one who held the Platonic role of leader from darkness to a state of enlightenment. Ayany champions historical modernity.

Yet even Ayany's legacy exhibits the ambiguous and ambivalent attitude of African artists and thinkers to the appeal of the modern. Ayany was known in Kenya, and especially among the Luo people, whose culture he criticized, as a master of "traditional" rhetoric. His predilection for litigation was accompanied by a mastery of oral skills and the use of invective and insult (Ayany translates from Dholuo as "insult") that made him the hero of many stories. At the same time as Ayany criticized unthinking devotion to custom and belief, he made himself the master of tradition and used tradition in a vigorous defense of the modern. His ambivalent legacy stands as a simulacrum of the profound ambivalence and outright contradiction that characterize so many African discourses on development and which the essays in this section seek not so much to deconstruct as to reexamine for their relevance to the present. The authors in this section argue that the recent past, with its uncritical rejection of culture and ethnicity and its ambivalent and even nostalgic embrace of what it rejects, should not be a prologue to the present.

REFERENCES

Apter, David. 1987. *Rethinking Development: Modernization, Dependency, and Postmodern Politics*. London: Sage Publications.

Bayart, Jean-François. 1979. *L'etat au Cameroun*. Paris: Fondation Nationale des Sciences Politiques.

———. 1981. "Le politique par le bas en Afrique Noire." *Politiques Africaines* 1: 53–81.

———. 1986. "Civil Society and the State in Africa." In P. Chabal, ed., *Political Domination in Contemporary Africa*. Cambridge: Cambridge University Press.

Bidima, Jean G. 1994. *Théorie critique et modernité négro-africaine*. Paris: Publications de la Sorbonne.

Callaghy, Thomas M. 1984. *The State-Society Struggle: Zaire in Comparative Perspective*. New York: Columbia University Press.

Chazan, Naomi, et al., eds. 1988. *Politics and Society in Contemporary Africa*. Boulder, Colo.: Lynne Rienner. 2nd ed., 1992.

Davidson, Basil. 1992. *The Black Man's Burden: Africa and the Curse of the Nation-State*. New York: Random House Times.

Dubois, Claude-Gilbert, ed. 1991. *L'imaginaire de la nation 1792–1992*. Bordeaux: Presses Universitatires de Bordeaux.

Eboussi-Boulaga, Fabien. 1993. *Les conférences nationales en Afrique noire: une affaire à suivre*. Paris: Éditions Karthala.

Gellner, Ernest. 1992. *Reason and Culture*. Oxford: Blackwell.

Geschiere, Peter, and C. Fisiy. 1994. "Domesticating Personal Violence: Witchcraft, Courts and Confessions in Cameroon." *Africa* 64, no. 3: 323–341.

Kohn, Hans. 1967. *Prelude to Nation-States: The French and German Experience 1789–1815.* Princeton, N.J.: D. van Nostrand.

Mbembe, Achille. 1989. "La naissance du Maquis dans le Sud-Cameroun (1920–1960): Esquisse d'une anthropologie historique d l'indiscipline." Doctoral thesis, Université de Lille.

———. 1992. "Provisional Notes on the Postcolony." *Africa* 62, no. 1: 3–37.

Migdal, Joel S. 1988. *Strong Societies and Weak States.* Princeton, N.J.: Princeton University Press.

Potholm, Christian P. 1988. *The Theory and Practice of African Politics.* 2nd ed. New York: University Press of America.

Richards, Paul. 1996. *Fighting for the Rainforest.* Oxford: James Currey for the International African Institute.

Ronen, Dov, ed. 1986. *Democracy and Pluralism in Africa.* Boulder, Colo.: Lynne Rienner.

Rothchild, Donald, and Naomi Chazan, eds. 1988. *The Precarious Balance: State and Society in Africa.* Boulder, Colo.: Westview Press.

Rowlands, Michael, and J.-P. Warner. 1988. "Sorcery, Power and the Modern State in Cameroon." *Man,* ns 23: 118–32.

Shafer, Boyd C. 1955. *Nationalism: Myth and Reality.* New York: Harcourt Brace.

Sitton, John F. 1989. *Marx's Theory of the Transcendence of the State: A Reconstruction.* New York and Bern: Peter Lang.

Young, Crawford, and Thomas Turner. 1985. *The Rise and Decline of the Zairian State.* Madison: University of Wisconsin Press.

Zartman, I. W., ed. 1995. *Collapsed States: The Disintegration and Restoration of Legitimate Authority.* Boulder, Colo.: Lynne Rienner.

7. Our Problem of Knowledge: Brief Reflections on Knowledge and Development in Africa

Kwasi Wiredu

Knowledge is necessary for action. That is axiomatic. Action is necessary for survival. That too is axiomatic. Therefore, most certainly, knowledge is necessary for survival. So what problem do we have when it comes to knowledge? The most obvious problem is that much of the knowledge we need in Africa now is in the hands, and sometimes in the heads, of non-Africans. This part of our cognitive needs is that part which can only be fulfilled through science and technology. There are all sorts of problems in the mechanics as well as the politics and economics of the needed transfer of knowledge. But there is a psychological problem in the very idea of the need for such knowledge transfer, a problem which arises from the fact that we came to be in such need from the unpleasant historical fact of colonization. If it had not been for colonialism, Africa might now, perhaps, be in the forefront of the acquisition and application of scientific knowledge. Who knows?

But as things stand now, pressing for science and technology in Africa is apt to give the appearance that Africans simply want to imitate their erstwhile colonizers. And this seems to be why there is a certain ambivalence to science in the attitudes of some African intellectuals. Ironically, this attitude brings them into alignment with those intellectuals in the Western world who are disenchanted with science and technology as a result of having too much of it in their society. Perhaps those Africans too are imitators. But since it may not be a bad thing to imitate a good thing, the question might be "Which imitation is the more sensible one?"

Perhaps it may not be a question of imitation at all. The quest for knowledge of any type is a characteristically human endeavor. In the changes and chances of human history some peoples may come to be ahead of others at some particular point in time in some particular area of investigation, but there is nothing to indicate that such situations must be permanent, and there is also no reason why any form of genuine knowledge should be attributed to any peoples in any proprietary sense. And what warrant is there for the pessimism that would permanently debar our imaginations from foreseeing Africa as an eventual theater of state-of-the-art science and technology, yielding ground to none in the advancement of scientific knowledge for the promotion of human well-being? Imagine how puzzled the Africans of that era would be to learn that some of their ancestors seemed to think that there was something un-African about science.

I am in no danger of forgetting that this is pure utopianism. But one good thing about utopianism is that it may give us a clear idea of the things worth struggling for. And that may be quite a fraction of the battle won. In the present connection, what we need to be clearest about is that the best-case scenario does not include only the cultivation of science and the technical applications of its results but also the actual practice of such applications in the promotion of human well-being. By this I mean creating conditions under which individuals will have the chance to realize their own interests, which are conceived of as being intrinsically bound up with the interests of others in society.

Now it is almost as clear as daylight that scientific and technological advancement do not of themselves ensure the attainment of this humanistic ideal. It is an ideal that is humanistic in the sense that it defines itself in terms not only of human but also of humane values. If anything, technical development seems to have a tendency to generate conditions inimical to the ideal in question. The logic of the process goes something like this. Science and technology lead to industrialization, which in turn is apt to lead to extensive urbanization, which in turn is apt to lead to that restriction, in individuals, of the sense of human sympathy that is likely to manifest itself in the form of crime and all sorts of social inclemencies. Even given the modest degree of science, technology, and industrialization that we have realized in Africa to date, anybody with eyes can see the workings of this logic. Elsewhere they can see that logic writ large.

Yet there is no going back on the commitment to technical development. That commitment was made in Africa by the political leaders who fought and won independence for us. They were motivated in part by the desire to empower Africa to exploit the resources of science and technology to improve the living conditions of its people. Abbreviation is a useful device of language, and people often call this motivation simply the motivation of development. But this phrase has the unfortunate tendency to suggest that technical development is the essence of development. The resulting fallacy is one which fosters the impression that the more technologically advanced peoples of the earth are developed in more senses that can be legitimately claimed. In fact, if you open your eyes a bit, you can see that a technologically advanced country can be severely underdeveloped morally. So the really important question facing anyone who makes the commitment in question is "How may technical development be used to achieve a well-rounded development?" Or, more specifically, "How may technical advancement be used to promote humane values?"

Notice that this question generates its own problem of knowledge. If technical development consists of the exploitation of scientific knowledge, then our question raises the need for knowledge about how to handle certain uses of knowledge to achieve our purposes. Is this second-degree knowledge also scientific knowledge? If it is, then certainly it is a different kind of scientific knowledge than the kind that is associated with physics or biology. Still, it is often important to see the unity in diversity, and we may use an enlarged concept of the scientific to introduce a helpful unity into our cognitive endeavors. A natural proposal here would be to use "scientific" as a synonym for "rational."

This proposal is not at all arbitrary. One does not need to meditate too long to see that the kind of science you have in, say, physics is but a specialized phase of some of the procedures of inquiry that are inseparable from human existence. It is, presumably, not for nothing that human beings have been called rational animals. Rationality is so essential to our species identity that, indeed, in order to be able to be irrational, one has to have a certain minimum of rationality. I keep my fingers crossed, though, that not too many of us would limit our cognitive ideals to that minimum. Certainly, there *is* a great scope in life for development and refinement of that rationality which is intrinsic to the human mentality.

An even more significant reflection is that if, besides all the mathematics and physics in the world, we need the more informal kind of rationality in order to bend the knowledge attainable in disciplines of those kinds to the higher purposes of human well-being, then that form of rationality is, in a certain sense, more important than any other. Furthermore, it is an endowment of which we are not short in Africa, either in our traditional or semi-modernized condition.

Of course, some of the types of inquiries that are conducted in the social sciences are directly cognate to the kind of rationality that we are talking about. Let us call this rationality humane rationality, in contradistinction to the type which is immanent in the natural and some parts of the social sciences, which we might call technical rationality. Then it can be said that in the social sciences, the closer we are to issues of humane rationality, the less quantifiable or formalizable are our considerations and the more we are thrown back upon our native resources of rational reflection on the ends of life.

Philosophy has important conceptual concerns with the two types of rationality, but its role is especially important with respect to humane rationality, because in that connection, that role becomes ethical in a strongly normative sense. Here philosophical thinking may be dedicated not only to securing a clear and coherent picture of the first principles of social existence but also to venturing concrete suggestions on social action. In our fluid situation in Africa, the importance of this role of philosophy is impossible to overemphasize. Evidently some illustrations will help.

Consider, then, the moral basis of social existence. It seems clear that you cannot have a human community without the observance, to some degree, of rules for the adjustment of the interests of the individual to those of others in the community. But though this adjustment is necessary for human fellowship, it is unlikely to be enough to allow human flourishing. A society of rational egoists could have the necessary minimum of the adjustment of interests to keep human community going. But such a society would be an emotionally desiccated environment, one largely without love or sympathy. Even if human beings could prosper materially in significant numbers under such circumstances, that kind of flourishing would be incomplete, being starved of the emotional dimension.

In order to secure this emotional dimension, there is need for an element of altruism in human motivation. That is, we must experience the necessity for the adjustment of interests not as a prudential imperative but rather as the result of an inner drive of human sympathy. Morality without this sense of sympathy may be called mere prudential morality; with it, it may be called pure morality. Objectively, both species of morality may revolve around the same set of rules. But subjectively, these types of morality are worlds apart: one is motivated by self-interest, the other by altruism. The quest for morality in human affairs is the quest for this latter, richer standpoint of action. It is, however, a fact, although an easy one to miss, that even pure morality is not adequate for all purposes of human flourishing. There are many extremely important questions of social existence that cannot be decided by principles of pure morality alone. Think of issues such as the following: How best may a community organize and regulate production and reproduction and, especially, the preliminaries leading to the latter? How may it optimally arrange for the securing of peace and order? How may it define social success or failure on the part of an individual? And how shall it organize itself to meet such contingencies as the tragedy of bereavement? These are a few of the questions that go beyond pure morality into the regions of custom. The sorts of answers to these types of questions that are thought and practiced in a community determine the character of the community's ethic (now I am obviously using this word in a wide sense). It goes without saying that in this respect, there can be variations from culture to culture or even from subculture to subculture—a fact, by the way, which anyone ought to be able to contemplate without falling into the error of relativism.

Communalism is a well-known variety of social ethic. It is often attributed to Africa. I am inclined to think this attribution a just one, provided that uniqueness is not precipitously assumed and provided that the complementary contrast with individualism is not overdrawn. Certainly, my own society—that is, Ghanaian society—is communalist in its traditional orientation. Indeed, sojourning for the time being in an American city, I might even say that I feel a nostalgia for that ethos in my bones everyday. A communalist society is one in which an individual is brought up to cultivate an intimate sense of obligation and belonging to quite large groups of people on the basis of kinship affiliations. This inculcation of an extensive sense of human bonds provides a natural school for the enlargement of sympathies, which stretches out beyond the limits of kinship to the wider community.

In all probability, every social ethic has its strengths and weaknesses. This is assuredly true of the communalist ethic. But for the purposes of the question I wish to raise, it is only relevant to advert to its strengths. These are obvious. To content ourselves with but a brief indication, the sense of belonging and the feeling of security which the network of kinship support provide to the individual is a precious characteristic of this kind of society.

Alas, nothing is more painfully clear in our urban areas in Africa than the fact that this ethos is under the most severe strain from the impact of science and industrialization, as the remote and immediate causes, respectively. Given that it is not a judicious or even a real option to turn our backs on industrialization, the great question facing Africans is how to have it both ways—namely, how to eat our industrial cake and also have, more or less intact, the virtues of our traditional communalism. It may be that this is not possible. Or, on the other hand, it may be quite possible. Perhaps there are some none-too-recondite considerations that might motivate the less dismal conjecture.

We might note, for example, that industrialization has made inroads not only into the communalist ethic but also into basic morality itself. Clearly, it would be insupportable defeatism to yield morality to the force of any human-created circumstances. But if this were so, it would be a trifle pusillanimous to yield the blessings of communalism too readily to the rigors of industrialization, for the pressures assailing the latter are of a piece with those assailing the former. It should, in any case, be apparent from the little sketch of the springs of pure morality attempted above that communalism is a natural, if not invariable, concomitant to the workings of morality, given a suitable disposition of material conditions.

What kind of knowledge or reflection, then, is required for confronting our major question? It is almost tautological, given our previous considerations, to say that what is needed, in this particular connection, is not the hard sciences, with their technical rationality, but rather the softer parts of the social sciences and philosophy, with their humane rationality. Philosophy is in the picture because, as already noted, reflection on our most basic ideas about society is needed for an understanding of our problem in the first place, not to talk of what is required to solve it. But the social sciences, history, economics, anthropology, political science, etc., are all in the picture not only because the empirical assumptions of philosophy are subject to their scrutiny but also because insights arising from these areas of inquiry are directly relevant and, in fact, essential for any very fruitful treatment of the problem. And, apart from anything else, if you push any discipline hard, philosophy will be there to find.

It is not difficult to appreciate also that in dealing with a problem, such as the one under consideration, which involves the interplay of large systems of artifacts on the one hand and human nature and conduct on the other, not only are particular forms of knowledge needed, but wisdom is needed as well. Here is a good reason for respectfully seeking the cooperation of our traditional sages, philosophical or otherwise.

Since the ethic of a culture is a most important aspect of it, we may reformulate our problem as one that is concerned with how to exploit all the resources of the modern world for the benefit of our society without jeopardizing the strong points of our culture. But this is also exactly our problem of development. It is probably not controversial to suggest that a very significant proportion of the terrible reverses that Africa has suffered in the decades after independence have been due to ill-conceived programs of modernization.

8. The Topic of Change

F. Eboussi-Boulaga

QUESTION OF METHOD

With the title "The Topic of Change," I propose an analysis of the idea of change, thus aiming at elucidating, by argumentation, the nature and relations between other ideas which constitute and relate to "change," first as a pure or universal idea and then as an instance of particular processes or series of occurrences in reality to which the idea refers. To do this, I further propose to use the term "topic" (a rather unusual but now standard English translation for the Latin technical term "locus," designating a logical concept with roots in ancient and medieval traditions) in its narrow and technical logical sense, which derives from the Greek *Topika* (English translation, *Topics*), the title of one of Aristotle's logical treatises (comprising a total of eight books), which he devoted to a method for the discovery of arguments and in which he presented the strategies and principles which guide the art of dialectical (also commonly referred to as Socratic) reasoning. Although they were part of the treatises which made up Aristotle's works on Logic (Organon), since the Scholastics, *Topics* have received (relatively) less attention from later scholars. Like Aristotle's own treatise, my discussion here "proposes to find a line of inquiry whereby we shall be able to reason from opinions that are generally accepted about every problem propounded to us," in this case, about the meaning of change (*Topics*, Bk. I, 100ª: 18). In organizing his arguments on dialectical reasoning, Aristotle grouped his material into convenient *topoi* (plural of *topos*), or "commonplaces" of argument (that is, arguments that are generally agreed upon and which, when used, are means for clearing a disputed claim within a larger argument), which are useful in examining opposing assertions. Aristotle says, for example, that "If the question be put in a particular and not in a universal form, in the first place the universal constructive or destructive commonplace rules that have been given may all be brought into use. For in demolishing or establishing a thing universally we also show it in particular: for if it be true of all, it is true also of some, and if untrue of all, it is untrue of some . . . for public opinion grants alike the claim that if all pleasure be good, then also all pain is evil, and the claim that if some pleasure be good, then also some pain is evil. Moreover, if some form of sensation be not a capacity, then also some form of failure of sensation is not a failure of capacity . . . ," and so on (*Topics*, Bk. III, 119ª: 32–119ᵇ: 4). These exemplary passages demonstrate Aristotle's regard for dialectics as the science of first principles. He believed the study of the dialectics to be a crucial undertaking because, he further believed, other sciences came to rest on its defined first principles, which, in his rendition, open the window to the rest of understanding. Such understanding revealed the degree of distribution of predicables between members of genus and species (that is, between universals and particulars) by means of the *differentia* which mediate between them. He referred to dialectics as "the copingstone of the sciences"—that is, the highest (because the clearest and hence the ultimate) sort of knowledge. By thus defining dialectics in relation to "topics," Aristotle underscored the primacy of philosophical or conceptual understanding that is required for all non-demonstrative reasoning.

The view that the theme of change has been at the center of Africans' theoretical and practical preoccupations during the past one hundred years hardly needs emphasis. The peak of such preoccupations has occurred in the last decade. These preoccupations have not been without justification, for indeed an account (topic) of change is critical for understanding how Africa has developed and been managed, since in both the colonial and postcolonial periods, Africa has been defined as a space that is lacking change and exhibiting tradition or as a space in which change has to be introduced and managed by an external apparatus. This essay is a contribution to that ongoing debate about change to which I already have added my voice in previous work (see Eboussi-Boulaga 1993). I use the term "topics" to propose an organized outline of my understanding of the concept of change by recovering some of its classical senses and theorizations and applying them, somewhat obliquely, to an evaluation of the idea as it applies to Africa. The questions which I posit in the course of the discussion will therefore include the following: What is change? How and why does change occur? What are the ideal conditions of change in the sense of socio-political transformations? These questions aim at providing the grounds for elucidating the meaning of the concept, and my attempted responses to them try to recuperate much from Aristotle's theory of causation in a way that builds, through metaphysics, an analogical linkage between material change on the one hand and socio-political and cultural change on the other. In other words, if we can establish that certain principles are attributable to the idea of change universally, then they can be (but have not been) attributed to some views of change as they are applicable to Africa.

PRESUPPOSITION: POLITICAL GOOD AS CIVILIZATION

We must state, in light of our own experience and according to Aristotle, that the supreme human science which orders all others is politics. "The fundamental purpose of the social sciences," writes E. Weil, "becomes understandable only with the start of politics and by reference to the philosophical category of rational action. In fact, the social sciences work to analyze POLITICAL data, that is, the data which help political man to act and to react. The concepts of economic equilibrium, social tension, group behavior, classification of a population by age-groups, and variation of average life span would never have been formulated and would be of absolutely no interest at all . . . if they did not provide directions for possible [political] action." I would apologize for the length of the quotation if this evidence were not so often forgotten or ignored. We are therefore forced to insist and say that "Rational action is based on the knowledge of conditions, and it is the social sciences which reveal these conditions; but we would make no attempt to know them if it were not in light of action and starting from its point of view."[1]

The political good which provides direction to the research and elaboration of knowledge is, however, not immediately that which defines a particular regime or a given nation. The political good is not the reason of state, in the usual cynical sense of the term, but instead defines what, on occasion, authorizes rising up against might and defending ourselves against the state. It defines what permits arbitration in every conflict, without one of the parties having to be judge at the same time. Political good is the architectonic science of the social sciences known as civilization; it is the one which confers the power of state and the one which justifies it.

In a site of civilization, the process of socializing and personalizing the individuals or the groups that the civilization encompasses is recognized as having an unconditional (sacred) value which seals and sanctions beliefs, rites, and prohibitions. Individuals are considered within the civilization to be veritable men and women, endowed with language, who cannot be treated either as animals, foreign enemies, or as barbarians or brutes (with human faces) that can be killed or reduced to slavery in the service of true men and women.

A site of civilization prohibits, in principle and on principle, perjury and failure to honor a promise. It also prohibits violence, murder, and, lastly, extortion in relationships. Institutions in a site of civilization create a sphere of confidence where individuals can move about without fear that at any instance they might be surprised in their good faith, attacked and violated, and despoiled of their property and their livelihood.

Put another way, civilization is a metalanguage of politics in which politics discovers its grammar and its constitutional requirements. "It's the point of view from which we can grasp each system as a whole and from which we can ask questions relating to our internal cohesion, to our pertinence or adequacy to historical circumstances, to our adaptability."[2]

Where societies and states are not based on civilization or where the idea of civilization is not postulated as a principle and an end, these sites must be termed pre-political or "returns" to the state of nature. Without the idea of political good as civilization—that is, as an institution of veritable man in a given socio-historical space—the social sciences would lack direction, orientation, and sense. They would become futile and incoherent.

THE DIALECTICAL APPROACH

In the perspective envisioned here, we begin with the discussions in which members of our society actually engage in relating to their condition, their destiny—that is, the questions and the problems they ask about their condition and their destiny and the solutions they apply to them. The most general propositions on which they are based, the most frequent types of arguments to which recourse is made (or those which fit), are called commonplaces, *TOPOI*, to which we must add the questions to be raised, the viewpoints not to be neglected (insofar as coherent discourse is sought), as well as the objections to be formulated (in order not to leave oneself exposed to refutation).

As I indicated earlier, what Aristotle referred to as *topic* is part of the logic of invention and is used for the reconstruction and establishment of theories, or simply for positive critical explanations. But as a tool for organizing discourse or dialectical reasoning, *topic* does not yield its themes or its objects of research. The *topic* approach takes seriously those who engage in conversations and controversies. It has its starting point in what is commonly accepted and enjoys an authority and an importance which are quite relative to each society. The *topic* leads, no less, from categories of discourse to discourse on the categories of reality; it identifies and defines those rules which direct discussion and give it sense.

CHANGE

Change, or its absence, is a preoccupation of our societies, a subject of constant discussion. The successive ideologies of development and democratization are ideologies of change. However, as applied to many essential fields, like economy and politics, we have heard the paradox, "the more things change, the more they stay the same." At the same time we are undergoing upheavals without precedence, veritable cataclysms.

Our situation calls for distinguishing two sorts of change: change within a system which itself remains unchanged and which does not and cannot have rules for change and change of the system, the change of change by passage to another regime, or to another speed, by qualitative leap. We have discussed the first type elsewhere.[3]

Here, I wish to consider those changes which are upheavals. Economic crisis, bankruptcy of the state here and there, democratization and the multiparty system, and human catastrophes by wars and famines have all been dubbed the chief causes of current mutations in Africa. We ask ourselves in amazement: "How have we come to this?"

INTERNAL CAUSES OF CURRENT MUTATIONS IN AFRICA

The task of researching the internal causes of current mutations in Africa could benefit from the previous epistemological reflections and critiques. What questions, tasks, and methods should be investigated?

In this essay I propose that those who wish to offer solutions to Africa's problems need first to understand the idea and ideal conditions for the process of change. For this reason, I offer for discussion some first principles, in the form of an explanation of the terms for meaningful change, and thus generate new themes for further discussion. Because Aristotle believed that dialectical disputation works on the basis of provocation, or propositions, refutations, and counter-refutations, I believe that my own approach to debating change in Africa will pay off in some way or other. It is the price of avoiding confusion, vagueness, and, consequently, insignificance.

Terminology, Analogies, and Models

Through an examination of words, we attempt to bring to light questions, problems, and viewpoints as well as the type of "solutions" to be tested. This exercise in terminology is a process of the logic of invention. It is carried out in part by making an inventory of "commonplaces and special terms" and by proposing "a grid, a tablature of boxes on which the subject under consideration is plotted."[4] Also, it offers a repertory of general principles on which argumentation will be based, the aspects of the question about which we must think. This is what Aristotle himself meant by *Topika*. As P. Veyne observes, "The goal of *topics* is to allow invention, that is, to (re)discover all the considerations which are necessary in a particular case; it does not permit discovering anything new, but rather allows mobilizing accumulated knowledge, not to overlook the right solution, or the right question, not to omit anything."[5] In fact, it is a question of looking at the subject from every angle, although still in a general way. I now turn to the practical application of *topics*—that is, to the examination, by dialectical reasoning, of the nature of the idea of change and its cognates.

1. "Causes." What do we mean by cause? We identify and describe causes by first accepting that a change has occurred which has resulted in a sequence of different and discernible states. Such states serve as our evidence or data from experience, and they allow us to search for an explanation by comparing and contrasting those conditions which characterize different states. In other words, mutations, whether in the physical or social world, constitute the final state; they are the results which must lead back to an initial state. From there, we can measure the transformation which has occurred: its object, its operation and its agents, its form, its means and its instruments, its place and its time, its justifications and its consequences. It is what must be described, explained, made understandable. As Schopenhauer puts it, "As long as a change has not occurred, there is no reason to seek a cause . . . , because where nothing changes, there is no action, there is no causality."[6] Change, and also action, can only be conceived with full knowledge of the facts. As Largeault adds, "To cure an illness, we must know the causes. When the concept of cause is lacking, no matter how imperfect it may be, we won't get very far. We will be unable to set forth problems. We practically will not be able to describe anything or communicate about what we see. We will barely be able to act."[7] Must we invoke the authority of famous physicians to rehabilitate an idea which seems consubstantial to human reason and language? Not all that long ago, any discourse on cause was referred to contemptuously as metaphysics. Maxwell maintained, however (and rightfully so), that we were unable to imagine a series of ideas without a dependence on "reasons." Maxwell explained, "When we speak of them in relation to objects, these reasons are called causes. And when the objects are mechanical or considered from a mechanical point of view, the causes are defined with greater precision and are called forces." Einstein raised the

ante by affirming that he would have preferred "to be a cobbler or even a worker in a casino," if he had been forced to renounce strict causality in his field. The invocation of physics, the favorite field of causality and of researching causes in their strongest sense, has the objective of calling attention to models in order to use them analogously in approaches where only the weak sense applies. Rigor and speculative imagination have everything to gain from this displacement, which re-injects vigor and pertinence into what, according to Aristotle, is recognizable as cause: efficient cause or "force," material cause or "physical–chemical substrate, the initial condition," formal cause or "form," final cause or "goal, teleonomy." In considering the mutations which affect our continent today, it is the historical and social order which prevail. Here, our understanding depends on the account which furnishes the most satisfactory, the least arbitrary, plot; that which continues with a simple description or classification (anatomy, zoology) to the explanation which reduces things to their most elementary and most fundamental state; or that which derives from these without always succeeding in arriving at an approach which comes from theory and modeling.

2. "Internal." The inside (which is contrasted to the outside) is at once this indeterminate whole that is called Africa. It is the field of transformations of its states. It is the framework which circumscribes the mechanisms promoting the birth of new forms, the different modes of their propagation. It is the realm of trajectories of systems or subsystems which extend from an organized and stable state to one that is chaotic and unstable (and vice versa). The internal causes can therefore be ecological in nature or of economic, social, political, or cultural order.

What is located outside this field is said to be an obstacle, a stimulant, or simply a condition. Properly speaking, there are no "external causes," as this fragment of Nietzsche's *Will to Power* insinuates: "Against the theory of influence of milieu and external causes: internal force is infinitely superior; much of what seems influenced by the exterior is only an adaptation, of endogenous origin, of this force. Milieus which are rigorously the same could be interpreted and used in rigorously opposite fashions."[8]

What is external becomes efficient only if it encounters a host internal milieu, only if it is integrated into the capacity of a functional element of the field or the system. The notions of operation and system exceed the rigid contrast between outside and inside. They allow one to dispense with making the difficult differentiation between an external cause and its internal effect. The choice of insisting on internal causes assigns priority to the material cause or initial datum and to the formal cause, to the form, before dealing with the triggering mechanisms, with the permanent conditions. By ending with what concerns the goals and the intentions, we do not underestimate the final cause in the field of action and history. We mark only a preference for "the initial datum, the individual variation. The formal cause which is the conceptualizing element that resides in the object itself."[9] Internal causes are intrinsic and ultimate—inherent—and without them, the object would not exist.

3. "Current mutations." The causes of changes are the ones to research. Mutations are changes, but of a particular type, often called "structural transformations." Mutations presuppose a discontinuity, solutions of continuity between the initial situations and the final result. The changes involved in a mutation are of a qualitative size, such that they bring about transformation of the system, rewriting the original code. In a living organism, a new characteristic appears suddenly; it calls attention to a change which affects the gene. It is called upon to reproduce and therefore leads to the evolution of the species.

In a useful analogy, biology teaches us that mutations are rare in nature. Their frequency is increased or accelerated by artificial means. Despite their importance within evolution, they rarely produce improvements which render the species better adapted to its environment. The majority of mutations (99%) are harmful, not to say lethal. We would add that mutations which are slightly harmful wind up disappearing with the passage of those generations they have weakened, but not before they have inflicted great suffering on these generations.

With new mutations, each species thereby becomes the bearer of a burden of genetic defects. To the extent that what occurs in history and in the social arena have analogies within these biological findings, the current mutations in Africa will doubtlessly prove rare; their frequency will signal violence and artifice. Finally, there will be very few mutations which will show an improvement in our capacities to adapt to the natural and human environments of our era and of our time.

Finally, we must comprehend the two meanings of the expression "current mutations." We will take note of completed mutations—the result of previous evolution—but we will also consider mutations that are under way—already set in motion and still in motion—and their acceleration, their probable development, in a foreseeable future.

4. "In Africa." It is difficult to derive from the word Africa the designation of an assembly of heterogeneous countries and realities so as to eliminate the minimal presupposition that this geographical "cont(in)ent" bears, virtually speaking, the integration of its components or of its contents. Without this wish of unity, it would be contradictory to speak of its mutations and to research their causes. We must postulate that Africa has a tendency to claim to be an autonomous assembly of internal dependencies in which we can observe

the concentration of the global at the local level, the passage from an ordered state to a chaotic state, and the reverse of this passage. It is in the interests of such a project that we determine which mutations are beneficial and which ones are malignant. We should be even more specific and precise concerning the cardinal point from which we judge and measure according to *before and after*, where we can capture an initial situation in order to follow its deployment, its turns, and its development up to explosion or implosion. Without doubt, such a fixation transforms the geographical expression into a historical space in which destinies unfurl with human stakes of life and death, conflicts of interests and of sense.

What should we glean from this journey with the passage of words? Assuredly there are program indications which could not be followed and developed in the following pages. We will return to them partially under the form of theses that are to be cleared up in such a way as to take into consideration the particular and specific situation which clearly beckons us.

The essential lesson bears on the notion of *mutation*. It is the object which determines the method and the adequate types of causality.

1) A mutation can be distinguished by the appearance of new properties which are fundamentally different from those of the original system following a transformation of code or system.

2) Mutations therefore occur when the "gene," or whatever is its homologue, is affected. But the agents or factors involved in this modification can be internal or external. Mutation itself resides in neither the program nor the milieu.

Research into the causes of mutations poses special problems and paradoxes: these comprise continuity and discontinuity. By definition, mutation is the forgetting or wiping out of initial conditions. We cannot go back to these initial conditions from the new state effected by mutation without creating interruption. Mutation has something of the unique, transitory, and unrepeatable in its genesis and trajectory. But once a mutation occurs, it is able to reproduce in stable fashion. It becomes the object of systemic approach, endowed with a stable structure.

Mutations seem to prescribe two irreducible but apparently complementary approaches which leave the observer dissatisfied. To the question, "How do these forms appear?" it seems that we must answer "Only by history"—the account of what happened in the understandable form of a summarized plot, a weaving of material causes, of purposes and of chance encounters as well as of heterogeneous categories which give the best, most probable, and most plausible understanding of an event which has already happened. We can answer nothing more. For complex phenomena, the explanation reveals its limits and the vicious circle which radically curses it: it gives an account of the origin on the basis of and from the inside of forms and structures which regularly reproduce themselves.

On the other hand, the answer to the question, "How do these mutations reproduce?" calls on laws and blueprints of invariability through translations, transformations, inversions, symmetries, and all sorts of combinations. The principles of homogeneity and of continuity ensure the conservation of production and reproduction. We have multiple internal changes on the interior of a system which remains invariable and stable. We can thereby arrive at the rigor of formulations by proposing quasi-sociological laws. However, a system described in this way excludes, at the risk of being contradictory, the conditions of its own change, the "rules for changing its rules." In a word, what we are lacking are the mutations; we make an inventory of them when they no longer exist, when they are through, but not when they are under way or in the future. How, then, can we get past this difficulty or logical dilemma? We can look for solutions in three directions, even in the form of metaphors and analogies.

RANDOM EMERGENCE

Biology, which has suggested clarifications to us regarding the phenomenon of mutation, happens to have a proven blueprint for explaining specific causality, a blueprint that is neither in the program nor in the milieu but rather that results from their interaction. This is called random emergence. The concept of random emergence explains that although such an emergence is the product of the interaction of its former states, it is in no way precontained in these states: "We are not dealing here with a type of causality which would obey a law of probability, and which would therefore have in itself a character of nomologic regularity, but with a causality which is intrinsically random, and therefore unpredictable. Such causality bears not only on the moment where the observed effect can appear but on the very existence and on the nature of this effect. Its appearance can be determined after the fact and its content analyzed, but we can in no way trace it back to its antecedents."[10] When the emergence occurs, with its truly new determinations or mutations, it inserts itself immediately into the situation while modifying the configuration of the entire system, and the interactions will occur, from this point on, differently in the new framework: "And from these interactions will result, always in random fashion, other emerging determinations which, from interaction, have led to the observed final state. Although each step may be random, the whole will appear to form a perfectly coherent link." [11] We must insist on this phenomenon, which is simultaneously at the center of life and life itself; it allows us to better understand how life is woven and how it unravels.

This phenomenon makes us overturn our "ontological" scale. Let us repeat: "Emergence is a new quality in comparison to the constituents of the system. It therefore has the virtue of a HAPPENING, since it surges forth in discontinuous fashion once the system is constituted; it of course has the character of IRREDUCIBILITY; it is a quality which cannot be broken down and which we cannot scale down from former elements." [12] Random emergence concerns a question of a veritable jump in the phenomenal order, as in that associated with logic. We are surprised to see it at work in apparently elementary but basic notions such as matter, life, sense, and humanity. These "in fact correspond to emerging qualities of the system. . . . Matter has consistence only at the level of the atomic system. . . . Life . . . is the emanation of living organization. . . . Sense, which linguists seek, groping their way along in the depths or the nooks and crannies of language, is nothing else than the emergence of discourse, which appears in the deployment of global units, and which acts back on the basic units which made it appear. Finally, the human is an emergence befitting the hypercomplex cerebral system of an evolved primate. Also, to define man in contrast to nature is to define him exclusively in function of his emergent qualities." [13]

Emergence supplies us with a sort of connecting thread in the analysis and comprehension of complex and fundamental realities. What is qualitatively (ontologically or logically) first is not what is the most elementary, primitive, and timeless. Emergent properties are chronologically last; they are the products of synthesis. Hegel would say that they are always "becoming" and therefore are not what was at the beginning, always, as it is now and forever. They have the fragility of what is associated with the fruit of interaction and time: "We wish to see these exquisite virtues as inalterable essences, as ontological foundations, when they are the most recent fruits. In fact, at the most basic level, there are only constituents, earth, fertilizer, chemical elements, the work of bacteria. Consciousness, liberty, truth, love are the fruits, the flowers. . . . They represent what is the most fragile, the most alterable: the slightest thing will deflower them, degradation and death will strike them first, [even] when we believe or would like them to be immortal." [14]

To apply and transpose the preceding remarks, we may state that the current mutations of Africa tend to be emergent phenomena in the manner in which they emerge or collapse, in an interaction (the constituents of these systems—among themselves or with others—coming from what we still agreed to call the exterior). It is advisable to try to grasp these mutations in their vivacity without reducing or destroying them.

INTERACTION

The phenomenon and the notion of emergence leads us to turn quite naturally to the general theory of dynamic systems, which gives the best explanation for emergence. The common denominator here comprises the fact and idea of interaction. These are at the base of the appearance of new forms. Interactions are the reciprocal actions of objects, of elements of a system or systems, which modify the respective nature and behavior of phenomena which are present and which give rise to a third, original and stable reality. As an illustration, we can recall E. Morin and his idea of the "relational interactions" which generate "stable forms." As fruits of random encounters, these relational interactions produce the necessary effects and the regimes of laws. In this way, they cause "to be born and to endure these systems which are cores, atoms and stars":

- "Strong" interactions binding protons and neutrons, and their binding force, dominating the electrical repulsion between protons, gives formidable cohesion to the core.
- Gravitational interactions determine, act on, and accelerate the concentrations of galaxies, the concentration and lighting of stars.
- Electromagnetic interactions bind electrons to cores, bind atoms in molecules, and play a complex role in all the stellar processes.[15]

The point of evoking the facts of interaction is that there exist well-defined mathematical concepts which allow a description of these facts with more or less accurate approximations. In this way there is causality between the individual or the species and its environment, causality which takes into consideration the evolution of the species. This causality resides particularly in the originality of representing the interaction closer to experience and in a manner that is both more verifiable and of a formal power which allows the weak and yet fertile use in areas which reject quantification and numbers but which do not allow rigor and minimization of the arbitrary nature of descriptions.

The models typifying dynamic systems are first contrasted to the models derived from the rationalization of mechanical construction, which constitutes the basis of most of our concepts of economic, cultural, and biological development.[16] Everything can be represented according to the following evolving and cumulative blueprint: in the beginning, there are various elementary modules. Among the many figures that their free association produces, many disappear. Left are only those which are stable, those which resist randomness of all sorts.

The forms thereby spared and favored form complex structures through coupling. By connections and interrelations, these forms become integrated into a vast organism, which develops according to the criteria of immanent optimality, according to its own law—escaping individual mastery and intent. This constructionist approach lends itself easily to a deliberate ideology, to the "Taylorism" of the division of work and to the linear rationality of many doctrines of progress (i.e., evolutionism, social Darwinism, dialectic and historical materialism, and liberalism), all of which issue out of the Enlightenment. It seems that the Enlightenment has attained its explanatory limits and that failure has unveiled the violence that it inflicted on the majority of realities that it touched.

The interactional model seems better adapted to describing emergent phenomena, with their solution of continuity and their morphogenesis—that is, their irreversible, non-linear, and non-constructed character, which signal the absence of homogeneity of their spaces and times. Here, it is impossible to proceed by adding up similar elementary modules or by having recourse to an assembly and interconnections which are remotely controlled by a preexisting program or code. It is instead a question, in a luxuriant and undifferentiated reality, of exploring and occupying that reality in order to make it our area: in seeing interesting zones there or in extending and bringing them along progressively; of eliminating what is harmful, fragile, and contradictory; or simply by meandering, detouring, recycling, and making wrong turns. In other words, by "doing it ourselves."

Before enumerating the typical cases of interaction, we must define the basic notions which come into play. There is interaction between objects. An *object* is distinguished by a form of stability. In this way, the whirlwind is the symbolic object of the theory of dynamic systems, which dread "thingism" and the stasis it implies.

One characteristic of the object is that it is a stable form or structure. Its stability is relative and revolves around a fixed point of equilibrium via an attractor—that is, a system of forces, a minimum of potential, from which are derived the forces which act on the object.

The field of influence of an attractor can be designated as a basin of attraction, and it is inside this basin where we will observe figures of dynamic equilibrium of the type that we see in the case of whirlwinds. As the illustration of the interfaces between diverse zones of stability, the effect produced by such interfacing in the field of influence of an attractor is called a catastrophe. It is the buffer zone which delimits the basins of attraction and is like a step at the frontiers of these attractions, under their more or less great dependence. Each of its points is not only the intersection of spatial and temporal coordinates; it includes other sizes and the representation of all possible states of its figure.

The points of catastrophes, or "crossings" of the real with the virtual, are termed singularities. These are the structures of the entirety of the possible states of the system that correspond to the field of catastrophes, to the range of their possible combinations. A point of singularity of a higher order concretizes and polarizes the simplest singular points. These are like its radiation, its vibration all around. It is, in this way, an organizing center and best exemplifies the notion of deployment. A singularity is a power which expands up to the limits of its capacity. By doing so, it appropriates a space and sets limits—frontiers—but it also gives rise to interferences, to conflicts, to fringes of uncertainty, to interactions.

These interactions appear in four cases of principal figures, as follows:

• First case: the same force field differentiates itself into several separate basins of action.
• Second case: by interaction, two objects are transformed into a single object.
• Third case: the conflict of two attractions has as an outcome the coupling into a third object, while the two initial objects become profoundly modified.
• Fourth case: the resonance between two dynamic systems has the effect of an original process that results in new figures of stability.

Inversely, resonance sets into interaction and in motion systems which had been stable up to that point. We have here, it seems to me, some useful applicable analogies which provide the necessary linkage between, on the one hand, all phenomena which can be characterized by "the destruction of a symmetry or of a homogeneity" and, on the other hand, any area for which the local dynamic was invariable under the action of an attractor. Such areas are those which cease being invariable and toward which "the liberated trajectories of attraction" first go, before going toward other attractors. There is now every reason to take advantage of the works of René Thom, such as his *Structural Stability and Morphogenesis* and *Mathematical Models of Morphogenesis*,[17] for an examination of current mutations of Africa.

TELEONOMY

There remains the third and last orientation. This orientation is going to provide the plan and criteria according to which we determine what is and what is not a mutation and how we distinguish a beneficial from an evil mutation. Several special indications to guide research of this axiological level are presented in the preceding section. First, we noted that we would presuppose "Africa" as the object of these mutations. We thereby gave this object a form and a certain stability. And, linked to a minimum of potential, this last characterization implied an optimum. Africa, as object, is its own end in itself. It tends to move to its optimal form of stability in a fluctuating environment.

From there, it follows that the mutation appears and is grasped in its form and only in it. Chapter 5 of René Thom's *Mathematical Models of Morphogenesis* gives an inventory of elementary catastrophes, which are divided into two groups or types: catastrophes of conflict and catastrophes of bifurcation. The inventory deals with forms.

In order to determine whether a mutation is beneficial or evil, we must have chosen stability or the optimal form of the object "Africa" as something good and desirable, and it follows that we must favor mutations which render Africa more adapted to its environment. Emergent forms must have the capability of reorganizing themselves, of rediscovering a new coherence and a new efficiency. *Adaptability*, then, refers back to other requirements. *Internal coherence* provides the unit with a plurality of centrifugal elements. It achieves the compatibility of these elements; it is the power integrating their constituents into a stable optional form. In dynamic living forms, *efficiency* is expressed as a great capacity of the form to externalize itself, through much transformational presence in space. Efficiency manifests itself also by simple diffusion, "a great transmissibility, promptness and exactness in prevision, to which, in the realm of human things, we must add the explanatory and anticipatory power with respect to the unknown and to adverse potentiality." These requirements guide one's judgment in the detection of emergent forms or beneficial mutations. These are formal criteria in the sense that they are only a thematization of what is a form. In point of truth, it is the criteria of the second order, the metacriteria, which belong to the level of foundations or presuppositions which are not directly inspired by experience precisely because they render it possible. All systems, whether they are of organic forms or of social-historical action in production or selection, manifest this double layer of criteria and metacriteria; one set of conditions makes it possible for another set to emerge from a new reality brought about as a result of beneficial mutations of the former order of things. But blindness to evil mutations, indifference to them, or positive participation in their production must also belong to transcendental negative categories. If evil mutations are not the simple negation of formal metacriteria, they must be located in the sphere of motivations.

Evil mutations are no less transcendental operators of failure to recognize reality, confusion, or the categorical inversion of what does or does not depend on us. Their positive counterpart will be their removal into categories that issue from the option for the comprehension and preference that are continually presupposed in the analyses and descriptions of stability, that which is optimum and beneficial.

What is it that must be stated more clearly? Research on the causes of mutations leads to determining the very nature of mutation and then to determination of whether the mutation is good or bad. These two types of determination are different in nature; they are distinct, although they are linked.

The first type of determination is decided in light of the formal characteristics of mutation. This type of determination follows calculations. The farthest it can go is with the notion of *cost*—while not leaving the confines of form, which is considered to be an end in itself, to be, itself, its own end as a stable structure. This type of determination therefore goes back to the formal axioms of intelligibility.

The second type of determination refers us back instead to the norms, based on the preference that we show for a given form over another. The interest and the preference are justified in the deliberation and decision which weigh the cost in terms of the function of the stakes and the objectives pursued. The second type of determination presupposes that there is room for maneuver and play. It leads quite naturally to action. This occurs in order to promote good mutations, to eliminate bad mutations, and to make couplings of causal series that have little chance of encountering one another, such that they give rise to new forms, those which have never before been seen and which are favorable to mankind.

This realm of conventions and norms, therefore, does not seem to be reserved for intuition and arbitrariness. We can set into play the models of calculation and the theory of measurement, with its cardinal notions of coupling and cost, in order to emphasize the requirements of coherence, efficiency, and adaptability. To favor the norms, we can have recourse to game theory in order to maximize gains, to minimize losses, and to choose the best couplings with regard to special human interest and finalities.

The area of human interest and finalities is that of foundational liberty as supreme emergence. It is not without the other areas that supreme emergence integrates while transforming them, offering metacriteria to their criteria.

We are thereby back to our point of departure. What we presuppose under the terms of political good for civilization appears here as the realm of emergence of conventions and norms, as a reality of second order. With its cognitive and performative metacriteria, which are like its properties of quasi-object, this reality plays the role of regularizing the horizon. It is the happening of the moment in which knowledge reflects on itself and estimates the value of itself by linking itself to the categories of action and sense. But these postulations or presuppositions, which are not immediate objects of determination, have an operational value as emergent properties. Through the mediation of models of calculation, of the theory of measurement and that of games, these presuppositions are transformed into concrete requirements that are proportionate to their field of application, with their particular and calculational constraints.

For this reason, the notions of efficiency and performance assume form in the functioning of the idea of goal, what we must attain "despite perturbations and random chance which occur along the way." And when it is a question of the form in quest of its optimum manifestation, of the act which is itself its own end, final causality comes into play to take into account these processes which produce autonomy, with its decisions, its strategies, and its possibilities of "liberty."

But, we must insist, form is invented by itself as it gropes its way along, and form's final point or end does not preexist its undertaking, its progressive accomplishment: "Finality is consequently an emergence born of the complexity and living organization in its communicational/informational characters." Finality is not a prerequisite character to this organization. It is, in fact, "teleonomic" not to say "teleologic." While teleology starts from a well-designed intention, teleonomy swims in an obscure zone of imminent finality, and the recursive circle is itself immersed in a zone of physico-chemical interactions without finality, wherein operates the disorder/order/organization dialectic.[18]

We have, therefore, come full circle. The only thing remaining is to present several general propositions in the guise of prescriptions that we might use to guide the determination between simple changes and real mutations, and especially in order to perceive the causes of mutations, so that we may either avoid these or promote or accelerate them.

Application: Rules and Examples

The task which now falls to us consists of associating all new morphological appearances with the dynamic situations which engender them and which therefore designate them as mutations. Independently of any consideration of substrate or origin, the speed and the form resulting from the interaction of phenomena speak for themselves and serve to characterize the nature of changes. In this exploration, it is sufficient to aid ourselves with what the dynamic of forms, the inventory of elementary catastrophes, and the models of epigenesis and emergence can teach us.

We must be satisfied with announcing this heuristic approach by formulating several general precepts, which will be commented upon, explained, and illustrated with appropriate examples. I set them forth in the form of "theses."

1. When we cannot separate the variables in order to resolve independently the economic, socio-political, technological, and ecological problems (in turn and successively, as previously), then there has been a mutation.

Non-separation leads, as we have noted, to the phenomena of coupling, which do not respect a linear development in which "the effect is directly proportional to the cause." It is no longer necessary to begin with the evidence of a substrate, to reduce reality to its forms or its elementary modules and to synthetically reconstruct everything with them. This method has been substituted for with the method which entails "coupling . . . among phenomena which, with some bringing the others along in united fashion, in turn do not cease increasing their effects, sometimes up to divergence; phenomena of increased or reciprocal neutralization which lead to the collapse of modes of reasoning of traditionally linear thought."[19] The famous precepts of *Discourse on Method* (by Descartes) are the greatest expression of this method:

> The first [precept] was to never take anything as true that I do not evidently know as such . . .

> The second [precept was] to divide each of the difficulties that I would examine in as many parts as possible and as would be required to best resolve it.

> The third [precept was] to conduct my thoughts in order beginning with the most simple objects and the easiest to know, in order to show little by little by degrees up to the knowledge of the most complicated . . . And the last [precept was] to make so complete a census and such general reviews that I would be assured of omitting nothing."[20] Apparently it is wise to substitute pertinence with respect to the individuals who are performing the research. The reductionist approach will be preceded by a global approach in relation to the environment of a system which cannot be closed. Research into reputedly linear efficient causes, with their long chains of reasoning, will cede its place to the updating of figures of regulation, to "singularities" with the entire range of deployment of their forces, with each stable structure having its basin of attraction, its attractors. . . . These notions comprise the idea of entirety and require that priority be given to the "teleonomic" perspective, the imminent finality of forms and systems. Finally, we will choose "an aggregate" over an exhaustive approach, which is often impossible and which is most often sterile.[21]

2. Increasing complexity is a mutation if it results from the non-separation of variables which it multiplies and from which the interactions increase.

The disappointments and the setbacks of African politics "of development" come from their ignorance of complexity. We were content to fabricate slogans to extract a variable and to make of it the theme of an annual five-year or ten-year campaign. We have been worn out by this game, which continues. Today, it's the structural adjustment, multi-partyism, privatization, democratization, following a hundred other "hodgepodge of slogans which, by dint of being prostituted, have made us skeptical, skinned, half-deaf, half-blind, aphonic, in a word, more niggers than we were before them" (A. Kourouma,

Monné, *Outrages and Challenges*). The systemic economist says nothing different than the novelist when he writes "Traditional development plans have wound up creating more problems than they helped resolve, but especially by creating them at the crisis level."[22]

It is an understatement to say that in Africa, there is no "reform of understanding," that the directors and their foreign mentors, including the organizations of international cooperation, proceed according to the most timeworn ideas. These directors and mentors believe that they are using common sense, when in fact the knowledge they claim and the policies they preside over are the result of the debris of obsolete theories that have become prejudices. Their realism is blindness, the greatest obstacle to understanding their mutations, their accelerator for the worst. Given the current marginalization of Africa, we are inclined to think that the absence of ideas or the predominance of false and worn-out ideas carries a greater weight than does the ferocity of vested interests, which is undeniable. We must meditate on the considerations with which Keynes ends his *General Theory:*

> At the present moment people are unusually expectant of a more fundamental diagnosis; more particularly ready to receive it; eager to try it out, if it should be even plausible. But apart from this contemporary mood, the ideas of economists and political philosophers, both when they are right and when they are wrong, are more powerful than is commonly understood. Indeed the world is ruled by little else. Practical men, who believe themselves to be quite exempt from any intellectual influences, are usually the slaves of some defunct economist. Madmen in authority, who hear voices in the air, are distilling their frenzy from some academic scribbler of a few years back. I am sure that the power of vested interests is vastly exaggerated compared with the gradual encroachment of ideas. Not, indeed, immediately, but after a certain interval; for in the field of economic and political philosophy there are not many who are influenced by new theories after they are twenty-five or thirty years of age, so that the ideas which civil servants and politicians and even agitators apply to current events are not likely to be the newest. But, soon or late, it is ideas, not vested interests, which are dangerous for good or evil.[23]

The cultural mutation inspired by the sense of danger is the awareness that underdevelopment and marginalization are first and perhaps foremost a state of mind. The mental status of this mutation suggests that intellectual tools are the primary means by which we are capable of taking control of the complexity of our situation and giving form to our institutions. Evidence shows that emotion and intuition shall for us be neither efficient nor reasonable solutions to our problems.

3. The current mutations are like the reappearance of diversity, of conflict, and of metabolic forms where we were expecting homogeneity, calm (peace), and static forms.

Thirty years of independence have made abundant and almost exclusive use of ideologies and paradigms of homogeneity, of uniqueness, and of identity. In politics, we based what passed for action on the denial of regional differences, ethnicities, and conflicts of layers, not to mention social classes. Divergence of opinion was prohibited. In culture, we postulated the continuity of a historical time and we internalized evolutionary postulates by applying them rigorously in dealing with "inferior classes" of our own society, in the servile attitudes vis-à-vis the Western masters, and by finally reducing all problems of all conflicts, not to say of all individuals of our country, to the "tribal" factor—that is, in truth, biological and racial factors. The contradiction therefore wound up shattering the suicidal nature and powerlessness of this way of doing things. Must we invoke ancient Heraclitus in order to return to wisdom and to recognize what nature has never stopped putting before our eyes? "We must know that conflict is generalized (integral), that justice is a brawl, and that all things are produced at the moment of the brawl and of necessity." The appearance of the anthropological and social complexity of Africa, which has caused all attempts at "simplification" and at cultural, religious, and economic reduction to collapse, has never stopped contrasting its diversity, even while it called for unity. We have tried to disassociate unity and diversity as being incompatible and contradictory: Become homogeneous or perish. We were identifying homogeneity with organization. However, it is accepted in physics and in biology that "one of the most fundamental traits of organization is the aptitude to transform diversity into unity, without canceling the diversity (association of protons, neutrons, electrons in the atom, associations of diverse atoms in the molecule, of diverse molecules in the macro-molecule), and also to create diversity in and by unity. . . . Cellular organization produces and maintains diversity of its molecular constituents. . . . Everything that is a living organization, that is, not only the individual organism, but also the reproductive cycle, the ecosystems, indeed the entire biosphere, illustrate the linking of this double proposition into a circuit: diversity organizes unity which organizes diversity."[24] The equilibrium between these two poles will comprise a dynamic tension and not a well-balanced mixture of averages. We know what the cost is when one pole is favored to the detriment of the other. Dispersion is impotence pushed to annihilation. The tyranny of unity ends in the same result: "anthropological pauperization," which translates as "poorly organized and poorly appearing systems."[25] Denial of diversity indicates a refusal of the principle of competition, the motor of creation of new forms, the principle of living totalities capable of reproducing and of redoing themselves. Von Bertalanffy takes on a Heraclitean accent when he proclaims, in his *General System Theory*, that "Every whole is based upon the competition of its elements, and presupposes the 'struggle' between parts."[26]

4. Mutation resides also in the figure that takes on the mode of regulation which passes from hierarchy to homeostasis and vice versa.

Managing diversity has its own requirements, its particular constraints, depending on whether we are seeking promotion or suppression of diversity. What is called the crisis of authority, the political spectacle of a state which no longer has a grasp on realities and which is content with its mimicry of the archaic ceremony practiced by the king magicians and miracle workers (with the abdication of parents and the impossible education), attests to the inadequacy of the mode of vertical and hierarchical regulation, of the authoritative principle. The prevalent model is pyramidal, contrasting a summit and a base. Between one and the other there are degrees or elements of a progressive series, which can be ascending or descending. The important thing is that there is a starting point for the impulsion of the series, which is propagated step by step, with an increasing or decreasing intensity or value depending on whether we are moving away from or toward the head, the "chief," or the "principle." It is this summit from which departs the energy which is diffused throughout the entire body, according to a direction, a sense, but also a modulated output, a rhythm. This summit is the one which has the idea of everything and can therefore adjust the proper operation, just like the conductor of an orchestra. Authority is at the same time head of the series and outside the series. It enjoys a sort of uniqueness and a transcendence. All the subordinated echelons depend on authority. It is the "first cause" of their being, of their efficiency, of the form without which there would be only an incoherent multiplicity.

The principle of authority lets its difficulties be seen when it is incarnate in an individual, as soon as we leave the plane of linear propagation for a pluridimensional and multipolar space, which has neither up nor down. It then becomes impossible to see the individual who exerts authority as different by nature from others, and it is also impossible to see his position as an excellency. In the social realm, the relationship of command and obedience (in order to avoid passing through an unjustifiable arbitrator) is going to feed on what Hegel calls "the equivocal displacement." The ethical authority will let it be understood that it is based on a cognitive excellence, on an epistemic authority; both social authority and ethical authority will have us believe that they derive from an ontological superiority or from nature. The authority which experience denies or cannot confirm will not succeed. But induction, the reduction of its force to the concatenations of an objective area takes from authority all transcendental, "sacred, value," leaving it with only a structural and functional character. Authority is intrinsic where it is not, and an authority which is no longer indisputable is always ruined. Beyond the "metabases" of one type of authority to another, there is constantly the absurd to-and-fro, which is paradoxical and devoid of significance, of "the ensemble which includes itself as an element," of "the element which divides the ensemble that it supposes," and of the element of the series which is taken as outside the series, for the element outside the series, with its successor, is that which is said to be the first.

Homeostasis proposes another model. Homeostasis is the ensemble of the processes which act to maintain all the internal consistencies of an organism in such a way as to preserve it as a distinct internal milieu and morphology, despite the perturbations or external aggressions. This makes a reality something that is undivided, with its own essence, something that is distinct from all the others. This is what philosophical tradition precisely calls form, which provides for it not only an internal milieu but also an integral existence. Here there is no specific, locatable inductor agent of this act of existing. The mode of ordering and regulation is global and is the fact of the interaction of all the components, of

> the generative organization/reorganization from which homeostasis is constituted and ceaselessly reconstituted. But in turn homeostasis becomes for it the generative action which constitutes it. We find here again, in complicated but always fundamental fashion, the circuit of recursion: the organization of regulation must be itself regulated by the regulation which it creates. The living regulation therefore includes a recursive regulation of the regulator by the regulated. In other terms, homeostasis comes full circle, regenerating the circle that generates it. In this way, genes produce and cause organisms to exist, which produces them and gives them existence.[27]

The crisis of the principle of authority is in fact the crisis of the authority of principle, understood as immutably fixed in its nature and uniqueness, the transcendence of a maximum and optimum value which appears in a dominant relation to subordinates or derivatives. Such a relationship reduces the subordinates to the status of nothing, because they are frozen in a relationship of order; they become asymmetric, and they presuppose a hierarchy of degrees of being. It is vain to wish to restore or to reestablish that which is tottering, like the traditions and manners of creating the order which engenders chaos and arbitrariness.

5. Time is the substance and the form of mutations.

We can therefore inventory and describe mutations like coupling, resonance, and the competition of different evolution curves, or simply the characteristic speed of such and such among these. Mutation connotes a change of regime or speed in time, a sudden jump in acceleration or deceleration which brings with it other behaviors, other ways of being, upheavals, and reformulation of all connections. In mutation, time is not an empty container that leaves unchanged whatever enters. Time is a force—a power of configuration—and not a rigid, inert identification which simply furnishes a coordinate for an event. From this point of view, time requires translation into terms of interaction of differentiated temporalities or rhythms, the case of general figures referred to above. We may then say that in the first case we are dealing with a temporality (rhythm or evolution) which breaks down into two different temporalities in the same field. The second case is one in which two different evolutions (complementary or antagonistic) fuse into one, for better or for worse or without particular consequences. The third case involves coupling, which results in a third evolution. The fourth case considers the backlash of the resonance of two speeds: the result can be new stabilities, new forms of development, or destabilization (by the acceleration or braking of stable structures).

We can also diagnose mutations in general terms, in the same temporal perspective, based on their symptoms, which are crises. Those crises that we experience appear in two principal modes—as anarchic growth or non-growth, unbalanced and undifferentiated; as the non-anticipated, unforeseen acceleration of an area, which it leaves behind, lagging behind other sectors and thereby placing the entire structure at risk.

The absence of coordination of life rhythms is of little consequence in a community which is only an aggregate, one with independent components which have a lot of space between them. This is not the case in a closed space or in a system made of functional and closely interdependent parts. The latter situation (composed of closely interdependent parts), then, requires an "organic growth," by which diversification occurs according to the requirements of the different organs, of which the functions are determined by the needs of the organism in its entirety. Mutation occurs when the system is constituted. Then, the undifferentiated and incoherent growth becomes the evil. "As long as in certain regions . . . , undifferentiated growth proliferates like a real cancer, moreover, it's the absence of growth which places the very existence of man at risk. . . . *It's this mode of unbalanced and undifferentiated growth which is at the heart of the most grave problems that threaten humanity—and the way leading to the solution is organic growth.*"[28] Mutation is distinguished by the fact that what is said here about the worldwide system holds rigorously true for the more restrained systems which constitute our "nations" and our continents. The whole has an effect on the parts that it determines and transforms; the outside has an effect on the inside, which is relative, through and through, to the outside and vice versa. Problems arise from the very moment that there is divergence and bifurcation, for which coordination would require convergence and complementarity; when there is forced homogenization and convergence where differentiation and competition should prevail; when there is reversal of process such that what should accelerate and increase in fact slows down and lessens while what should slow down, stop, and disappear in fact increases in monstrous fashion, like a cancerous tumor.

6. In order to give a more concrete character to these remarks on the formally temporary nature of mutations and to comprehend graphically the speed and the upsetting consequences of several of these mutations, we can comment on the well-known evolution curves.

a. The most simple curve is the linear model. Acceleration here is zero. Growth occurs in equal increments and in equal durations. Increase in size is represented as a straight line whose slope is a function of the fixed added increment in the unit of time. This is the favorite "curve" which common sense and "sages" use to describe social changes and transformations, those that occur individually and those that are taken together. Increase in size is used right away to represent the type of change which occurs inside a system which itself remains invariable. Change is the result of an association or disassociation of unchangeable elements or of the fact of the increase or reduction of same substance or passage from the potential to the actual. Change of the system, change of change, is feared as the nonsense and the chaos which it is. Plato and Aristotle think this way. The latter writes, "There can not exist a motion of motion, a becoming of becoming, or, in general, a change" (*Physics*, Book V, lines 14–16). Changing the concept of change, which permits accepting mutations positively, is a difficult conquest of the physical sciences and the modern age. This change has not yet been acquired by common sense, which continues to reign in the social sciences, not to mention in academic, administrative, and political practices. However, without change, modern reality remains hermetically closed. What the philosopher and logician Arthur N. Prior said about science holds true in a general manner: "It would scarcely be an exaggeration to say that modern science began when we got used to the idea that changes were changing, that is, when we got used to the idea of acceleration, as contrast to simple motion."[29] The marginalization of Africa therefore also has this significance—that this continent functions and plans only according to a single regime of change, the linear model. It does not take into consideration the exponential model which is so typical of modern times. Africa is moving away from this mindset more and more quickly in many respects. In doing so, it fails to recognize the characteristic effects of a world that is in the process of integration, where what is local can have its source elsewhere. "Diffusion, contagion, bouncing back, boomerang effects, linking effects are today the aspects of reality for the most backward backwater in the world."

Africa's marginality consists, therefore, in the fact that it is suffering because of modernity rather than because it is being deprived of it.

b. The other curves which we have selected belong to the same type and are variations of this type. They translate different sorts of acceleration.

b1. There is the exponential model, which intervenes in varied and also ordinary areas, including the increase in savings with a constant rate of compound interest and the demographic growth of a human or amoebic population. The evolution of a quantity which doubles at the end of a set time is represented by a curve with a constant exponential or "geometric," undefined rate of growth in an open system.

b2. In a closed system, growth is rapid at first, with the curve having the speed of an exponential curve, then growth slows until it stops at an impenetrable ceiling. The ensemble produces an "S"-shaped curve.

b3. There is the case in which the rate of growth is itself growing instead of maintaining. Doubling is accomplished in smaller and smaller units of time. The same is true for demographic growth and for certain sectors of technical evolution. The curve which represents such a growth is flatter than the exponential curve: it no longer has the speed of a parabolic branch but rather that of a vertical asymptote. This curve suggests the paradox of undefined growth in finite time, which is, in fact, unimaginable.[30]

These brief reminders suggest interesting elucidations of the phenomena of crisis and mutation. I will enumerate a few as chapter headings of a research program, but I will not be able to treat them in depth. There is a qualitative leap in the passage from a linear model to an exponential model with a constant rate of growth, and there is an even more significant qualitative leap between the latter and that with a rate of growth which is constant. In this way, there are veritable mutations in the order of populations, artificial memory, and information.

What is called underdevelopment can be interpreted as the non-coordinated juxtaposition of different growth rhythms and the bouncing back or backlash of the most rapid with the slowest. In the transmission of knowledge—beginning without a link between generations—real breaks occur. As the saying goes, there is an entire world between fathers and sons. Changes are such that in most areas, parents do not have any experience to transmit—nothing which might be of immediate use—unless they find a way of reinventing this experience. The crises of authority and of education are linked as the impossibility of delivering an acquired and objectivized fund of experiences and knowledge. This marks the end of heritage.

Finally, this is the laying bare of the illustration according to which we can resolve vital problems of population, of food, of the environment, and of public health by postponing them for as long as possible. We have here areas in which acceleration occurs at an ever-increasing rather than constant rate of growth. The slightest delay aggravates the situation and requires the most costly solutions. The accumulation of delay leads to irreversibility and to irremediable catastrophe.

There is no way to conclude. In order to comprehend mutations in terms of their full scope, it seems indispensable to envision them essentially in their forms and in their interactions within a system which is integrated in the long term. The analogies taken from biology, from the general theory of dynamic systems, and from mathematical models are valid if we make them capable of "reducing the arbitrary nature of descriptions" and of the characterizations that are called crisis, mutation, and marginalization. These analogies refer to tools, to quasi-formalizations which give a better grasp of the realities. We can then anticipate and reflect, in a deliberate fashion, on certain evolutions before it becomes impossible either to brake them or to stop them. Intuition and spontaneous good sense are not adapted to the situation that Africa faces. We must give them a formulation which reinvents them at the level of the problems of modern times and of a world which is simultaneously inexhaustibly diverse and yet singular.

NOTES

1. E. Weil, *Philosophie politique*, p. 13.
2. F. Eboussi-Boulaga, *National Conferences in Black Africa: A Matter to Follow*, p. 166.
3. F. Eboussi-Boulaga, "The Political Economy of Cameroon: Historical Perspectives," Leiden, June 1–4, 1988. Meeting notes: A summary of my presentation is included.
4. R. Barthes, *Sade, Fourier, Loyola*, p. 63.
5. P. Veyne, *Comment on écrit l'histoire*, p. 146.
6. Cited by J. Largeault, *Principes de philosophie réaliste*, p. 138, note 14.
7. Ibid., p. 118.
8. Cited by P. Veyne, *Comment on écrit l'histoire*, p. 240.
9. J. Largeault, *Principes de philosophie réaliste*, p. 118.
10. J. Ladrière, *Vie sociale et destinée*, p. 127.
11. Ibid.
12. E. Morin, *La Méthode, 1: La Nature de la Nature*, p. 108.
13. Ibid., p. 107.
14. Ibid., p. 111.
15. Ibid., p. 51.

16. G. W. Kowalski,"Calcul, mesure, jeu, évolution: la transformation de la dialectique fin-moyen dans le développement de la pensée scientifique," pp. 225–70. Following developments owe much to this article. It decisively guides our entire approach.

17. R. Thom, *Stabilité structurelle et morphogenèse, Interéditions;* R. Thom, *Modèles mathématiques de la morphogenèse.*

18. Morin, *La Méthode, 1. La Nature de la Nature,* pp. 262–63.

19. M. Masarovic and E. Pestel, *Stratégie pour demain, 2ème Rapport au Club de Rome,* p. 9.

20. R. Descartes, *Discourse on the Method of Rightly Conducting the Reason and Seeking for Truth in the Sciences,* p. 17.

21. D. Durand, *La systématique,* collection Que sais-je?, p. 8.

22. Masarovic and Pestel, *Stratégie pour demain, 2ème Rapport au Club de Rome,* p. 9.

23. J. M. Keynes, *The General Theory of Employment, Interest, and Money,* pp. 383–84.

24. Morin, *La Méthode, 1. La Nature de la Nature,* p. 116.

25. Ibid.

26. L. von Bertalanffy, *General System Theory,* p. 66.

27. Ibid., p. 193, 195.

28. Masarovic and Pestel, *Stratégie pour demain, 2ème Rapport au Club de Rome,* p. 29.

29. P. Wetzlawick, J. Weakland, and R. Fisch, *Changements,* p. 29.

30. P. Antoine and A. Jeannière, *Espace mobile et temps incertains; nouveau cadre de vie, nouveau milieu humain,* pp. 15–16.

REFERENCES

Antoine, P., and A. Jeannière. 1970. *Espace mobile et temps incertains: nouveau cadre de vie, nouveau milieu humain.* Paris: Aubier, Montaigne.

Barthes, R. 1971. *Sade, Fourier, Loyola.* Paris: Seuil.

Bertalanffy, L. von. 1969. *General System Theory: Foundations, Development, Applications.* New York: G. Braziller.

Descartes, R. 1971 [1952]. *Discourse on the Method of Rightly Conducting the Reason and Seeking for Truth in the Sciences.* Part I. Britannica Great Books, vol. 31. Chicago: William Benton Publishers for the University of Chicago.

Durand, D. 1979. *La systématique.* Paris: P.B.F.

Eboussi-Boulaga, F. 1988. "The Political Economy of Cameroon: Historical Perspectives." Meeting Notes, Leiden, June 1–4, 1988. (A summary of presentation is included.)

———. 1993. *National Conferences in Black Africa: A Matter to Follow.* Paris: Karthala.

Keynes, J. M. 1991 [1953]. *The General Theory of Employment, Interest, and Money.* San Diego, Calif.: Harcourt Brace Jovanovich.

Kowalski, G. W. 1980. "Calcul, mesure, jeu, évolution: la transformation de la dialectique fin-moyen dans le développement de la pensée scientifique." *Recherches de Science Religieuse* 6.68/2: 225–70.

Ladrière, J. 1973. *Vie sociale et destinée.* Gembloux: Duculot.

Largeault, J. 1985. *Principes de philosophie réaliste*. Paris: Klincksieck.

Masarovic, M., and E. Pestel. 1974. *Stratégie pour demain, 2ème Rapport au Club de Rome*. Paris: Seuil.

Morin, E. 1977. *La Méthode, 1: La Nature de la Nature*. Paris: Seuil.

Thom, R. 1977. *Stabilité structurelle et morphogenèse: essai d'une theorie generale des modeles*. 2nd ed., rev. and enl. Paris: InterEditions.

———. 1980. *Modèles mathématiques de la morphogenèse*. Paris: C. Bourgeois.

Veyne, P. 1977. *Comment on écrit l'histoire*. Paris: Seuil.

Weil, E. 1956. *Philosophie politique*. Paris: J. Vrin.

Wetzlawick, P., J. Weakland, and R. Fisch. 1975. *Changements*. Paris: Seuil.

9. Chéri Samba's Postcolonial Reinvention of Modernity

Bogumil Jewsiewicki

No contemporary visual artist working in Africa has had greater success and broader appeal than Chéri Samba, the artist-painter from Kinshasa. His works have transcended the informal roadside exhibitions along the streets of Kinshasa to claim both formal space and formal audiences in the exhibit halls of museums in Paris and New York. Drawing on multiple influences derived from African sources such as recent history and forms of popular culture available on a global basis, Samba has created a body of work that combines moral discourse, biting satire, and commentary in a way that has caught the imagination of art worlds on three continents. Samba comments on the role of the nation formerly called Zaire in the contemporary world and on the broad gap between rhetoric and aspiration on the one hand and the experience of everyday life on the other hand. Modernity and its promises and claims are inserted as a dominant theme throughout Samba's *Oeuvre*. Undoubtedly, at least from a chronological point of view, Chéri Samba's art is postcolonial. Who then could mediate the interpretation of the postcolonial better than the colonial? In order to deconstruct the invention of the modern, one should first look at the invention of the primitive as art category. In my opinion, Paul Gauguin's

This essay, under the title "The Modern and the Primitive: In Search of Ourselves," was presented as the Annual Michael Wade Memorial Lecture at the Harry S. Truman Research Institute for the Advancement of Peace, The Hebrew University of Jerusalem, on May 10, 1993. A different version, one which stressed Chéri Samba's search for the essence of modernity, was read at the International African Institute seminar entitled "African Philosophy as Cultural Critical Inquiry," in Nairobi on April 26–30, 1993.

project is the best way to understand Chéri Samba's project, since the latter, at least from an interpretative point of view, is not possible without the former.

On the Postcolonial

Inventing what no longer is, and perhaps never was, but what must be in order to legitimize our presence, to give it a meaning that insures the link between what no longer is and what is not yet, constitutes the most important feature of postmodern invention of the present. Nowadays, our postcolonial world seems postcolonial only because the colonial project has ceased to lend its narrative meaning to both the present and the future. It disappeared with the last empire; it became a trace of the past, which was indeed colonial but which no longer is, either as a substantive or as an adjective. From the relative ease of being in referential terms, we have shifted to the reality of being that indeed exists but which, for want of self-expression and self-invention, is likely to miss its own existence (without even noticing it). The postmodern fear of being ill-conceived in the representation that the other could make of us made it so important for us to have the self-representation that circulates in the image market, that ensures our existence, no more after death, but in real life and in the here and now. And so nowadays, the failure to have one's self-image in circulation signifies nonexistence.

On Postcolonial Aesthetics

Pareyson provides a methodological basis for comparing Paul Gauguin's and Chéri Samba's projects. Whereas the artwork may seem to be an object, one discovers a whole world in it. The facts of a material object open onto what previously seemed to be the impenetrability of a spiritual universe. According to Pareyson, the finished work is both the finishing point of a movement, since the work can be determined only when finished, and a constant plea for interpretation. Every work demands active reappropriation, not for what it is but rather for what its objective was.

It is therefore useful and even necessary to examine the artist's project without actually postulating that it be identical to the work's project. The work that systematically feeds on other works, whether they are the artist's own former or prospective works or the works of other artists, is original. As a project within a dynamic sum total of other projects, each being a finished project in its immediate relation to the subject and a project liable to be appropriated by the spectator (and differently interpreted by the author himself/herself as well as by other authors), a work of art is thus quartered between exemplarity and congeniality. Thus, "one can resemble others while remaining oneself, and be oneself while resembling others" (Pareyson 1992: 4).

COLONIZING AS KNOWLEDGE: GAUGUIN'S INVENTION OF THE PRIMITIVE

He is always poaching on another's fields; today he is robbing
from the savages of the South Sea Islands.
—CAMILLE PISSARRO (1950: 126), commenting
on Gauguin's 1893 exhibition

Leaving the impressionists to join the symbolists, Gauguin was in search of
a unitary representation of the world, of which the primitive was the principal
component. Gauguin's pictorial work, his writings, and his correspondence
clearly demonstrate the importance of this concept (see Citti 1992 for its
meaning in the 1980s) in his quest for aesthetic knowledge. For the symbolists,
as well as for Gauguin himself, art was global knowledge. In 1885 Gauguin
wrote: "In my opinion, the great artist is the formula for the highest intelligence" (Field 1977: 198). This statement should be understood in light of
Charles Morice's exhortation (Field 1977: 199) that "art must be brought back
to its principle—to thought."

Gauguin tried to reproduce the fundamental truth of the world—that is,
in the form that compels relentless search (Riconda 1980). One of the ways
of pursuing this quest was Gauguin himself, his thought, his memory. Thus,
Gauguin rejected models and geometric perspective; he refused to copy nature.
To devote himself to painting alone, he concentrated on a mediated approach,
and as far as possible, he saw the world only through existing images, through
interpretations/appropriations of images produced by other artists. Gauguin
literally stole images. Buisine (1992: 115) describes his painting as a "particularly vast and varied collection of other artists' paintings." Gauguin himself
(1989: 65, letter dated 1891) wrote to Odilon Redon about his departure for Tahiti: "I am taking with me pictures, drawings, indeed a small world of friends."

Gauguin hoped to discover liberty and truth by getting to the heart of
origins—"his own, which he longs to have as 'savage' and Indian, and humanity's, which he imagines as idyllic" (Cachin 1989b: 223). Steeped in Japanese,
Indonesian, Peruvian, and Egyptian art, in Epinal's images, in stained-glass
church windows, and in the Christian art of Brittany, Gauguin invented Tahiti
on idols. Buisine (1992: 112) suggests that these idols are indeed images of
Gauguin himself, reborn primitive. Pissarro said that Gauguin was collecting
curios (Cachin 1989a: 230), and it is worth remembering that many of his
fellow painters did the same without leaving Paris.

To paint "La orana Maria" (Fezzi 1982: 32–427), Gauguin drew his inspiration from the frieze in the Borobudur Buddhist temple at Java, of which
he had photographs. Octave Mirbeau (1986: 126) describes this picture as a
"disquieting and racy mixture of barbaric splendour, Catholic liturgy, Hindu

reverie, Gothic imagery." Gauguin's dream of a spiritual communion with the primitive, which the woman best represents, into a truly carnal union which does not seem to distinguish clearly between the spiritual and the erotic.

Endless Painting and Endless Book

In (re)painting Manet's Olympia in 1890, Gauguin was rewriting *Don Quixote de la Mancha* three-quarters of a century before Jorge Luis Borges. Gauguin's writing—through the lines and colors he draws—announces his project, which is his desire to part with the linear passage of time, with progress. Gauguin's project isolates him from his old friends, among them Pissarro, who accuses him of being antisocial. The act of writing, in its broader sense of drawing a chain of arbitrary signs to indicate that the world has meaning, is for Gauguin—as it will later be for Borges—a rearrangement of the library or the infinite museography of all times and cultures. The Olympia—like other images—dwells in Gauguin. He repaints it in, among other works, "The loss of virginity" of 1891, in "Manao tupapau" of 1892, in "Te arii vahine" of 1896, and in "Nevermore, O Taiti" of 1897. For Gauguin, his works are part of the museology in the making; he often quotes himself (Buisine 1992: 114 lists such instances), somewhat as a scholar—a writer of reality—using virtual quotations to make visible his relationship with the 'tribe' of those who know. To produce the "effect of reality" (Barthes's *l'effet de reel*), he anchors the act of painting in the world around him. He hangs his own paintings on the walls he paints, as in the case of the 1893–94 "Self-portrait with a hat" (Fezzi 1982: 48–187), featuring in the background "Mamao tupapau." He revisits the same images, as in the case of the "Self-portrait with Yellow Christ" and the "Yellow Christ," both of 1889.

Let us note another way of revising an image, which takes Gauguin through a spiral movement to a global painting. A single painting is only a word of the formula, an attempt to establish the representation as global knowledge. In 1892, Gauguin paints the "Self-portrait with an idol" (Fezzi 1982: 38–452) by revisiting the idea of a "Self-portrait with Yellow Christ," yet he switches from religious symbolism to the primitive. The latter passes from Brittany Christian folklore to the primordial primitive. Gauguin presents himself with the idol, implying the very purpose of his travel, the search for primitive Gauguin. Three years earlier, in the middle ground of yet another painting ("The Beautiful Angela" of 1889), the image of Gauguin's own handmade pottery prefigures his first idol.

Like an ethnographer of his time, Gauguin collected documentary evidence (Buisine 1992: 116) thanks to regular visits to the Paris 1889 Universal Exhibition, an abundant visual documentation: here could be found pictures cut out from illustrated magazines, photos from the frieze's bas-reliefs in Boro-budur Buddhist temple in Java, a fresco drawn from the tomb of the eighteenth century Theban dynasty conserved in the British Museum, and travel accounts. Gauguin's limited knowledge of the language and culture indeed significantly affected his construction of the primitive. For instance, he did not seem to be aware that "ta matete"—the title given to one of his Tahitian paintings, comes directly from the English "the market" (Danielsson 1988 [1964]: 81, 102, 105). While at Papetee, he visited the small museum of the Catholic mission, which then held some writing tablets from Easter Island, from which he incorporated hieroglyphic signs in the "Merahi metua no Teha'amana." This painting constitutes a kind of anthology of images: Teha'amana assumes a sitting posture typical of a Tahitian woman at the photographer's studio, but the composition is inspired by a Hindu-inspired fresco. The title, which means "Teha'amana has a lot of relatives" (Danielsson [1988: 143] lends it an ethnologic significance), initiated a kind of dialogue with the image; like the primitive woman Teha'amana, this painting, which tells the very essence of the primitive in modernity, also has numerous kin.

Travel is only a pretext, a way of giving rise to the primitive. The pictures Gauguin owed to Egypt, Indochina, Brittany, and Tahiti and the words he appropriated shamelessly were only a way of calling forth the primitive from the depths of his innermost being. In his way of inscribing the Tahitian words, without paying any attention to the integrity of the language, there is indeed a colonial attitude of deliberate disregard. The recourse to the exotic written word has two essential functions in Gauguin's project. First, it authenticates his expertise—the Tahitian words and phrases inscribed on the paintings correspond to a list of words that many travelers incorporated in their narratives. Second, this writing, of which he is both the inventor and the translator, gives him the chance to consider himself an expert, a master of the word, the demiurge who recreates the world. The polyphony opened a space in which everything would henceforth be possible and dared.

Often interpreted in anecdotal terms, the painting "Aita tamari vahine Judith te parari" of 1893–94 constitutes the most elaborate example (*The Exotic Eve* [Fezzi 1982: 390] gives us a foretaste) of Gauguin's research that presents the primitive as embodied in the modern, the "place elsewhere" hidden under the "place here"; this work contrasts the desire supposedly free elsewhere with the norm here, the spiritual with the erotic. The monkey at Annah's feet makes us think of the crucifix of the Brittany self-portrait or the idol of the Tahiti one. The colors of this monkey bring to mind some of Gauguin's self-portraits and remind us that, for Gauguin, "color is, to the same degree, music, polyphony, symphony" (Gauguin 1989: 27, undated text). The little monkey—Annah had the monkey mascot—prefigures "Oviri" (savage), a ceramic, strange, barbaric, and androgynous sculpture (Guerin's presentation of Gauguin 1989: 10). Gauguin wanted to have this figure erected on his tomb. It is Gauguin himself as savage, exiled in Paris, while Annah's portrait carries the caption "Judith is still a virgin." She was the daughter of his Parisian neighbors at the time and she was of the same age as Annah and his Tahiti vahines—all minors and all objects of his desire.

The play between the inscription in Tahitian and the image introduced innovative changes but was not unprecedented in Gauguin's painting. In "The vision according to the sermon or Jacob's struggle with the angel" of 1888, Gauguin was already proceeding in the same manner: the composition is inspired by a Japanese engraving, yet the neighborhood of both scenes, which depicts Brittany women coming out of church (which is stylistically inspired by folkloric imagery) and Jacob's struggle with the angel (also stylistically derived from the Christian imagery), creates a counterpoint between what is before our eyes and what our culture teaches us.

Gauguin does not despise the use of "mechanic" images; photographs, especially those of Charles Gustave Spitz (Danielsson 1988: 81), are used in paintings such as "Pape moe" (1893) and "Tahitian women" (1899) (Walther 1988: 80; also known as "red flower breasts" [Fezzi 1982: 76–555]). Gauguin also uses photographs to paint portraits, as often of models that are inaccessible (because they are dead, as in the case of his mother in "Exotic Eve") as of those in his immediate environment, such as the Tohotana portrait (1902). It is impossible to interpret this recourse to photography as an affirmation of his willingness to paint only those images mediated by others. Gauguin pursues his search for a polyphonic construction of painting and of knowledge, through which he hopes to build the space of liberty. In his unending painting, models and sources of inspiration are implicit instead of hidden.

Before he painted Teha'amana's portrait, there were "The loss of virginity," his self-portraits—especially "The Wretched," which he sent to Van Gogh—and another entitled "Christ in the Garden of Olives," which corresponds to a poem by Aurier (Cachin 1989a: 127). The most synthetic of his paintings, "What is our origin . . . ," of 1897, which closely resembles Wagner's aesthetic program and Verdi's *Aida*, was called "a great immemorial opera of humanity" (Cachin 1989a: 235).

The "Primitive": Anthropophagous Colonialism

It seems that Gauguin loved playing with identities; recall his 1890 painting "Exotic Eve" (Fezzi 1982: 16–390), with his mother's face (Dorra 1953; Danielsson 1988: 37–38). Eve, absentmindedly plucking red fruit from a paradisiac tree, looks as if she is directly reproduced from a painting by Douanier Rousseau or from a Persian tapestry. After his Brittany experience, Gauguin returned frequently to Eve, giving her multiple faces; he said to Eugene Tardieu, "The Eve I have chosen is almost an animal; that is why she is chaste, though nude" (Danielsson 1988: 202). For Gauguin, Eve is the primitive woman since she is primeval; that is why he gave his first Eve his mother's face. Indeed, she is plucking red fruit, a Christian symbol of sin, but the entire painting is calm and serene, and red fruit can also mean blood and therefore birth, the coming into this world, the passage from the paradisiacal security of his mother's womb to this world, which is only sin. The nude woman holding a fruit in her hand, who indeed symbolizes new life and fecundity, is often repeated in the Tahiti paintings (e.g., see "Te aa no te areois" of 1892, which is very "Egyptian" in outlook [Fezzi 1982: 34–439]). It is therefore possible that "Exotic Eve" represents Gauguin's fantasy of leaving for an exotic and primitive island (that is almost all he knew about Tahiti before his departure; Danielsson 1988), the fantasy of his return to his origin, his mother's lap. Shouldn't we therefore see in his invention of the primitive a move for absolution from the original sin? Painted two years later, the Tahitian Eve of "Te nave nave fenua" of 1892 (Fezzi 1982: 36–446), which evokes an oriental divinity, plucks a white flower. Does Gauguin mean to imply that at the end of the journey, with the attainment of the primitive, the paradise (the country in which living is cheap and love is free, qualities which Gauguin was seeking all his life) was to remain for good?

Comparing the spouse of a French policeman and a Tahitian woman, Gauguin wrote: "It was total decay and new bloom, law and faith, artifice and nature" (quoted by Walther 1988: 39). We must also remember Theo Van Gogh's remark about "The Beautiful Angela," that she resembles a young and beautiful cow (Cachin 1989a: 115). Gauguin sees the female nude as an ideal mediator between nature—which is closest in resemblance to the female nude—and civilization. More primitive and animal than man her begetter, woman's body opens onto the primitive; it was by steeping himself in it that Gauguin hoped to find not only pleasure but also the truth about himself. Annah the Javanese is another of the many mistakes, sometimes laughable but more often tragic, made by the painter in search of the true primitive: is it Annah, whom the painting represents, or Judith, whom the inscription calls forbidden desire (and why not a nude Tahitian woman symbolizing wanton pleasure?). In the primitive land, aren't they all multiple figures of the artist's desire to dissolve himself in the pure primitiveness? Thinking of himself as both monkey and spirit, alluding to "Oviri" and the pure desire, would eventually free Gauguin from the identity of the civilized person.

Gauguin's project has been colonial since its Brittany period insofar as it reserves for the other only a generic identity that signifies and represents what the essence of the traveler no longer entails: a "virgin land," a "primitive race," as Gauguin explained to Eugene Tardieu (Danielsson 1988: 202). Thus, the haunting presence of his face and of the nude female's body may mean especially the desire to redeem civilization through the colonization of the most primitive human body, the naked body of the native woman. Isn't that the essence of the first "Exotic Eve," the return to the maternal lap? "What is our origin? Who are we? And what is our destination?" inquires one of Gauguin's paintings.

Gauguin is both colonial and modern, but he is neither colonialist nor modernist. Walther (1988: 39) is mistaken in saying that "he came as a colonizer, not with the intent to enslave politically the indigenous people, but to steal from their culture what he thought the old world lacked," just as Pissarro was wrong to blame Gauguin, after the Brussels exhibition of the "XXs," "for not applying his synthesis to our modern philosophy, which is absolutely social, anti-authoritative and anti-mythical" (Walther 1988: 29). Gauguin is rather a lay missionary (like the present-day Africa scholar; Wallerstein 1973) "who might have meddled his life with the Maoris' so much that he accepts all this past as his own. All he has to do is to translate it into a work" (Octave Mirbeau, in 1893, as quoted by Danielsson 1988: 165). Gauguin thus becomes like the anthropologist, both assuming that their knowledge is more authentic than the knowledge the savage can have about herself or himself. Gauguin may be conscious of it; Buisine (1992: 112) suggests that the idols that are arbitrarily positioned in his paintings "constitute as much hieratic and immemorial figures of the primitive artist."

The colonial essence of Gauguin's aesthetic project underlines the authoritarian and mythical character of bourgeois modernity, especially its anthropophagous character. It was in the name of this project, dividing the world between us, the Westerners, and them, the primitives, that Gauguin imposed his search for the primitive on women and on the whole of Tahitian society. His life on the island, his painting and writings—especially Noa-Noa—are buried in the colonial binomial of ourselves and the other, of the primitive and the West, which Appiah (1992) denounces. Gauguin wanted to be a savage among the civilized and the civilized among savages, which is the paradox of every anthropologist. It is an essentialist binomial by which only the failure of the colonial project of modernization is possible. As Barbara Fields precisely notes (1982: 149), the Westerner believes that a white woman can give birth to a black child, whereas a black woman can bring forth only a black one. In the colonial culture which is still ours, the only quest for identity that is open to the mulatto is the ancestry of his non-Western parent. The young Alex Haley's claim (1976) to the Irish half of his ancestry (Hollinger 1992: 80) provoked laughter, whereas his *Roots* claim to the African half of his ancestry seemed perfectly legitimate (Reed et al. 1989: 227).

The Trap of Authenticity

Gauguin had no successor in the West, since in the meantime, the primitive has reached our shores as African idols and other works of primitive art thought to be more authentic than the cultures of colonized peoples. Primitive art was and still is considered to be the expression of a timeless tribe genius that has been corrupted forever by the civilization brought by colonialism. Gauguin himself found it very difficult to hide from the public his Tahitian disappointments, the fact that his Tahitian women were often Christians—dressed like Westerners, ignorant of the traditional culture that Gauguin would find only in ethnography books and museums. For Matisse, Picasso, and Braque, art provides a mechanism for going back to the origins of Western civilization without necessarily leaving Paris. This art has no individual author, no concrete cultural attachment to an existing society. Matisse, who bought a "negro" object, presented it as Egyptian (Cachin 1989a: 109).

Gauguin made his own identity a compromise between his imagination and Western representations. Savage by his Peruvian mother and living in Brittany as a peasant, he endowed himself with this inimitable "in-spite-of-my-savagery" attitude (Gauguin 1989: 11). The desire to be seen like "Oviri" (the savage)—this is what he called his self-portrait in gypsum (Guerin's presentation of Gauguin 1989: 10)—and to enjoy the advantages of a savage and a civilized individual had a double price. Gauguin's returns to civilization became possible only on pain of destroying the "inimitable" attitude he created for himself. In 1903, while Gauguin was thinking of returning because of his illness, Daniel de Monfreid wrote to him: "It is feared that your coming will disrupt some work and an incubation that occurred in the public opinion about you. You are currently the extraordinary artist who sends from the depth of Oceania his disconcerting and matchless works [. . .] you enjoy the immunity of great deaths, you have gone down to art history" (Danielsson 1988: 309).

A critic of the 1893 exhibition wrote: "We are awaiting in Paris the arrival of a Tahiti painter who will stay at Jardin d'Acclimatation,"[1] "while his work will be at Duran-Ruel or elsewhere. I mean a true Maori" (quoted by Danielsson 1988: 163).

Fig. 1. Chéri Samba, left, with Moke in Kinshasa. Courtesy of Louis van Bever.

CHÉRI SAMBA AND THE INVENTION OF THE MODERN

"I mean a true Maori!"

A century later, almost day in, day out, a "true Maori," "His Eminence the Artist Samba" (this is the title of one of his self-portraits) disembarked in Paris in the 1989 "The Magicians of the Earth" exhibition's van. There is, however, a distortion of the prophetic vow of the modernist adventure in painting. The "primitive" of the end of the twentieth century did not go to lodge at the Jardin d'Acclimatation, and Samba's art tracks down modernity instead of the primitive.

Ms Mitterand inaugurated Chéri Samba's 1989 individual exhibition, but the doors of the Louvre remain closed to the contemporary African artist and to African "primitive" art. Does Chéri Samba's presence in Paris and New York really inaugurate the end of the monopoly of Western bourgeois taste? Paradoxically, Gauguin announced a century ago its absolute rule, thus preparing the ground for the coming of the aestheticized primitive, encapsulated in the concept of art, with no relation to society other than a tribal style, in the custody of a recognized interpreter, a professional of primitivism, an anthropologist or African art museum curator. Stendhal (1932 [1824]: 6) clearly announced the new trend: "My opinions about painting are those of the *extreme left*" (italics in the original). *Madame Bovary* was received and rightly so, regardless of its author's denials of any but aesthetic purpose as an ideological crime (LaCapra 1982). Since the mid-nineteenth century, art has become more and more conservative, bourgeois, or proletarian, particularly when it bears on the definition of collective identities which have meanwhile become the monopoly of the State. And so the fact remains that aesthetics and ethics are truly political subjects.

Chéri Samba is aware of this fact, even if he avoids discussing the topic, unlike a writer such as Yambo Ouologuem, who plays in literature the comparable role of the provocateur turning against the colonial master the scorn for norms that he does not consider to be his own. Pierre Alexandre (1981: 127) has laconically expressed the view about the ethics that, as aesthetics, has always been eminently political: "Africans were nude and Europeans were shocked: today it is the other way around." This is not the first time that a transfer of knowledge has surprised the colonizer, who cannot distinguish between provocation and revolution. The Western university, in its institutional as well as in its human components, finds it difficult to admit that it is as much the object as the subject of a primitive Oedipus complex (its ex-object). The "primitive" has been imposing itself during the last quarter of this century as the subject of knowledge. It is the triumphant Western bourgeois culture that has set up the Oedipus complex as an initiatory rite of political and cultural modernity; today the ritual murder still seems to be the only access to the heritage, up until now the sole monopoly of the jealous father.

The Postcolonial Dislodges the Primitive

It seems that Chéri Samba is the one who has succeeded—the claim could also be made that his recognition was attributable to a few critics and to a small number of collectors, like Jean Piggozi—in that these few introduced into the contemporary art museum the painting of self-taught artists living in Africa. André Magnin (1991: 15) wrote, "it is a fact that African art has always been absent from the large international exhibitions and museums of contemporary art. What was involved was a failure to recognize or, worse, ignorance or contempt."

It is no accident that institutions like the Georges Pompidou Center and the Museum for African Art and individuals like André Magnin and Susan Vogel have undertaken, at the risk of their professional reputations and credibility, to overturn the canons of judgment, the norms of recognition and evaluation. Confident in his experience of contemporary music in international circles, the owner of a small Paris gallery, Jean-Marc Patras, made himself the painter's agent, taking his promotion in hand and imposing on it the discipline needed to develop the public personality of a star. There is nothing wrong with that; quite the contrary. On what principle, if not the old tenacious racist ideas about Africa, a reservoir of old forms, should an African artist not be entitled to the services of a Western agent? The promotion deal is necessary for parting with the myth of primitivity and of works produced by an abstract tribal genius. Chéri Samba comments on this in the painting entitled "The contract, why did I sign a contract?," an excellent example of the interview he grants a public whose question he anticipates. He ends the imaginary interview by saying, "I will remain Chéri Samba," and he signs the interview with "Chéri Samba in Paris June–July 90 (acrylic)."

Chéri Samba was the ideal person to become an international star. For fifteen years he has applied himself to constructing and cultivating his own public image, a step which is part of his temperament and culture as a Kinshasa man. "The artist Samba and the siren" (1978), a painting which exists in at least ten versions and which dominates his work of the late 1970s, is explicit on the subject. In this painting 'Mami wata' (whom he is always careful to call by her French name), the siren, holds a magic book in the left hand and a snake, symbol of sin, in the right. Chéri Samba appears through the clouds, flanked by two angels, one of who holds a Bible. The other promises him that with the help of God he will become a great artist. Yet the siren—who gives her lovers power and wealth, according to Kinshasa popular culture—haunts Chéri Samba so much that he paints himself dreaming of an imminent consummation of his love for her, though he is fully aware of the fact that she is merciless in destroying those who fail to keep her commandments. For Chéri Samba, as for Moke, Mami wata is the prototype of a prostitute, a barren woman, a creature of physical love who forsakes her social procreative role. She is the one who inspires the women in "The fiancés in the wind and fire" (1989), "Effects ya masanga" (1988; *masanga* means beer), and "Pity! The prostitute" (1980).

Like many men of Kinshasa, Chéri Samba is egocentric, a man who cares about his clothes and looks like a self-proclaimed master of the impossible, one who, in Kinshasa parlance, would like to eat the chicken as well as the egg— an allusion to rumors in Kinshasa that accuse, with a hint of admiration, the privileged personalities of the regime of pushing their defiance of social norms to the verge of incest. Chéri Samba mocks this penchant for taking up the most absurd challenge in "tembe ezali mabe" ("I can do it too"; 1984), which does not prevent him from erring on the side of pride. The painting "Death by hanging" refers to these rumors: the suicide admits in his farewell note that he

Fig. 2. Jean-Marie La Haye, *Samba the Stampmaker*. Courtesy of Jean-Marie La Haye.

slept with his sister-in-law, with his niece (bear in mind that Chéri Samba comes from a matrilineal society, in which men have paternal responsibilities toward their sisters' children), and with the wife of the friend who put him up.

The difference between Chéri Samba and some ten other very talented Zairian artists is that Chéri Samba, thanks to his own boundless ego, which is on a par only with that of the president of his country, remains himself wherever he is. In this way he gets the best out of all of his friends, who are also his advisers, without ceasing to be the essential postmodern man, since he carries his culture with him wherever he goes, retaining his personal integrity and the ability to impose his will, to bow to no authority, money, nor fame. In New York as in Paris, Samba remains a typical Kinshasa man, always resorting to subterfuge to avoid the enemy he cannot confront, only to reappear elsewhere as himself again. It is his deep-seated pride in the politics of cultural authenticity that gives him the ease with which he paints: "Since 1989 Chéri Samba has taken the entire world as his theme: New York, Chicago, Paris, London, Frankfurt. . . . And he also comments on our weird art world that he has found

Fig. 3. Chéri Samba, *Paris as Seen by Chéri Samba*. Courtesy of Chéri Samba and Nestor Seewus.

out all about and which bothers him. He does this by portraying himself directly on his canvases, the man from Kinshasa who has made it, a self-taught artist" (Magnin 1991: 21).

There is no doubt that Chéri Samba's self-confidence and its manifestation in all his work owe much to the milieu in which he grew as a young painter. Toward the late 1970s in Kinshasa, as a popular painter, Samba frequented the company of an informal group of foreigners and Zairian intellectuals who were best distinguished by *Analyses Sociales,* the journal they started publishing in the 1980s. Whenever they met in the Didier de Lanoy's (Ana Lanzas joined him later) postcolonial salon, the group mocked the colonial taboos, trivializing racial prejudice: indeed, holding up to ridicule and scoffing at bourgeois culture, drinking beer, having fun, and glancing through comic strips. In the midst of this apparent disorder and casual atmosphere they talked politics freely and expressed their concern about the fate of Zairian society. This salon, very much in the Kinshasa style (de Lanoy's first wife was Zairian) as regards its open door as well as the entree it gave to many antechambers of power, was helpful when real problems arose. In this circle Chéri Samba enjoyed fundamentally disinterested and respectful patronage and advice in the development of his personality. This environment accentuated his inclination to mingle the narcissistic style of a Kinshasa snappy dresser with the manner of a preacher, which had been inherited from his father's Christian village culture. His irresistible desire for shtick, which was tinged with voyeurism and eroticism (both of which were in search of moral justification), found there fertile ground. To a very large extent, he owes his present self-confidence, the ease with which he navigates the universe of contemporary masters of the arts, to this milieu, which forced him to improve his standing. There it was always necessary to be on one's guard, to be quick at repartee to avoid exposing oneself to witty and caustic jokes. Thanks to this salon, as well as to the patronage of Nestor Seewus and Jean-Marie La Haye—an amateur painter himself—Samba came up against Western art. With respect to this issue, J.-P. Jacquemin (1990: 31–32) quotes Chéri Samba's characteristic reaction. To Seewus's question as to what he thought of the Brueghel paintings on show, Chéri Samba answered, "I can do that."

In this salon, Chéri Samba was present at and took part in the political discussions and ideological disputes. The 1979 painting "Heaven, purgatory and hell are all here on earth according to Mr. Didier" precisely echoes these discussions. At the center of the canvas, Didier de Lanoy and Chéri Samba, each glass in hand, display a small flag, chanting, respectively, "Hurrah for hell" and "Long live the kingdom of god." They are surrounded by an empty chapel and many people enjoying sexual pleasures. Another painting, "Is there life after death?," takes up the same theme, with Jean-Marie La Haye as the central character.

In this circle, Chéri Samba was known particularly for cracking jokes, and sometimes he was even the target. His painting allowed him to play tricks on his friends/patrons, who encouraged him in the quest for an ambivalent pictorial and verbal discourse. In "The unfaithful woman" and "The naughty cats" (1989), Samba represents his friends/patrons in rather embarrassing situations, calling them by their first names, Ana and Didier. He ceaselessly insists, sometimes with subtle mockery and an undertone of moral didacticism, on his white friends' inexhaustible interest in young Zairian women and on their taste for change (see "Transferred love"). He rejects the role of a painter who merely executes orders meant as a joke. He participates in his friends' social life, contributing his moral sense, which values male chauvinism at women's expense on the condition that his immediate family stay away. It is striking that the only time Samba painted his spouse was when he represented the classic middle-class salon of Kinshasa, complete with wedding photo on the wall, refrigerator, TV, and fan. "Woman and her desires" is a portrait of the salon, one which enables man to win social recognition, and it features Fifi (his wife's familiar first name) wearing a wristwatch, earrings, and a locket on a gold chain around her neck. He leaves only one disturbing impression, probably unconsciously: the very posture of the body and the adornments of a woman whose husband can afford to satisfy her desires evoke the image of a siren. Is such a woman—she who bears his children—at the same time one of the attributes of a man's respectability and the one who channels his wealth from the devil of modernity in exchange for the lives of members of his family?

Jean-Pierre Jacquemin (1990: 31), a frequenter of the salon and a friend of Samba's, who promoted the exhibitions of Zairian painters, including those of Chéri Samba, tells the story of a painting left by J.-M. La Haye in a sorry, debauched state. Friends entrusted the canvas to Chéri Samba for alterations and finishing touches. The new painting was entitled "I'm made for African women." A notice at the center of the painting read "An exercise by the student Jean-Marie La Haye, corrected by this teacher, Chéri Samba, who gave him 35/50." The original nude on the left of the canvas corresponds to a portrait of Jean-Marie La Haye on the right. This opposition underlines, through a moral message, the gratuitousness of including an unjustified nude. Was that what Chéri Samba was offering as a penalty—awarding his "student" poor marks? At the upper center of the canvas, Samba corrects La Haye: the same nude becomes an evocation of the flanked siren of another portrait by La Haye, whereas the ambiguous title proclaims "I'm for African women." This theme is taken up two years later in "No longer in agreement with the greybeard." A lengthy legend reveals, among other things, that the subject of the painting, this same painter and friend, is unable to "forsake the paradise of young girls of sixteen to twenty years of age." A third painting, accomplished in a classic style of Kinshasa portraiture, a painted reproduction of an identity photo, "The grandfather's love," reminds Samba's friend of his age, and both paintings evoke an indirect comment on the joys of Africa, which, despite the sense of old age, allow white men to enjoy the gracefulness of young girls. This last painting promotes the image of Chéri Samba the star; in French, the legend, attributed to La Haye, speaks of "glorifying my grandson with Chéri Samba's painting."

But Chéri Samba was never a full member of the Didiers band, since he was not an intellectual in the classic sense of the word. In the salon he would have a drink, take advice, have his texts in French or English corrected for a painting in progress. His 1979 painting "Heaven, purgatory, and hell are all here on earth," the "Let us immortalize the friendship" of 1980, or "Bameli Bangi" (1984) set the scene and the principal characters. In "Let us immortalize the friendship," Samba does not necessarily present himself as a guest; he is surrounded by the girlfriends of his white female friends, one of whom, Philda, appears in several paintings. To Didier, who slips his head to the upper left corner of the painting and whose wife Ana is among the group, Samba yells humorously, "Mundele [White man] . . . come out of my painting at once."

None of his background has ever prevented Chéri Samba from living the real Kinshasa life or from thinking in Kinshasa *lingala* (the main language spoken there), a language in which what is said can be clearly understood only through an association of terms whose simple grammatical structure yields no more than a general meaning; Kinshasa is a culture in which modern popular songs and the Bible have replaced proverbs without actually obliterating them. Want of space precludes analysis of the written texts here; suffice it to say, however, that Chéri Samba gives, as faithfully as possible, an account of different levels of the language and attributes to each character the appropriate speech between the vehicular *lingala* mixed with, for instance, *kikongo*, creolized French, standard French, English, etc. Samba is the child of a city in which cure and death fuse in a powerful metaphor which gives meaning to daily existence, however absurd it might seem by Western standards. He is that Kinshasa male whose ego, though bigger than the Chinese-built local People's Palace, is so fragile that it must ceaselessly be offered beer, girls, and especially other males' envy. For such a male, whose aim is to boost his own ego, another man's girlfriend or wife is merely prey, whereas his own wife remains a property, more personal than his own shirt. Samba explicitly addresses this issue in "I embrace French women as much as Philda"; he addresses it better still in "Ya ozalaka boye?" ("Big brother, you are like that").

In the true Zairian sense of the term, Samba is doing his best to "eat" the others—in other words, to promote himself at their expense—and in turn, he runs the risk of being eaten, day and night (especially at night, which is the time for sorcerers). Nothing conveys the socio-cultural universe in which Chéri Samba evolves better than the Zairian songs and his paintings. The atmosphere of complicity between the governors and the governed, the situation in which everyone is an accomplice in his or her own exploitation (Jewsiewicki 1992b) because he or she hopes to someday become the one who "eats" the others, are vividly expressed in life stories (see Mbembe 1992).

The Extravagance of a Petit-Bourgeois

Chéri Samba consciously highlights what other artists do reluctantly. This is even the defining characteristic of his work as compared with that of his Kinshasa colleagues. He derives the maximum advantage from his piercing look of a cartoonist who takes things seriously. Endowed with a personality of

Fig. 4. Chéri Samba, *The Scoundrel* and *Big Sister, You Are Like That.* Courtesy of Chéri Samba and Jean-Marc Patras.

the Andy Warhol type, Samba claims that caricature is far too easy a genre. Yet his work is all extravagance and exaggeration, the complete opposite of his life as head of a family that he leads in conservative *petit-bourgeois* style. In painting, however, Chéri Samba has no sense of moderation. His canvases are very large in an environment in which almost every painter works on canvases made of fifty-kilogram flour bags, which are cut in half and are usually stamped "US AID." He hangs his paintings on a tree near his shop and selects controversial subjects so as to attract a mob in a corner of a busy thoroughfare.

The shop and the two avenues are crowded with people who admire the only painting, entitled "Rebellion (Lulua against Baluba)" exhibited in front of the shop. The roads are closed to traffic. The artist Samba meanwhile has a bone to pick with the local authorities. He is forced to remove the painting and fined for recalling the unhappy memories of the pre-independence era. He paints another picture under the name "Happy the people who dance" to win back the confidence of the authorities. (Samba 1990: 79)

Of necessity, all Zairian painters work in public for lack of space and because avoiding the public eye will certainly invite the suspicion that the artist is up to something underhanded (i.e., pornography, sorcery, etc.). As good artists, they exhibit in the front of the shop small "classic" paintings: sirens, animals, landscapes that testify to their ability without getting them into trouble. Testing the limits that are considered acceptable to different institutions of State power is not without its dangers. Chéri Samba escaped these dangers by paying a fine; another Kinshasa artist, Pap'Emma, suffered weeks of imprisonment for exhibiting at the French Cultural Center a painting which represented a gendarme making love to a married woman. The police thought they were being insulted.

Almost all painters inscribe a legend or elements of dialogue that are inspired by cartoons, which are very popular in Kinshasa. Chéri Samba writes entire stories on his canvases. Every painter tries to attract white customers by referring to his collective imagination of Africa. Chéri Samba is bold enough to attract these customers through their penchant for masochism by caricaturing their male obsessions with the bodies of black women and the "primitive" pleasure that these bodies promise. In his heart of hearts, Samba is an artist, but he does not deny himself the craftsman's pride in a piece of work well done. The lettering of his texts is over-polished, just as he strives to represent other people's faces with photographic precision. It is in this context that Jean-Pierre Jacquemin (1990: 14) shares a highly significant anecdote. He confided to Chéri Samba that he had as much difficulty depicting his own face as he did in faithfully representing those of others. Pushing his regard for perfection to extremes, Chéri Samba incorporated his photograph into the painting "The tree that is barren, or bears bitter fruits, is never the target of stones (Matt. 7: 17–18)." This 1986 painting is part of a new series in which Chéri Samba is the hero, as the subject of other people's covetousness; in this series, Samba embarks on a critique of the tradition that endorses the exploitation of those who are successful. The series includes "The dowry" (1979), "The art of lazybones" (1989), and "Condemnation without judgment" (1990).

Chéri Samba mocks everyone—his eyes always ferret about; he respects nobody but himself, the great lady-killer, the international star. The work "I embrace French women as much as Philda" of 1984 portrays Samba in the arms of two white women and gives an account of his conquests: "I knew 394 offices, which means I made love five to eight times a day".

> I love making self-portraits so as to reproduce myself, since I am not a TV star. I love to make the artist known. If the mass media do not come to me, I should be the first to make myself discovered. (Samba, as interviewed by Marcadé 1991: 10)

This middle-class man, who is careful in the management of his wealth, who invests only in assets—he did not have a car before owning a house and two plots in the urban area—respects the political and religious authorities. Let us consider, for example, his painting "The Marshal Bridge" of 1984, which reflects the official propaganda to such an extent that it conveys the false impression of impertinence. Many artists have painted this bridge, as Mobutu's (Zairian president) propaganda was successful, at least for a while, in suggesting notions of regal pride, before it was dislodged by the growing misery. Chéri Samba has always been sensitive to ongoing events in his city, as I have shown elsewhere (Jewsiewicki 1991b). In other respects, he fills his canvases with naked female bodies, paints acts of copulation without always hiding them behind a prudish removable curtain. His nudes always have a moral justification: the correction of a social evil; his social critiques always come across as an apparent endorsement of the government.

> In Africa nudity is a shocking thing. The fact that an African, a Zaire citizen for instance, can see a woman's thighs up to her slip, is deemed scandalous. . . . Similarly, hugging in the street is obscene. . . . When I am painting scenes of this nature, I am actually violating prohibitions. . . . My solution to this is to critique these reputedly scandalous scenes and behaviors in the texts that come with the paintings. (Samba, as interviewed by Marcadé 1991: 86)

Whenever the subjects of the critique are identified, as is usually the case when Samba is concerned that he may be accused of criticizing the government, they are related to his white friends, as in "The unfaithful woman" or "A suspected *kiompukeur* [one who penetrates] . . ." or again, the subject is himself, as in "Chéri Samba implores the cosmic" (1979) and "The lake street" (1990). Indeed, Samba represents himself as guilty but penitent, as regretting his mistakes even before he makes them, as searching for pleasure less often than he stands up to the challenge of the Kinshasa male: "give me the courage to display my machismo to this woman" ("Yo ozalaka boye?" 1983). His only guilt, therefore, is his desire to distinguish himself, which is a serious infringement of the "traditional" society's morality but a proof of election in the urban postcolonial society, if blessed by God. Chéri Samba claims that he deserves this benediction in "Artist Samba and the siren." In "Pity! The prostitute," the business card dropped on the floor serves as a signature, suggesting that the client who dared to leave without paying because he gave sexual pleasure to the woman who directly evokes the siren is none other than Chéri Samba himself. Similarly, "The lake street" represents Samba as guilty, since the street full of potholes passes in front of his house. However, this painting gives him the opportunity to assert himself as the owner of such a beautiful house. Whenever he comes on stage, he has to show off as the strongest, the one who has achieved the impossible. For example, "Chéri Samba implores the cosmic" suggests that he made love to two women at the same time. "The tree" displays after its title the verse which was identified as Matt. 7: 17–18: "The tree that is barren, bears bitter fruit, is never the target of stones." At the center of this painting, Chéri Samba's face sprouts from the trunk of the tree, leaving no doubt about the metaphor, whereas higher up is inscribed "The immortal Samba wa N'Zinga ('Chéri Samba')." Could anything be more meaningful?

> I have always said that I never painted for the sake of beauty but to convey a message. But it is not so simple. For me there are three fundamental principles in my painting: to improve the work to create humor and to tell the truth. (Samba, as interviewed by Marcadé 1991: 85)

The Painting and the Knowledge

Chéri Samba's project has three distinct characteristics. First and foremost, his painting explores modernity, tracks it down everywhere, examines it, critiques it, and caricatures it in an effort to capture its formula and key and to possess it. This is Samba's obsession, which he cannot escape in Paris any more than in Kinshasa. His early paintings that are preserved in private collections search for the key to modernity in keeping with the siren's body, that aquatic spirit, half woman, half fish. It should be noted that in Chéri Samba's Kongo culture, aquatic spirits intervene in healing, whereas Kinshasa culture interprets poverty as an illness. The key to success is depicted in this culture to lie somewhere between evil (the magic book) and God (the Bible), between the individualistic pursuit of pleasure—the woman who offers herself—and respect for social norms. After his big hit with the exhibition of "The Magicians of the Earth," after a long stay in Paris and a visit to New York, Samba said, "After all, we are all the same [Africa and the West]. There is misery in the West also" (Samba 1991: 87). His quest for the formula for modernity challenges social disparities and the exploitation of man by man: "Paris is clean," "Frontier Airport, a developing country."

Secondly, Chéri Samba paints human beings as a moralist, as a preacher who stands up as a teacher and a knight-errant whose mission it is to save humanity. However, we should understand that it is all about an official figure,

Fig. 5. Chéri Samba, *The Border Airport to the West*. Private collection. Courtesy of Chéri Samba and Jean-Marc Patras.

a mask worn by a dancer before a public which connives and participates in the ceremony. Samba defends himself for deviating from this path whenever the spectator realizes that he or she is the cheerful accomplice of a voyeur, of a collector of amusing items, of a journalist on the lookout for a sensational event. Chéri Samba, forever in truth an adolescent in the big city, has an insatiable passion for the eventful life of the neighborhood, for adultery and other types of immorality, accidents, any kind of police operation, etc. He is also a true local moralist whom the people follow because his words touch them. He therefore has to be on the lookout for such events in order to base his teaching in real experiences and to enable everybody who participates in the preaching, every passerby who hears his harangue, to feel personally challenged. He is a great amateur of the social pathology he would like to scan with his speech.

I am convinced (unlike Jean-Pierre Jacquemin 1990) that his painting is erotic. He finds painting a naked body delightful (see "Effects ya masanga" [1988] or "Crazy love" [1989]), and in spite of himself, he cannot refrain from painting such bodies. There are sensual pleasures and that mark of Kinshasa culture which Samba does not forget to underscore—the propensity for anything challenging. The greater the risk, the more exciting the challenge while rumor constitutes the best possible *Guinness Book of Records* (see "Tembe ezali mabe").

Unlike Moke, a former protégé of Pierre Hafner, who depicts scenes of urban life like a photographer, Chéri Samba paints discourses and tells stories that have several narrative levels. He declares, "*The truth is most often told in my paintings.* That is why there are a lot of texts in my canvases" (Samba 1991: 85, italics in the original). If I had to suggest the unique formula that captures the essence of the way he expresses himself in painting, I would say that every painting is an oral interview that Samba has granted himself, the transcription of which he leaves to the spectator. It is a production, a typically Bakhtinian performance, staged under similar political conditions. The carnival representation of society's submissiveness to authority, "The march of allegiance" is a cruel farce which naively pretends to confuse political allegiance to the regime with a brassiere. (In French the term *soutien*, "support" or "allegiance," is also a component of work; *soutien-gorge:* brassiere.) Samba painted several versions, some with the subtitle "Comic Please," and he stretched this notion to the fight against AIDS.

Let us take another look at one of the versions of "The march of allegiance." The master of ceremonies is roaring the usual political slogans from the platform. The transcribed song at the foot of the painting is a parody of the "Zaroise," the national anthem of the new regime. The first participant in the parade insists that "it is a parade of allegiance and not of shoes," an allusion to the economic crisis and the problem of poverty, because the people marching are barefoot, whereas those in the stands wear shoes. Finally, it seems, this parade of allegiance is also an allusion to the habit of the local authorities of a small town of choosing from among the girls forced into the parade those who will warm the invited politicians' beds that night. Isn't the work also an occasion for proclaiming that cultural authenticity is imposed upon the people, who are forbidden to wear dresses that are declared non-authentic and to take Christian names? Is it authentic, then, that bras and panties be removed to please the powerful men in the stands? Several of Chéri Samba's paintings deal with the prohibitory politics of the "return to [cultural] authenticity."

Third, Chéri Samba's paintings give prominence only to the person most important to him, Chéri Samba. In the first place, there is an abundance of self-portraits, which, apart from the siren engaged in a dialogue with Chéri Samba himself, dominated Samba's works up to his big success in the West. During the 1980s, Jean-Marie La Haye seemed to be not only his favorite model but also the white man who served as his figurehead and perhaps even as a new incarnation of the siren. Later, this presence of the self becomes less direct, more discreet, assumed especially by the written word, in Samba's way of constructing the verbal and pictorial discourse by making reference to himself. It could be said that from a naive and unconscious narcissism, Chéri Samba moved to a more intellectual, sophisticated, but also a more perverse, egocentrism. The paintings of the 1990s represent Chéri Samba's world, the modern world he conquered, which henceforth belongs to him.

Chéri Samba not only composes his paintings with the help of images and ideas drawn from the environment, as I have pointed out elsewhere (Jewsie-wicki 1992a), but he also seizes on these images and ideas to bring out the meaning behind an unfinished painting composed of references. Thus the usual interpretation of the 1990 painting entitled "The fight against mosquitoes" has to take into account the fact that the principal character with a drawn bow was borrowed from a 1989 postage stamp which played a role in the campaign against AIDS. The mosquitoes that the old couple desperately chase around before going to bed represent retroviruses. To add another pun to the text, Chéri Samba resorts to a quotation which he does not even acknowledge. In the form of a souvenir photograph or a tourist painting, "Renouncing prostitution" evokes a typical black beauty with naked breast and is entitled "The era of prostitution." The beautiful half-naked girl is carrying books on her head. Are we to conclude that for Chéri Samba, both prostitution and girls' education are the white man's legacy? On the painting itself, the same girl is dressed like a poor Zairian woman; the naked breast this time suggests maternity as she watches a pot boiling on a charcoal fire. The very fine confrontation of symbols should be stressed: it turns the painting into a real polyphonic composition. Finally, the girl refuses money from her former white lover, who brings out of his pocket a huge bundle of banknotes, and this evokes one of his paintings, of which Samba made many versions in the 1980s, "Madeso ya bans" ("Corruption"). Need we recall that in 1990 Samba said, "the West now accuses us of corruption, and yet it was the West that implanted these values in our land" (Samba 1991: 86)? Should we see in "Renouncing prostitution" Chéri Samba's farewell to the siren?

Borrowing from others does not, of course, prevent Chéri Samba from denouncing, in the painting called "The copyist," the artists who supposedly copy his works while all revert to the urban popular culture images. I have already remarked on the development of the siren as a signifier: it allows Samba—just as it did Moke and other artists—to paint the prostitute, the barren woman, the love that aims only at sexual pleasure and that avoids procreation. Another visually signifying sketch was made into the very successful Kinshasa painting "Inakale" (Biaya 1989), which represents, according to Chéri Samba himself, "a palm-wine drawer who meets a snake on top of the palm tree. He decides

Fig. 6. Chéri Samba, *MPR's Dish*. On the 1990s political transition in Congo-Kinshasa (Zaire). Collection of C. Bonau. Courtesy of Chéri Samba and Jean-Marc Patras.

to jump in to the river below, since the palm tree is on the bank, but finds crocodiles on the surface of the water" (Samba 1990: 79). Samba used this story to paint "A suspected *kiompukeur*," whereas Moke used the image to paint (in 1991) "The Gulf War" (*Africa Now*: 173).

> If western artists no more tell stories, perhaps they've simply run out if ideas!
> (Samba, as interviewed by Marcadé 1991: 87)

I think I have demonstrated the validity of a reading that views with equal seriousness both aesthetic projects, that of Gauguin, which, chasing the primitive, brings modernity into painting, and that of Chéri Samba, which opens into postcoloniality by searching for the modern. The colonial project, in its epistemological sense, is impossible without the primitive. Gauguin travels to the ends of the earth only to discover the other in himself, because, as Musil writes, "the object subsists only by its limits, that is, by an act of hostility toward its entourage [. . .] there is no Pope without pagans" (1969: 33). But, once identified with the primitive, Gauguin consumed himself, since "man only resolutely asserts his fellow man by rejecting him" (ibid.: 31). Chéri Samba's project, the irruption in the West of the primitive, tracks down modernity and announces the possibility of "looping the loop." Doesn't Gauguin's negative, the primitive that assumes the modernity, announce Musil's paradox? In "Renouncing prostitution?" (1990), an anthology of paintings by Chéri Samba over a period of ten years, Musil affirms that one cannot be better asserted than when he is rejected. Would the distinction be the key to true knowledge, the key to the questions asked by Gauguin in his painting "Who are we? What is our origin? What is our destination?"? In "I am made for African women," Chéri Samba seems to be picking it up by appropriating La Haye's unfinished painting. May it be that the answer emerges through the assertion of oneself, however narcissistic this action may be?

However arbitrary it seems, I cannot resist juxtaposing "The draughtsman Chéri Samba" and "Annah the Javanese," wanting to be right in seeing in the latter the self-portrait of the savage/modern Gauguin, an announcement of "Oviri." This juxtaposition, which is more a matter of setting up two boundary posts than of drawing a straight comparison, draws its meaning from what Victor Bol writes about Segalen: "This entry into the absolute, which archaic societies and elaborate religions achieve through ritual [here Bol quotes Eliade describing Kierkegaard's efforts to be Jesus' contemporary as a normal attitude of an archaic man], is what Victor Segalen wants to achieve through a poetic act, which is to represent the very essence of man" (1972: 242–43). Gauguin's painting, Segalen's writing, and, of course, Chéri Samba's work are as much poetic acts aspiring to express "the very essence of man."

NOTE

1. The zoo in the Bois De Boulogne, near Paris.

REFERENCES

Africa Now. 1991. Groningen: Groningen Museum.

Alexandre, P. 1981. *Les Africains.* Paris: Ed. Lidis.

Appiah, K. A. 1992. *In My Father's House: Africa in the Philosophy of Culture.* London: Oxford University Press.

Badi-Banga Ne Mwine. 1989. "Texte." In *Art contemporain bantou. Deuxième biennale du Ciciba.* Kinshasa, juillet 1987. Libreville, Africa: Ciciba.

Bessieere, J. 1992. "Primitivisme littéraire et rhetorique temporelle et *scripturaire.* A propos de Segalen, Michaux, Butor." *Revue des Sciences Humaines* 227: 143–63.

Biaya, T. K. 1989. "L'impasse de la crise zairoise dans la peinture populaire urbaine, 1970–1985." In B. Jewsiewicki, ed., *Art and Politics in Black Africa.* Ottawa: CAAS, pp. 95–120.

Bol, V. 1972. *Lecture de Steles de Victor Segalen.* Paris: Minard.

Bouillier, H. 1961. "'Peintures' de Segalen." *Cahiers du Sud* 51, no. 361: 378–88.

Buchloh, B. H. D. 1982. *Formalisme et historicité.* Paris: Ed. Territoires.

Bugnicourt, J., and A. Diallo, eds. 1990. *Set: Des murs qui parlent. Nouvelle culture urbaine à Dakar.* Dakar, Africa: Enda.

Buisine, A. 1992. "L'originel et l'antérieur: Paul Gauguin." *Revue des Sciences Humaines* 227: 99–118.

Cachin, F. 1989a. *Gauguin.* Paris: Hachette.

———. 1989b. "Gauguin vu par lui-même et quelques autres." In *Gauguin.* Paris: Editions de la Réunion des Musées Nationaux.

Citti, P. 1992. "La figure du primitif dans les années 1890." *Revue des Sciences Humaines* 227: 67–77.

Compte, A. "Cours de philosophie positive, première leçon." In *Oeuvres choisies.* Paris: Ed. Montaigne.

Cornet, J.-A., et al. 1989. *60 Ans de peinture au Zaire.* Brussels: Les Editeurs d'Art Associés.

Danielsson, B. 1988 [1964]. *Gauguin à Tahiti et aux îles Marquises.* Papeete: Ed. Du Pacifique.

Diouf, M. 1992. "Fresques murales et écriture de l'histoire. Le set / setal a Dakar." *Politique Africaine* 46: 41–54.

Dorra, H. 1953. "The First Eves in Gauguin's Eden." *Gazette des Beaux Arts.* Paris (March).

———. 1967. "More on Gauguin's Eves." *Gazette des Beaux Arts.* Paris (February).

Dumon, D. 1989. "Maîtres des rues. Les peintres populaires du Zaire." Brussels: Cobra Films, video.

"Elements d'une hagiographie." In *Chéri Samba/Le peintre populaire du Zaire.* Ostend: Provincial Museum voor Moderne Kunst, pp. 9–33.

Eliade, M. 1953. *Traité d'histoire des religions.* Paris: Payot.

Fezzi, E. 1982. *Tout Gauguin, la peinture.* Paris: Flammarion.

Field, R. S. 1977. *Paul Gauguin: The Painting of the First Voyage to Tahiti.* New York: Garland.

Fields, B. 1982. "Ideology and Race in American History." In J. M. Kousser and J. M. McPherson, eds., *Region, Race, and Reconstruction.* New York: Oxford University Press, pp. 137–55.

Frodon, J.-M. 1992. "Un entretien avec Serge Daney." *Le Monde* 7 juillet: 2.

Gates, H. L. 1992. "Pluralism and Its Discontents." *Contention* 4: 69–78.

Gauguin, P. 1989. *Oviri. Ecrits d'un sauvage.* Paris: Gallimard, choisis et presentés par D. Guerin.

Guenther, B. 1991. "Chéri Samba." Chicago: Museum of Contemporary Art, Exhibition, January 26–March 17.

Guillerm, J.-P. 1992. "Primitifs et origine de l'art. Autour du discours des Symbolistes." *Revue des Sciences Humaines* 227: 79–98.

Hollinger, D. 1992. "Postethnic America." *Contention* 4: 79–96.

Huyghe, R. 1977. *Gauguin.* Paris: Flammarion.

Jacquemin J.-P. 1990. "Saint Chéri Samba, vie et oeuvres (I. M.) pies: Elements d'une hagiographie." In *Chéri Samba, le peintie populaire du Zaïre. Exposition retrospective. Ostende 21 Octobre 1990–7 Janvier 1991.* Ostende: Provinciaal Museum voor Moderne Kunst, pp. 9–33.

Jewsiewicki, B. 1989. "Présentation: Le language politique et les arts plastiques en Afrique." In B. Jewsiewicki, ed., *Art and Politics in Black Africa.* Ottawa: CAAS, pp. 1–10.

———. 1991a. "The Archeology of Invention: Mudimbe and Postcolonialism." *Callaloo* 14, no. 4: 961–68.

———. 1991b. "Painting in Zaire: From the Invention of the West to the Representation of Social Self." In S. Vogel and I. Ebong, eds., *Africa Explores: 20th Century African Art.* New York: Museum for African Art, pp. 130–51.

———. 1992a. "Popular Painting in Zaire." In *African Art Events in Maastricht: Popular Art—Painting in Zaire.* Maastricht: Galerie privée Louis van Bever.

———. 1992b. *Vivre et mourir au Zaire.* Paris: Karthala.

Jules-Rosette, B. 1979. "Art and Ideology: The Communicative Significance of Some Urban Art Forms in Africa." *Semiotica* 28, no. 1–2: 1–29.

LaCapra, D. 1982. *"Madame Bovary" on Trial.* Ithaca, N.Y.: Cornell University Press.

MacGaffey, W. 1991. *Art and Healing of the Bakongo Commented by Themselves: Minkisi from the Laman Collection.* Stockholm: Folkens Museum—Ethnografiska.

Magnin, A. 1991. "Aka Soa, Udro-Nkpo, Srele . . . Art in Black Africa." In *Africa Now.* Groningen: Groningen Museum, pp. 15–24.

Marcadé, B. 1991. "Chéri Samba." *Galeries* 41: 84–87.

Mbembe, A. 1992. "Provisional Notes on the Postcolony." *Africa* 62, no. 1: 3–37.

Miller, C. 1983. "Le devoir de violence." *L'Esprit Créateur* 23, no. 4: 62–73.

———. 1990. *Theories of Africans: Francophone Literature and Anthropology in Africa.* Chicago: University of Chicago Press.

Mirbeau, O. 1986. "Paul Gauguin." In *Des artistes.* Paris: UGE.

Mudimbe, V. Y. 1994. *The Idea of Africa: Explorations, Conversations and the Politics of Memory.* Bloomington: Indiana University Press.

Musil, R. 1969. *L'homme sans qualité,* vol. 1. Paris: Seuil.

Niane, I. C., V. Savane, and B. B. Diop. 1991. *Set Setal. La seconde génération des barricades.* Dakar, Africa: Sud Editions.

Ouologuem, Y. 1968. *Le devoir de violence.* Paris: Seuil.

Pareyson, L. 1992 [1966]. *Conversations sur l'esthétique.* Paris: Gallimard.

Pissarro, C. 1950. *Camille Pissaro: Lettres à son fils Lucien.* Paris: Plon, edition etablie par J. Rewald.

Reed, I., et al. 1989. "Is Ethnicity Obsolete?" In W. Sollors, ed., *The Invention of Ethnicity.* New York: Oxford University Press, pp. 226–35.

Riconda, G. 1980. "La philosophie de l'interpretation de Luigi Pareyson." *Archives de Philosophie* 12: 177–94.

Samba, C. 1990. "La peinture populaire zairoise avec Chéri Samba. Citoyen SAMBA wa NBIMBA N'ZINGA DIT Chéri SAMBA (ex. DAVID)." In *Chéri Samba. Le peintre populaire du Zaire,* 78–81. Ostende: Privinciaal Museum voor Moderne Kunst.

———. 1991. "Memories of an African." *Raw: High Culture for Lowbrows* 2, no. 3: 12–19.

Segalen, V. 1978. *Essai sur l'exotisme.* Paris: Ed. Fata Morgana.

Shapiro, M. J. 1988. *The Politics of Representation.* Madison: University of Wisconsin Press.

Stendhal, H. 1932 [1824]. "Le salon de 1824." In *Mélanges d'art.* Paris: Le Divan.

Szombati-Fabian, I., and J. Fabian. 1976. "Art, History and Society: Popular Art in Shaba, Zaire." *Studies in the Anthropology of Visual Communication* 3, no. 1: 1–21.

Torgovnick, M. 1990. *Gone Primitive: Savage Intellects, Modern Lives.* Chicago: University of Chicago Press.

Vattimo, G., ed. 1988. *La sécularisation de la pensée.* Paris: Seuil.

Vogel, S., and I. Ebong, eds. 1991. *Africa Explores: 20th Century African Art.* New York: Center for African Art.

Wallerstein, I. 1973. "The Evolving Role of the Africa Scholars in African Studies." *Canadian Journal of African Studies* 17: 9–16.

Walther, I. F. 1988. *Paul Gauguin 1848–1903.* Cologne: Benedikt Taschen.

Wilenz, S. 1985. *Rites of Power: Symbolism, Rituals and Politics since the Middle Ages.* Philadelphia: University of Pennsylvania Press.

10. Luo Perspectives on Knowledge and Development: Samuel G. Ayany and Paul Mbuya

E. S. Atieno-Odhiambo

The early British administrators and missionaries working among Jo Luo in the period between 1895 and 1920 found a community with fully formed perspectives on knowledge (*rieko*), metaphysics (*Jok*), episteme (*piny*), and development (*dongruok*), perspectives that they readily articulated to the inquiring foreigners (Atieno-Odhiambo 1989b, 1992). As the first generation of high-school graduates from missionary schools emerged in the early 1930s, Beneaiah Apolo Ohanga ("Bawo"), Isaak Okwirry ("Jusa"), Mariko Ombaka ("The"), and Paulo Mbuya ("Olwal Ja Nyakongo") being foremost among them, debate soon arose as to the compatibility between what they understood as the Luo cultural values, on the one hand, and the missionary-Christian notions of progress, which they had embraced, on the other. For some the choices were easy: Ohanga became a Christian and an advocate of Western "progress" and "development" (Atieno-Odhiambo 1989a); Okwirry took the colonial administrators as his role model, complete with their contempt for the uneducated Africans, whom Okwirry condescendingly referred to as *Odiango-Abuk-Dhano-a-Dhana*—ordinary folks lacking book knowledge. (One of his nicknames also became Odiango.) Others problematized the whole issue of compatibilities. At the level of religion, Alfayo Odongo Mango was perhaps the most creative among this generation, creating not only a new theology but also an alphabet (Ogot 1971). This essay is concerned with yet another layer, that associated with those who sought a synthesis between the "good things Luo" and the "new good things Christian."

PAUL MBUYA ON CULTURAL SYNTHESIS

A luminary in this endeavor was Paul Mbuya, missionary, preacher, teacher, and later chief. Mbuya accepted the worth of both "sides of the fence." Having been educated by the Seventh-Day Adventists at Gendia, in the 1910s, Mbuya also sought Luo knowledge at the feet of Luo elders. Later he wrote:

> I often visited senior elders who were the custodians of substantial knowledge (*rieko madongo*) among the Luo. I can say that they were superior to (latter-day) Professors in their knowledge of culture (*timbe*) of the Luo. In 1913 I visited Gor the son of Ogalo and we stayed together for six months. Having asked me where I came from, and having recognized my lineage (*anyuola mara*), he consented that I should stay with him in his hut while he instructed me on such matters as we are now discussing. I also was a frequent visitor of another elder, Maena the son of Mboya II, a man who was famous for being wise (*riek*) in Karachuonyo. I also visited Omolo the son of Obop in the Ka-nyipir section of Karachuonyo. I used to teach school at his homestead, and regularly sat at his feet to hear teachings that he dispensed to me. Plus, I visited Oyugi the son of Mboya, an elder who was known as wise in all of Karachuonyo. I also met Chief Morira of Muksero in the land of the Aba-gusii.
>
> I also met with Owili Magak of the Kasipul section of Karachuonyo . . .
>
> I have visited elders who are wise in terms of the Luo developmental trajec-tory (*mariek kuom dongo mar Luo*) many of whose names I have not penned here. (Mbuya 1978: 8–9)

Having examined this indigenous archive, Mbuya sought a reconciliation with his own Christianity. He found it in a moral order that could integrate Christian teachings and Luo culture. He wrote:

> God (*Nyasaye*) gave the Luo FOURTEEN commandments. The Luo have upheld these commandments one generation after another (*tienge gi tienge*). The Luo adhere strictly to these commandments.

Whenever one broke any of these fourteen commandments, the elders met and denounced such transgression in loud cadences (*Ka gichok matek*), praying that their denunciation should bring affliction to the transgressor and to those that had sent him. These are the commandments:

1. Thou shalt offer sacrifices (*lisweche*) and invoke the name of the God of Migrations (*Nyasaye Nyakalaga*); thou shalt beseech him, with begging hands, to bless you with good luck, and to protect you fully from the shadows of devils (*jochiende*). In case of doubt, you will consult the ritual experts (*jodolo*).

2. Thou shalt offer sacrifices to invoke the names of your grandparents and your forefathers; you will also invoke the names of past senior Luo elders during this prayer.

3. Honor thy father and mother that you may prosper (*idongi*) on earth for many days; also be mindful (*dewu*) of elders.

4. Thou shalt not kill.

5. Thou shalt not steal.

6. Thou shalt not commit adultery, nor acts of bestiality (*gath*), nor *pogo liswa* (untranslatable). [Full text: *Kig iterri, kendo kik itim gath kata pogo liswa.*]

7. Thou shalt not be a perpetrator of perversity and profanity. [*Kik ibedi ja Mganga ma timo mirieri.*]

8. Thou shalt not lie, nor concoct lies, nor create conflict, nor bear false witness.

9. Thou shalt love thy neighbor, and any unexpected visitor.

10. Thou shalt not be a sorcerer (*jandagla*), nor a night runner–dancer, nor an evil eye, nor a wizard.

11. Thou shalt not make a breach on the land boundaries specified by elders, nor will you plant aloe (*ogaka*) on land designated as cattle tracks on your own.

12. Do not swear, nor undertake an earthly ritual oath (*mumb misiko*) in your hands without the knowledge of your clansmen; do not swear by the earth by licking it nor scattering the dust.

13. Do not swear by your thigh, by slapping it as you swear.

14. When a man dies in your village, thou shalt abstain from work for four days, three days for a woman; and one day if a dead body has been transported through your neighborhood. All these abstentions relate to tilling the land, not to any other work. In case of urgency, abstain on the day of burial, on the day of mock battle (*tero buru*), on the last day of official mourning (*yweyo liel*) which is the same day as a sports day. Also, abstain on any day that hailstorms fall during the long rainy season.

Mbuya found common ground between Luo prescriptions and the Christian concept of sin. In the Luo firmament, transgression led to mental and bodily suffering and even death (*Chira*). Mbuya equated *Chira* with sin and thus etched a compatibility between aspects of the fourteen Luo commandments and the biblical Ten Commandments.

In his canonical work *Luo Kitgi gi Timbegi* (1938)—*Luo Customs and Culture*—Mbuya wrote extensively on the cultural practices that informed his Fourteen Commandments. This work became the official Luo text, comparable in its internal impact to Apolo Kagwa's *Bassekabaka be Buganda* and Johnson's *History of the Yorubas*. In the works of Mbuya, the Luo, like their nemeses the Gikuyu and the Yoruba, were advocated for as a people who had strong sentiments about development (*olaju* in Yoruba, *dongruok* among the Luo). This *dongruok* first involved a process of acquiring proper indigenous knowledge, as demonstrated by Mbuya above and as confirmed by Odinga later (Odinga 1967: 1–16). But it was the praxis of this Luo–Christian synthesis that became troublesome, both to the missionaries, who regarded it as backsliding, and to mainstream Luo Anglican Christians, who accepted the missionary prescriptions related to faith, to "Churchtianity," and to development. As the tempo for economic development gained pace in the immediate post–World War II years in Luoland, spurred on by Oginga Odinga (Atieno-Odhiambo 1975), the very compatibility of some Luo cultural practices and the developmental agenda came to the fore in internal debates.

AYANY'S PLACE IN THE DEVELOPMENT DISCOURSE

An engaging text in these debates was the historical pamphlet entitled *Kar Chakruok Mar Luo*, authored by Samuel G. Ayany when he was a Makerere undergraduate in 1947 and published by the East African Literature Bureau in 1952. Until his death in 1992, Ayany had been an ebullient, self-conscious intellectual and a combative contestant for Luo public acclaim for forty years. As early as 1946, Ayany was engaged in advising the founders of the Luo Thrift and Trading Association (LUTATCO) on the merits of development (Atieno-Odhiambo 1975). By the 1950s, he was a noted history teacher at Maseno Secondary School, the quintessential Luo elitist school of the pre-independence years (Cohen and Atieno-Odhiambo 1989: 120–24). He taught British Imperial history but subverted the text by teaching bits of it in Dholuo: "Drake Oyange nogono saa ma koro ne eluoro piny gi rombo"—"(Francis) Drake, the lion-bandit, in those days circumnavigated the world like a witch-doctor dragging behind him a magical sheep casting a spell on mankind"— was his rendition of the "expansion of empire" theme, according to his former students (Awuor-Okullo, O. I. Powo Club, Awasi; October 13, 1983). He spent a lot of classroom time teaching against colonialism, and by the late 1950s, he had attracted a sufficient following to found and become the first secretary-general of the Kenya National Union of Teachers. By this time his *Kar Chakruok Mar Luo* text had become a widely read text in vernacular grammar classes at intermediate schools in Luoland. As we have argued elsewhere, *Kar Chakruok Mar Luo* had given the Luo a collective history. Ayany had sought a popular mode, in which potentially every Luo kinship line was represented in a narrative of continuous Luo history (Cohen and Atieno-Odhiambo 1987). By the end of the 1950s, Ayany had indeed become a *Mwalimu*. Reveling in the acclaim of the Luo reading public, Ayany acquired the *Nyadhi* (virtue-boasting) nickname of *Kundi ma Chwowo Jorieko*—the canker pricking at the sides of the educated class. He also saw himself as a leader whose opinions must be foregrounded: 'Nyathi Punda Ki dong'—the child of a donkey never stays behind—became another of his *Nyadhi* names. And a canker he was to all and sundry. When the guild historian B. A. Ogot co-authored a book, in which he averred that Ayany had at one time been less than wholesome as a practicing Christian (Ogot and Welbourn 1966), Ayany promptly took the newly installed head of the History Department at the University College, Nairobi, to the high court on the grounds of defamation. But Ayany was not content merely with courtroom dramas. He appealed to Luo public opinion by accusing Ogot of heinous impropriety: *Ogot Oyanyo Ayany gi Ayany ma ne pok Oyany-go Ayany*—Ogot had abused the Abused with such an abuse as had never been used to abuse the Abused (Ayany is here the Abused); thus Ayany onomatopoeically put it to his eager audiences at Shauri Moyo, the bar of his cousin Okoth Aliwa. In the 1970s Ayany went further, taking on Oginga Odinga himself over the question of legislative representation for the Bondo constituency. From 1969 onward, Ayany had allied himself with William Odongo Omamo "Kaliech" in Bondo, arguing that Omamo's politics were the politics of development, while Odinga stood for the politics of alienation of the Luo from the Kenyatta clan-state. Ayany took to writing letters to the daily papers using the pen name of Althea *Ohero Dongo*—Althea who loves development—during the 1975–78 period. At a memorable confrontation at the Rabango Bar in Siaya in 1978, I charged Ayany with moral cowardice for hiding under a pen name. Two months later I received a phone call: "I am going to Liberia (on duty), but when I come back I am going to take you to court for what you said at Siaya." That was Ayany for you—*Kundi ma chwowo Jorieko*. His mood in the late 1970s was quite consistent with the developmental agenda he had penned in *Kar Chakruok Mar Luo* nearly thirty years earlier. This text, which is still read, thus provides an instance of a discursive trajectory of one Luo participant in the quest for knowledge and development. Below I have translated sections from this work that are immediately pertinent to this twin agenda.

HISTORICAL TEXTS

S. G. Ayany, *Kar Chakruok Mar Luo* [*Luo Origins*], Preface to the 1952 First Edition

In the year 1947 there was a competition on the writing of books in Dho-Luo—the Luo language. I [entered the competition and] wrote about how the Luo moved from Sudan to their arrival in Kenya, and my essay won the first prize in that competition. For this reason the publisher was very keen that the essay ought to be transferred into a book. Since the essay, written specifically for competition, was brief, I took time to rewrite the whole work again, adding information here and there so as to make it more comprehensive and intelligible.

In these days, as we should all realize, there is a great thirst for access to (hi) stories (*sigendini*) depicting the lives of indigenous peoples (*jopiny*) in the days past. This demand is not limited to the Luo exclusively. Abaluyia, Kikuyu, Abagusii, [and] Abakuria, plus other communities as well, have this desire to write the (hi) stories of their ancestors. The Baganda have written theirs fully. Thus, old practices are guaranteed longevity if properly shelved, with no fear of total loss at all. In writing *Luo Kitgi gi Timbegi*, the worthy (*Migosi*) Paulo Mboya has made an investment for those who will land when we have spoilt all the good ideas (*weche maber*) about the Luo. Such visitors as the whites (*Josungu*) have introduced new ideas and a variety of thoughts (*paro mathoth*). These are different from how our ancestors lived and thought. Furthermore, these new ideas are proving very attractive to ordinary folks (*jopiny*), forcing them into forgetting totally the cultures (*timbe*) of their ancestors. For this reason, it is the committing of the written words in books that shall ensure indigenous victory in this struggle of the two cultures.

The Luo are a people who love (hi) stories. Our grandparents and parents committed these (hi) stories to memory, but often enough they found time to re-tell/re-enact (*gano*) them to those who had not totally mastered the stories. But now, the known Luo world has extended well beyond the parameters known by the generation of Podho (the founder of the Luo nation). How can one in Kongwa or Mega possibly find time to get to hear the Luo (hi) stories from the mouths of the mental repositories living in Luoland? But if these words were committed into the printed format in the form of a book, they would become accessible very easily indeed.

Chapter 3(c): The Luo Situation Today (December 1952)

In this small book I have told the story of the Luo, from their beginning until their arrival in Nyanza. I have also demonstrated the different developments within Luo tribes (*Ogendini*) together with their population sizes. We have also seen how the Kalenjin troubled the Luo in the past and how the Luo have lived at ease (*maber*) with the Abaluyia. We have shown that the Luo presence in Nyanza is a recent phenomenon. We know that white people have not been here for long; it is only 51 years at the time of this writing (1951). The missionaries built Maseno in 1906; Gendia too was built at the same time. That found when Mr. Hobley (Obilo) had already fought against the Uyoma and Sakwa peoples and also killed a number of people. I believe this would have been around 1899. So now let's have a look at the things happening in Luoland today.

The arrival of the white people brought in its wake the religion of Christ. At the beginning a lot of people joined in; it looked like almost the whole land had. People were walking from as far as Kadimo to Maseno just for the sake of receiving the Holy Communion. People began building villages, wherein all Christians lived, and within these villages people were joyfully glad (*ilo sidan'g*) because of the novel Word that had become manifest (*ma notuchono*). Do people still live in those villages as in the past?

Many primary schools have been built at these former village sites. And the founders of these villages moved back to their original ancestral homes, where they had belonged earlier when they were men of culture (*jopiny*), and now their numbers are dwindling. There are many reasons why these people migrated from their own constructions. These reasons still persist, and they make Luo *development* (*dongo Luo*) very problematic.

As is well known, there are very few Christians who do not consult Luo diviners (*ajuoga*). The biggest God for Jo Luo is the medicine (*yath*) that the diviner can provide. Whether he is at work, or in a position of authority/leadership over others, even if he is a church elder, or whatever other job he holds. However educated, or whatever else they may be—chiefs, clerks, traders, converts (*jolendo*), many teachers—all believe in the diviner. Rather than using one's intelligence to overcome the adversity (*chandruok*) that there may be, one runs to the diviner instead. This is a major backwardness (*dok chien*) among the Luo, and one that has made it very difficult for us to embrace the development trajectory of the foreigners (*dongo e yor jogo ma welo obedonwa matek putu*).

The trouble with this attitude is that it encourages laziness, the desire to harm your own kinsmen (*jowadu*), entertaining ideas that are outdated (*rieko ma chako chon loyo*), ruining the tribe by refusing to do your best at work while awaiting your own judgment day.

Many new ideas have arrived in our land. Education is one such [idea], employment is another, membership of various associations also. In all these endeavors there is only one real helper: hard work. It is not magic. It is not bribery. It is not visiting the diviner. It is not the boasting about one's wealth at music rendezvous. It is not speaking English. Once we realize that the quality of life (*yot mar ngima*) comes out of hard work, we must also know telling the truth is also a necessity. Hard work at theft will not bring about development. Plus, we must realize that we are working for the whole country. Nowadays many Luo have come to appreciate the value of money: for this reason, a lot of people dream about (*gombo*) becoming rich. People who think like this ruin the land when they hold high offices.

They nurse ill-will (*Gin kod guruguru*) against others, their sole preoccupation being arse-licking (*sombruok*) of their employers as their only guarantee for holding the job. It is hard for people to realize that jobs are not created because of the one person that wants to hold it. Jobs are created because of the needs of the whole community. This is why you may find that a man and sole wife will furnish their house with ten seats. They do this because they know that there will be people who will sit on them. This is why, when you build a shop, you should also know that it is likely the kind of resource that will be useful to both the community together with yourself. All jobs belong to the community plus you. There are many examples which show that all jobs exist because of the people. Wherefore, even if it means death, we should always strive to uphold the desires of the people.

There are other issues nowadays that tend to retard our development (*utho dongo marwa*). We must shun discrimination (*akwede*). It is a great pity that the foreigners in this land love discrimination; it is their wish that only they should hold all of the good jobs. We should not emulate this praxis; it is bad. Its mother is called Greed and its father is called Prejudice (*achaye*). On our part, if we emulate prejudice, we shall be "lost like a flight of swallows" (*walal miru*). Nowadays the times are hard and because of this the Luo must come to a meeting of the minds through discussion, at work and at play, in praise of working for the community and doing God's work.

In very truth, the one thing that waters the roots of prejudice so that it does not dry out is the dumbness (*dinruok*) of the people themselves. A lot of people unfortunately have not found the key to eye-opening: Good Teaching. They do not fully understand what is going on, and in addition, they are merely laid back (*gigalore agala*): they do not care about anything (*onge gima badhogi*). If a man is known as an adulterer, you might find people praising him for it and him laughing, being happy, and even feeling good about it. Even if a man is a thief, the same goes. You may well find that in some places he commands the kind of high respect that would not be accorded to you. Sometimes, at musical sessions, [a] lot of people go to the harpist, identifying him to the effect that "the man (the thief) is no ordinary person" (*ok en dhano-a-dhana*).

If a position arises well beyond the abilities of this bad man, you find that people will still vote for him.

If people persist in refusing to see the origins of the suffering they have, it is very difficult to alleviate that suffering. Even the medical doctor does not know what ails you, and if you do not tell him, he can never treat you. Similarly, we quite often do not know what good things we really want. For this reason, even if there is a job demanding a person with seasoned talents (*ngat mojin'g*), quite often the people themselves do not appreciate this. The individuals all genuflect and prostrate themselves (*umo mana iye piny*) in the hope that it should be their brother or their father that should accede to that particular job. Even if he has no special knowledge or merit (*rieko*) for the job, he still just lands the job on his bottom (*iredhe'e aredha*) because he belongs to this particular community! I once in the past witnessed a situation in a certain land where one clan came out unhesitatingly (*otitore tititi*) in the claim that it had to be their man who must be appointed as the clerk in charge of taxation records in a particular area. The chief of that land was himself a good man, so he accepted that the appointee should work. But the latter did not last long at his job. Just the writing down of the name of one person would take him a long time, and the task he could have accomplished in one day would take even as long as a week. This type of person wastes his own time and the time of all the people who have to do business with him, but more specifically he ruins the whole land.

He was appointed because of the demands of a blind community (*oganda ma muofu*) and which did not know the nature of the job he had been assigned to perform.

In many areas these days, there are a thousand and one opinions and performances (*weche gi timbe turi*) which come about because the people in their hearts only see through a film darkly (*neno mahuyuhuyu gi chunygi*). Sometimes you can find that certain sections of the community do not want the appointed chief of their land. Sometimes they do have legitimate justification. But often they entertain thoughts informed by greed and by prejudice. They may even tell you that they want the chief to quit his job because he has served for a long time, or sometimes because the chief is a poor man who therefore cannot lead. If you inquire as to whether this poverty of the chief makes him a thief, then they might tell you that his poverty limits his ability to entertain the sons of the soil with free food. Instead of looking for a chief, they are basically looking for a cook! Instead of searching for a lawmaker (*jabura*), they are looking for someone who may well agree to brew in such quantities that the supply may not run out!

Similar things are taking place within our schools. Sometimes there is a school in a specific neighborhood. Quite often the local people quarrel, even with the educational administrators, in case their own local son is not posted to teach in that particular school. Instead of seeking teachers, all they want is their own son.

It is necessary that the local people should know clearly what they want. Following this, they should look for any enlightened, steady person (*n'gat molony mojin'g*), and one who has the ability to carry that responsibility. I know that oftentimes it is not easy to get this type of man. I also know that it is possible to appoint people to learn on the job. But what should be obvious is this: To pick someone who cannot write even his own name and make him recording secretary of a meeting is like plucking one who has never watched a soccer match and making him the center-half in the Gossage Cup (football encounter between Kenya, Uganda, Tanganyika, and Zanzibar).

Although developmental matters are in poor shape, I think they will improve. In everyday life there must obtain a few faults. The major issue is this: People should have the eyes that can see these faults and the will to rectify them. Education has arrived, and as everyone knows the world over, it is a very good asset indeed (*sidan'g*). The love of God and having knowledge are the hope of the whole world. Therefore, if we were to get thorough education (*puonjruok mong'ith*), for the soul and for intelligence, I believe we shall win the war. There are many varieties of education. One can, for example, train to be a robber or to be a habitual thief (*abele wafuye*), one who does not see one's property without wishing to spoil it. Also, one can also learn to work for Were (the Luo God), for the people, and for himself. The education that we Luo seek today is not mere education (*puonjruok apuonja*) for the sake of doing arithmetic and speaking a foreign language but "EDUCATION." It is not a matter of having a higher *digri* (degree) only. Never. In truth we must have a degree if we can, and it is something a lot of people should obtain if we want to develop in diverse ways. But it is not the only way. "Bingo iro ok e tedo"— poking the smoke is not cooking. There are a lot of people with high qualifications indeed. But this has not stopped them from being petty (*josadha*), the kind of people who would not like to see ordinary people have access to the means of sustenance (*chiemo*) or prosperity (*konyruok*). It does not deter them from being a torment to fellow men, given the chance to do so.

The kind of knowledge we should be seeking should be that which enables us to honor our God (*Nyasaye*), to respect public property, and to undertake our work with keenness. It should be knowledge that enables us to love fellow men, deep-seated (*mar chuny*) [love] that brings about further development of our country (*matero piny nyime*). If you are a chief, act like a chief, not mixing with those who revel in perversity (*miganga*). If you are a clerk, act like someone who has some enlightenment (*ler*) to shed on the people; do not be the one to shout at those whose clothes are dirty or who have no wherewithal to offer as bribes. If you are a teacher, act as a leader from whom people may obtain education. That is the way through which self-improvement (*konyruok*) may come to us.

Having spoken about the negative consequences of sticking to the workings of medicines (*buru*) or magic (*bilo*), prejudice, and also about respect for the value of education and its potential for the prosperity of our land, there is one more thing that is really sinking (*chuanyo*) a lot of Jo Luo these days, about which I want to comment now. That is TABOO (*kwer*). "This is *kwer*, this is forbidden; we have never seen this before; this time around we shall see" (*wang'ni waneye*), and many more of such have overwhelmed people (*obemboji*) in the homesteads. And these prescriptions follow the Luo wherever else they may be, even in Uganda, Tanganyika, or wherever else they may be working. For the sake of absolutely meaningless taboo, a Luo will knock down a house that may have cost ten thousand shillings. Because of taboo, a widow without a husband may have no house. But all these taboos are meaningless. I personally have rejected many of these taboos, but I have not seen anything happen. I can recall about ten years ago. My mother's house was rugged, and it was necessary that we build another house. When we had made all the preparations for this, a message came to me requiring me to report at the Alliance High School within ten days. But since I was alone and my father could not build it without my help, it forced me to start work on the house right away without waiting an extra two days. My father had not yet made a clearing for the new house. Therefore, I started digging holes for the wall posts in the courtyard (*laro*) in front of the old house. My father thought that this act was taboo. But I tried persuading him until he agreed with me and so went ahead with the construction. But completing the house was not easy. It was a period of great difficulty. On every single day some elders would come and pity my father, saying, "You have done a sacrilege, you have killed yourself. Was ever a house built bang in the doorway of a previous one?" But I kept urging my father steadfastly, until we completed the structure, persuading him that his death would not come about merely because of the building of a house. His death would just be his own death (*thone wang'ene*). He agreed and we completed the house. But people swore that he would not eat the long rains (*chwiri*) harvests and the short rains (*opon*) harvests of that year. That was 1942. Now it is December 1952; my father is still alive. But many of those who were gleeful that he would not eat that *chwiri* are long dead. In truth, taboo is merely the fear that comes about because people themselves do not desire new ways of doing things. There are a lot of people wearing long beards who have very weird clothes (*lewni mayore*) and who carry reed-stalks full of medicines. People are afraid of these individuals, and whatever comes from their mouths is taken like the truth. But verily, accepting and enacting these utterances is like putting a stop to development such that people do not work, do not go to hospital, in order that things may come to ruin.

Finally I would like to address briefly on how Luo are doing in business and in creating wealth. Most people nowadays like business. People are pursuing whatever avenue exists for making money. Shop construction is going on apace. Lorries are being purchased tremendously (*sidang'*). People are trying all sorts of ideas so as to have money and wealth. Traders are marketing maize and cattlemen the same so as to make money. In truth, we shall obtain money, but the acquisition of permanent wealth will elude us because of our culture. These customs of ours will gnaw at our wealth like a squirrel gnawing at sweet potatoes until we become old, but we shall die without any patrimony to leave behind for our children.

There is nobody who can decree that people should not die. But we can put a stop to the practices of funeral reunion (*duogo e liel*), the brewing of beer for cleansing (*kong yawo dhoot*), the assemblage of hordes of people plus musicians and horn-blowers so as to go and entertain yourselves (*uchamo nyadhi*) in a place where someone has died. It is always a heavy burden on the part of those who are bereaved. I am not opposed to serving meals at funerals. But hanging out at a funeral site for even five days while you really have no obligations to fulfill there other than your anticipation of eating is a total waste of the wealth of the children of the deceased. Goats are slaughtered in addition to cattle, even for those coming from nearby, who can go back and obtain meals in their own homesteads. Chickens are roasted aplenty, and every married daughter (*migogo*), every single nephew (*okewo*), each and every type of relative demands as a right (*bandho*) that they should actually be fed. That is the way it will be when you die: they will waste your wealth. Your best chair will be ruined; your best clothes that your son should inherit will be looted (*giniyaki*) if your son is not yet a grown-up, and everything will be utterly destroyed (*nodunyre duto*). If such things are going on, it means that our children will have to start afresh exactly from where we ourselves had started, without any sound foundation that we have laid for them.

It would be good, regarding this, if we could change our custom, so that instead of going to demolish the property of the deceased, those of us who know him should help his widow with money, animals, and labor. Only a few people try to do this, but the majority of the people are merely consumers.

The other rat that is going to chew through our bunt-line (*nyabondo*) is this. True, some people may spoil our property once we are dead, but how about our own selves? Do we want merely to subsist or do we work to provide for a better future for our children?

As for this question, the majority of us who are employed, who are business people and who make money or wealth, have not provided an adequate answer. I know it is a marathon and that people have already kicked off the starting block (*en thecho ng'wech ji theche*). But even then, it is quite clear that the vast majority among those who are jogging along in this race do not have a clear grasp of where the end of it is, nor which turn it is taking. I think it has become difficult for us to know what to do with money. The foreigners have some ideas which we should borrow and try to put into practice. People should work, they should trade, they should farm and try every means so as to have good houses, eat good meals that sustain the body so that diseases do not find the opportunity to penetrate and cause permanent ailment (*hongni gi midekre*), and so that their children may receive adequate education. In addition to all that, they (foreigners) also believe that work should enable them to obtain clothing and wear (*ang'uola*) to cover their nakedness, to buy books to study so as to increase their knowledge.

But after accumulation of wealth it becomes difficult for us to regularly emulate these practices. Our culture tends to draw us toward adding on extra wives, buying witchcraft (*nawi*), to engaging in all sorts of hedonisms (*oyuma*), and because of this, our money is not going to enable us to live decently in the eyes of society and before God. Modern life comes with its own raging waves and thunderous storms (*apaka mathoth gi auka mager*). It brings along a lot of disruptive tribulations (tribulatio < tribulare) that have biting fangs and corrosive poison. If we do not try to follow the ways of modernity we shall not find the energy to bridge these rolling billows and the raging storms, and however much we dig in (*kata da wagur ondiro nadi*), we shall still skid and backslide.

We may debate the question of "Shall we abandon the old customs of our ancestors?" There is no one whose desire is that we should abandon our customs, if they are good. In the olden days we walked naked or donned a wrapper, raffia skirts (*chieno*), or beaded leatherwork (*olembo*). When textile clothing arrived, we did not insist, like the Lang'o (Maasai or Kalenjin) did, that we must exclusively continue wearing the old adornments. We used to sleep on the floor, on dried-out cowhides (*pien adela*) next to bonfires in places that were warmer than some white men's houses. Nevertheless, we have found that the utilization of blankets and sleeping on beds is a good thing, and for that reason, people are on the run, abandoning the way they sustained their former lifestyles.

Wherefore, having accumulated wealth, we should endeavor to encourage the preoccupation with farming in our land [so] that the food resources may increase. People should unite in matters of finance truthfully and with trust among themselves so that we may continue to explore new ways of conserving the very same wealth, so that it does not merely translate into consumer goods that we munch through like birds. It should be wealth held in trust, like the Luo Thrift and Trading Corporation. That is the only way through which we may fortify ourselves, that our progress may surge forward, our wealth expand, and be permanently secured.

All good things must come to an end. Let me bind my narrative (*goyo tinda*) with just this last word: let us work hard, making a distinction between sites of leisure and places of work. Let us be a thinking people, who take delight in borrowing ideas from others. Let us be eager to interrogate one another on the issue of development; let us not be people who are confused (*ji ma weche goyo obindi*); but we should be people who have a longing (*siso*) to know the wisdom of yesterday, of today, and [a people] who think about the future as well. If we do that, our churches will prosper as well as our local organizations, like the African District Council and Location Council; our educational system and other institutions will all prosper to our heart's content.

LUO DEVELOPMENT DISCOURSE AT THE END OF THE TWENTIETH CENTURY

In the texts cited extensively above, Ayany and Mbuya sought, at midcentury, to foreground the question of Luo culture at the center of the problem of Luo development. What is intriguing is the recurrence of these same themes, as this century now draws to a close, and the intensity with which these issues have been recently discussed, especially during the court contestations concerning the cultural identity of the lawyer S. M. Otieno (Cohen and Atieno-Odhiambo 1992) and at the January 1995 Colloquium on Luo Cultural Practices, which marked the first anniversary of the death of Jaramogi Oginga Odinga. Across the wider terrain, there have been contemporaneous disputations over culture occasioned by the death of the lawyer-politician Joe Appiah in Ghana (Appiah 1992) and over the propriety of giving the Kenyan boxer Wangila Napunyi a Gusii, Samia, rural, urban, Christian, or Islamic burial (Atieno-Odhiambo 1994). All these debates are about Africa's engagements with and reenactments of modernity on its own terms. The Luo of Kenya have unabashedly regarded themselves as "modern" in the twentieth century. Within the womb of their cultural debates lie some clues to the unfolding drama of African modernity in the coming century.

REFERENCES

Achebe, C. 1975. *Morning Yet on Creation Day.* London: Heinemann.

Appiah, J. 1990. *Joe Appiah: The Autobiography of an African Patriot.* Westport, Conn.: Praeger.

Appiah, K. A. 1992. *In My Father's House: Africa in the Philosophy of Culture.* London: Oxford University Press.

Atieno-Odhiambo, E. S. 1975. "Seek Ye First the Economic Kingdom: A History of the Luo Thrift and Trading Corporation (LUTATCO), 1945–1956." In B. A. Ogot, ed., *Hadith 5: Economic and Social History of East Africa.* Nairobi: East African Literature Bureau, pp. 218–56.

———. 1989a. "The Developed Corpse: Notions of Development in the Struggle for the Body of S. M. Otieno (Kenya, 1986–67)." The Red Lion Seminars, Chicago, November 21.

———. 1989b. "The Hyena's Dilemma." Workshop on Anthropology and Philosophy, Smithsonian Institution, Washington, D.C., April 17–21.

———. 1992. "From Warriors to Jonanga: The Struggle over Nakedness by the Luo of Kenya." In W. Graebner, ed., *Sokomoko: Popular Culture in East Africa.* Amsterdam and Atlanta: Rodopi, pp. 11–26.

———. 1994. "Burying Wangila, Kenya 1994." Bucknell University, Lewisburg, Pennsylvania, November 21.

Ayany, S. 1952. *Kar Chakruok Mar Luo.* Reprint, Kisumu: Equatorial Publishers.

Cohen, D. W., and E. S. Atieno-Odhiambo. 1987. "Ayany, Malo and Ogot: Historians in Search of a Luo Nation." *Cahiers d'Etudes Africaines* 27, no. 3–4: 107–108, 269–86.

———. 1989. *Siaya: The Historical Anthropology of an African Landscape.* Athens: Ohio University Press.

———. 1992. *Burying SM: The Politics of Knowledge and the Sociology of Power in Africa.* Portsmouth, N.H.: Heinemann.

Klitgaard, R. 1990. *Tropical Gangsters: One Man's Experience with Development and Decadence in Darkest Africa.* New York: Basic Books.

Mbuya, P. 1938. *Luo Kitgi gi Timbegi.* Reprint, Nairobi: Equatorial Publishers.

———. 1978. *Richo Ema Kelo Chira.* Nairobi: Equatorial Publishers.

Ngugi wa Thiongo. 1982. *Devil on the Cross.* London: Heinemann.

Odinga, O. 1967. *Not Yet Uhuru.* London: Heinemann.

Ogot, B. A. 1971. "Reverend Alfayo Odongo Mango, 1870–1934." In K. King and A. I. Salim, eds., *Kenya Historical Biographies.* Nairobi: E.A.P.H., pp. 90–111.

Ogot, B. A., and F. B. Welbourn. 1966. *A Place to Feel at Home: A Study of Two Independent Churches in Western Kenya.* London: Oxford University Press.

Onyango-Abuje, J. C. 1975. *Fire and Vengeance.* Nairobi: East African Publishing House.

Rodney, W. 1981. *A History of the Guyanese Working Class.* Baltimore, Md.: Johns Hopkins University Press.

Vaughan, M. 1993. "Colonial Discourse Theory and African History; or, Has Postmodernism Passed Us By?" London: School of Oriental and African Studies, February 10.

Contributors

Peter S. O. Amuka is an associate professor of literature at Moi University in Eldoret, Kenya. His main research interests include Luo oral literature and expressions, on which he has published several essays (as either journal articles or book chapters). He is currently working on a collection of his essays on Luo oral literature.

E. S. Atieno-Odhiambo is a professor of history at Rice University in Houston, Texas. His publications include *Siaya: The Historical Anthropology of an African Landscape* and *Burying SM: The Politics of Knowledge and the Sociology of Power in Africa* (both of which are co-authored by David W. Cohen); *Jaramogi Oginga Odinga*; and *Ethnicity and Democracy in Kenya*.

Fabien Eboussi-Boulaga is a professor of philosophy at the Catholic University of Yaounde, Cameroon. He has taught widely in Africa, Europe, and the United States. His numerous publications include *Les Lignes de Résistance; La Démocratie en Transition au Cameroun; Les Conférences Nationales en Afrique Noire: Une Affaire à Suivre; Christianity without Fetishes;* and *La Crise du Muntu*.

Bogumil Jewsiewicki is a professor of history and a researcher at the Centre d'Etudes Interdisciplinaires sur les Arts, les Lettres et les Traditions at Laval University and a researcher at the Centre d'Etudes Africaines, CNRS/EHESS in Paris. Previously he taught at several Congolese universities. His recent publications include *A Congo Chronicle: Patrice Lumumba in Urban Art* and *Chéri Samba: Hybridité d'un Art* (*Chéri Samba: Hybridity of an Art*).

Didier N. Kaphagawani is an associate professor of philosophy at Chancellor College of the University of Malawi in Zomba, Malawi, where he is also the vice principal. His latest publications include *Leibniz on Freedom* and *Determinism in Relation to Aquinas and Molina*.

Ivan Karp is a National Endowment for the Humanities Professor and director of the Center for the Study of Public Scholarship in the Graduate Institute of

Liberal Arts at Emory University. He was formerly curator of African ethnology at the Smithsonian Institution and is the author of *Fields of Change Among the Iteso of Kenya* and the co-editor of *Explorations in African Systems of Thought* and *Creativity of Power*. He is also the author of numerous articles on African systems of thought, social organization and social change, social thought, and museums and society.

Corinne A. Kratz is an associate professor of anthropology and African studies at Emory University. Her recent publications include *Affecting Performance: Meaning, Movement, and Experience in Okiek Women's Initiation,* and she recently completed a new book, *"The Ones That Are Wanted": Communication and the Politics of Representation in a Photographic Exhibition.*

D. A. Masolo is a professor of philosophy at the University of Louisville. Previously he taught at the University of Nairobi and at Antioch College in Yellow Springs, Ohio. Apart from his numerous articles and book chapters on African philosophy, he is also the author of *African Philosophy in Search of Identity* and a co-editor of *Philosophy and Cultures.*

David Parkin, a professor and director of the Institute of Social and Cultural Anthropology at Oxford University, has carried out field research in East Africa since 1962, much of it while he was with the School of Oriental and African Studies at the University of London. His current interests include Islam, medical anthropology, socio-material prosthesis, and cross-cultural rhetorics. His numerous publications include *Neighbours and Nationals in an African City Ward; Cultural Definition of Political Response: Lineal Destiny Among the Luo;* and *Sacred Void: Spatial Images of Work and Ritual Among the Giriama of Kenya.* He is also editor of *Anthropology of Evil* and co-editor of *Autorité et Pouvoir chez les Swahili,* a text which is the result of an ongoing collaboration with French colleagues.

J. P. Odoch Pido was born in Uganda where he received his early education. He was a pioneer student of the Department of Design, Nairobi University College, of the then University of East Africa. He is a designer, a Senior Lecturer, and is currently Chair of the Department of Design in the Faculty of Architecture, Design and Development at the University of Nairobi, Kenya.

Rosalind Shaw is an associate professor of sociocultural anthropology and African religions at Tufts University. Apart from her many articles and book chapters on religion, memory, and gender in Sierra Leone, she is author of a forthcoming book on ritual memories of the slave trade in Sierra Leone: *The Dangers of Temne Divination.* She is co-editor of *Syncretism/Anti-Syncretism: The Politics of Ritual Synthesis* and *Dreaming, Religion and Society in Africa.*

Kwasi Wiredu is a professor of philosophy at the University of South Florida in Tampa, and he is currently a visiting professor of philosophy at Duke University. His numerous publications include *Philosophy and an African Culture; Person and Community* (co-edited with Kwame Gyekye); and *Cultural Universals and Particulars: An African Perspective.*

Index

abstract theory, 7

Achewa people, 71–72

Acoli people, 85, 134; aesthetics of personhood, 133; languages of, 121; marriage
and divorce among, 118, 126–27; personhood and, 106–14; sex practices of,
124; songs of, 105–106, 114–18

adaptability, 201

adolescents, 108–109

adulthood, 138–39, 155

aesthetics, 111–12, 216, 225

Africa: artists in, 225, 228–40; capitalist penetration of, 32; change (mutations) in,
188–89, 191–96, 197–98; comparison
with India, 3; complexity of, 206; diaspora of, 2; languages of, 12, 32, 57, 134;
marginalization of, 210–11; nations of,
1–2, 13; science and technology in,
181–86

African philosophy, 1–4, 13–15; as cultural inquiry, 9–13; ethnophilosophy and, 4–9;
languages and, 12. See also philosophy

African socialism, 5

afterbirth, 107–108, 131

agency, 4, 10, 21, 23, 52, 136; autonomy and,
137, 155; change and, 7; clan and, 27; collective, 86, 143; complex, 137, 140, 147;
determinism and, 50–51; female, 38,
151, 163, 165; individual, 7, 28; male,
159–61; multidimensional complexities
of, 164–67; nationalism and, 175; negative, 146, 162, 166; negotiation of, 150;
paradoxes of, 45, 144, 151; personhood
and, 25–26; seeking, giving, and agreeing, 140–47; "wealth-in-people" and,
37–38; wedding advice and, 156–64

aggressiveness, 119, 121

AIDS (Acquired Immune Deficiency Syn-
drome), 10, 126, 134, 237, 238

Akan people, 76

Alexandre, Pierre, 225

Alfa, Pa, 38–39

Althusser, Louis, 10

altruism, 184

Alvares, Manuel, 33, 35–36

Amin, Idi, 96

Amuka, Peter, 83, 84

ancestors, 31, 92, 249, 256

anglophone culture, 12

animals, 76, 92, 106, 110

anthropology, 4, 13, 186, 224–25; colonialism
and, 9; knowledge and, 222; personhood
in, 21

appeal, 77

Appiah, Joe, 257

Appiah, Kwame, 2, 9, 13

Arabic language, 57, 59, 62

Arabs, 57

Aristotelianism, 6, 77

Aristotle, 187–88, 189; on causation, 193; on
change, 210; on dialectics, 191; on topic,
190, 192

artists, 177–78, 179; "primitive," 223, 224. See
also Samba, Chéri

Asante people, 30

ash, 109

astrology, 54, 64

Atieno-Odhiambo, E. S., 178

Atkins, John, 33

atomism, 28

attractors, 199

Australia, 5

authenticity, 223

authoritarianism, 7